PRIVATISATION & COMPETITION

A Market Prospectus

PRIVATISATION & COMPETITION

A Market Prospectus

Edited by

Cento Veljanovski

Institute of Economic Affairs

1989

First published in January 1989
by
THE INSTITUTE OF ECONOMIC AFFAIRS
2 Lord North Street, Westminster, London, SW1P 3LB

Hobart Paperback 28

ISSN 0309-1783
ISBN 0-255 36211-0

Typeset by Infograph Limited, London & Printed in Great Britain by
Billings & Sons Limited, Worcester

Filmset in Times Roman 11 on 12 point

CONTENTS

FOREWORD

Cento Veljanovski

Research & Editorial Director, Institute of Economic Affairs

NEARLY 30 years ago C. Northcote Parkinson concluded with the pessimistic assessment 'the process of nationalisation is more or less irrevocable'. He went on to argue:

> 'If we are to continue with two political parties and those the two we have, holding the views they do, we shall end with all industries more or less nationalised. For that is what one party seems to want and the other cannot prevent or reverse. The only obvious alternative is to end our experiment in democracy, confessing that it has been a complete failure'.[1]

Today both of these political parties agree that the 'experiment' has been a failure but not an irrevocable one. Remarkably, the party which could not 'prevent or reverse' state-ownership, and even engaged in its own fits of nationalisation, has as its key policy the sale of all the state-owned industries to the private sector, except, for some inexplicable reason, the Royal Mail, i.e., the letter post. The remarkable thing about the whole process is that it was unpredictable, and it followed no coherent over-arching strategy. Privatisation evolved, each sale was self-contained and each pattern of disposing of assets, from the legal arrangements to the terms of the sale, was *ad hoc.* The French have now done it faster and better than the British and the Japanese will in several years have done more than the British as measured in terms of revenue. Nonetheless the Thatcher Government led the way and is looked to all over the world as the example of a successful, extensive and radical privatisation

[1] C. Northcote Parkinson, *The Law of Delay*, London: John Murray, 1970, pp. 64-65.

programme. As an indication of the international popularity of privatisation, it has been estimated that before 1986 about $18 billion of state-owned enterprises and assets were sold. In 1987 five times this figure – $92 billion – were sold to the private sector.

While the success of privatisation in political and financial terms cannot be denied, the euphoria is tempered by a concern that serious deficiencies exist. This collection of essays explores perhaps the most profound weakness of the British privatisation programme – the failure to maximise the opportunites to introduce competition in those industries which were the heartland of the nationalised sector – telecommunications, gas, electricity, water and coal.

In 1984 privatisation was extended to basic infrastructure industries with the sale of British Telecommunications. This has thrust the policy into a controversial area where the scope for competition and the importance of the industries have raised serious doubts about the desirability of private profit-oriented operation. However, the debate slowly moved from a concern with this matter to a realisation that what the Government had done was to sell state monopolies virtually intact. In Parkinson's essay nationalisation was treated as synonymous with monopolisation. The nationalised industries operated as public monopolies with explicit statutory protection against competition. In many cases the monopoly privileges of the newly created private companies have been preserved, either by giving these firms overt legal protection from competition and/or failing to break them into separate units.

The contributors to this volume are agreed that the Government's privatisation programme has sacrificed the goal of greater competition and of introducing more market forces to the expediency of short-term considerations and that the programme relies to an excessive extent on the unproven ability of regulation to do what the market would have achieved costlessly. This is not to say that in the genuinely monopoly component of these industries there is not an important role to be played by the regulation of prices and terms in creating a 'fair trading' environment and protecting customers from monopoly abuses.

The benefits of competition can be stated in bold terms. The goal of maximising competition ensures that customers are provided with the goods and services they want at a price that reflects the opportunity costs of producing them. Competition acts as a self-regulating mechanism because the spur of profits encourages others to enter markets and provide services. The case against monopoly rests ultimately upon the discipline that choice puts on a producer. 'If the grocer is rude to his customers, they go to another grocer, and he is ruined; so grocers have to be polite – or more polite, anyway, than officials in a labour exchange'.[2]

In some areas of the utility industries – usually the physical networks – the prospects of competition are limited because they are

[2] Parkinson, *ibid.*, p. 66.

'natural' monopolies. While the relevance of this argument for actual privatisation policy, both as an explanation of what has happened and as a justification for limiting competition, is greatly exaggerated, the fact nonetheless remains that in the operation of the physical networks of the gas, electricity and water industries, and to a much lesser extent telecommunications, single-firm supply in a particular area is likely to be the norm. Obviously this does not support national utilities, only local monopoly networks. There is, therefore, tremendous scope for re-structuring some of the utilities. Where competition cannot be fostered regulation must ensure that the behaviour of the utilities mimics the results of the competitive market-place without at the same time creating offsetting distortions.

The challenge for policy-makers over the next decade or two will be to examine the mistakes which have been made in privatising the utility industries and how to foster more competition and less regulation.

There is one area of the nationalisation/privatisation policy which requires comment and offers an agenda for a future research programme. Economists have neglected the subject of why governments nationalise and then privatise. No one has yet offered a robust theory – a public choice analysis – of the conditions which are conducive to political and special interest groups seeing sufficient common interest to make privatisation a politically acceptable policy. The economic literature on nationalisation typically goes no further than to catalogue possible market failures and non-economic goals which may justify non-market provision. These do not, however, explain either actual nationalisations or the particular forms which state-ownership of industry take. Often the operation of state-owned industries indicates quite clearly that economic efficiency is not their principal goal.

This book arose from a conference organised by the IEA in September 1987 at which the papers by George Yarrow, Christopher Beauman and Professors Bryan Carsberg, Colin Robinson and John Hibbs were delivered. The remaining chapters have either been commissioned specially for the volume (Ray Evans, Howard Hyman, Dr Irwin Stelzer and my own) or are parts of works previously published by the IEA which the authors have been invited to amend. Two essays, by Professors Stephen Littlechild and Jack Wiseman, were written before the start of the British privatisation programme. They are included because they offer 'blueprints' for de-nationalisation before the policy became a viable political reality. By bringing together contributions from these three different sources it is hoped to achieve a self-contained and comprehensive discussion of the role of the market and competition in the privatisation programme.

I would like to thank all the authors for their co-operation in the production of this book.

The Institute of Economic Affairs dissociates itself from the views and analyses of the contributors to this book. Nonetheless, the independent and critical analyses of the contributors address one of the major policy issues surrounding industrial policy in the UK. Their scholarly discussion makes a major contribution to opening up a debate on the premises underlying Britain's programme of privatisation and addresses the continuing inefficiencies which it has fostered.

December 1988 CENTO VELJANOVSKI

PART I

A FRAMEWORK FOR COMPETITION

1

GROWING WITHOUT NATIONALISATION*

Jack Wiseman

Director,
Special Development Programme,
University of York

THERE HAVE BEEN frequent expressions of dissatisfaction with the internal performance of nationalised industries, but to a remarkable extent debate has concentrated in recent years upon the details of administrative and organisational change in the existing corporations, with little discussion of whether the scope of nationalisation might suitably be extended or existing corporations returned to the private sector. The enthusiasts of nationalisation and economic growth rarely recognise that the weaknesses of the nationalised industries may themselves have retarded the growth of the economy as a whole or that they must call into question the very principles of nationalisation if public corporations are to be judged by their past results.

The increasing weight of the nationalised industries on Britain's economic performance is clear. From 1938 to 1962 total annual investment in the UK grew from £656 million to £4,608 million, or about seven times. But the investment of the public corporations during the same period has risen from £10 million to £927 million, or over 90 times. The proportion of all investment has grown from about one-sixtieth in 1938 to one-fifth in 1962. (This fraction does not include investment by local and national government which was £1,013 million in 1962, or a further fifth.) The public corporations predominate in fuel and transport and also in communications of other kinds (telephones, broadcasting). They produce goods and services bought and used by the private sector of industry, whose own

* Reprinted from *Rebirth of Britain*, London: Pan Books, 1964.

efficiency in part depends on them. If the nationalised industries are inefficient, private industry will also be unavoidably inefficient.

THE CASE FOR NATIONALISATION

There can be no simple way to demonstrate how nationalised industries have influenced growth in Britain because we cannot know precisely what would have happened had the enterprises been in private hands. But it is clear that the efficiency of the large public sector must influence the whole economy. It is therefore fruitful to ask why the economic efficiency of public corporations should be expected to be superior to that of the private enterprises that might replace them. The advocates of nationalisation use arguments of a broader social character as well as narrowly technical ones. The two groups of arguments merge with each other, and the incautious critic is liable to find dissent about one of them countered by argument concerning the other. We shall begin with the broader arguments on the political and social ends of society and move to the narrower and more technical issues.

The nationalisers do not agree about first principles. Here is Mr C.A.R. Crosland in *The Future of Socialism*:[1]

> '...the ownership of the means of production has ceased to be the key factor which imparts to a society its essential character',

and

> 'monopoly, even when it is public, has definite drawbacks'.

Here, in the opposite corner, the late Mr John Strachey in the *Political Quarterly* in 1953:

> 'The British people must and will assume the ownership of the means of production which they operate...that entails the ownership...of vast and complex means of production, from the turbines of Battersea to the furnaces of Margam. Such giants' tools as these can only be owned in some collective way.[2]

This kind of difference continues to plague British socialists intellectually and emotionally. But the case for public ownership is weak. First, their arguments of principle against private property *per se* are implausible and unconvincing. (It does not follow of course that any given pattern of property distribution or any existing structure of property law is incapable of improvement. I myself would favour heavy inheritance taxes.) Second, the destruction of private property must imply the concentration of political and economic power in the same hands. This must be expected to result, and has in the past resulted, in a severe (and for me intolerable) curtailment of individual freedom. Third, even if the arguments of principle against private property were accepted, they would lead to

[1] London: Jonathan Cape, 1956.
[2] John Strachey, 'The Object of Further Socialization', *Political Quarterly*, Vol. 24, 1953, p.73.

support for universal public ownership rather than for the existence of a few public enterprises in a predominantly market economy. But no one proposes universal nationalisation in current policy for Britain. Fourth, and arising out of the others, nationalisation is to be judged by its results, and the onus is upon those who wish to destroy private property to show why their proposals are to be expected to bring advantages massive enough to outweigh the dangers and objections.

SOCIAL COSTS

A second line of approach has come into prominence. It does not attack private property as an institution but argues rather that free markets fail to take account of 'social costs' whereas public corporations can do so. The public discussion of social costs is wreathed in obscurity. Two broad strands of argument can be discerned, the one vague or confused, the other technically interesting but inconclusive in its support for nationalisation.

The most naive form asserts that markets function unsatisfactorily because the 'wrong people' get the goods. But if a rich old lady can buy eggs for her dog while a poor mother cannot get enough for her children, the reason is unlikely to be the imperfection of the market for eggs. The target of reformers should be the distribution of capital and/or income. To blame the market for the poverty of some who trade in it is to misunderstand what markets can be expected to do.

An apparently more sophisticated, but effectively more obscure, argument of this general kind is that private ownership of resources encourages 'social inequality'. Thus, Mr Michael Shanks claims that there is a strong *prima facie* case for believing that the transfer of big industrial assets from private to public hands would promote greater 'equality'. Equality, and even more social equality, appears to be something we should encourage, in the same way that we are against sin. But as in the case of sin, there is need for more precise specification if the moral imperative is to be a guide for action rather than simple jabberwocky. Since Mr Shanks does not explain what he means by 'social equality', it is a little difficult to make any judgement on the plausibility of his *prima facie* case. If he means *economic* equality, then the *prima facie* case is certainly not made out. The belief that the distribition of income is uniquely determined by the pattern of ownership is both technically implausible (no consistent economic model is ever suggested to support it), and in our present context disingenuous in failing to recognise that 'public ownership' is ownership by people: it is vested in those who can get and hold political power. Equally, the strong *prima facie* case is unsatisfactory if it refers to earned incomes. Wage differentials are wider if anything in the Soviet Union than in Britain: the spread between the highest and lowest paid workers in the early 1950s was commonly as high as 15 to 1.

SOCIAL COST AND THE COMMUNITY: PIGOU REDISCOVERED

The narrower form of the social cost argument claims that the values established in competitive markets do not take account of costs falling on the community or benefits accruing to the community, whose interests may therefore be bypassed. The modern formulation originated with the late Professor A.C. Pigou. Pigou has recently been rediscovered and the claim advanced that Labour thinking on social policy derives from his writings, as Mr Peter Hall claims in *Labour's New Frontiers.*[3]

> 'We have begun to grope our way towards a practical concept of economic planning which may prove, in a few years time, to be as revolutionary in its implications as was the Keynesian revolution in economics thirty years ago. It also originated many years ago with a Cambridge economist: Keynes' contemporary Pigou. It is the concept of social costs and benefits'.

But the claim that any unique relation can be traced between, say, Pigou's classic, *The Economics of Welfare*,[4] and a definitive social programme is preposterous, and can suggest only that those who make it are more familiar with, say, geography, than with the pioneering works of Pigou or the voluminous literature to which they have given rise.

Let us consider the nature of divergencies of private and social benefits and costs in more detail. The classic illustrations are well-known. My factory emits smoke which dirties your clothes, but I do not pay to have them laundered. Or my railway train runs past your wheat field, and emits sparks which burn your crops. But what to do? Recent discussions of social cost problems in economic literature have clarified the relevance of the concept to issues of public policy. The most significant development is that it has been convincingly demonstrated by Professor R.H. Coase, Professor J.M. Buchanan and Mr Ralph Turvey that, while so-called divergencies of social and private costs and benefits (essentially similar to the external economies and diseconomies of business enterprise) may affect the efficient use of community resources, they need not do so and frequently do not. For example, in the 'crop-burning case' the 'efficient' solution (depending upon the circumstances) from the point of view of the use of community resources might be, for example, to fit spark-preventing devices, to leave the land by the railway uncultivated, or simply to accept the risks of crops being burned. But that ideal solution can be reached by market transactions, whatever the particular rights of the affected parties. If there are no obstacles in the way of creating the market institutions, the use of resources by the community would be the same whether or not the railway owners have to compensate the farmers for burned crops. And similarly with

[3] London: Andre Deutsch, 1964.
[4] London: Macmillan, 1920.

the smoke nuisance case, which Pigou made famous. Essentially, therefore, the social cost problem becomes one of deciding on forms of compensation, which is in effect a decision about the laws of property.

The argument has several corollaries. First, social cost problems are not confined to particular industries but are relevant to all activities that involve the specification of property rights – in effect, the whole of economic activity. Second, the character and existence of social costs is less obvious than is commonly assumed. They may involve subjective assessments, and there is no agreed method of identifying and valuing them or of deciding which 'costs' are the proper subject of public policy. If I hang my weekly wash in my front garden, my neighbour may find the display offensive and argue that I have imposed a social cost upon him, but it does not follow that the *community* should take cognisance of it. Or consider the effect of cinemas upon members of the Salvation Army, to whom their presence was at one time an offence (a cost). By what criteria are we to decide upon the appropriate course of public action or inaction? Third, the existence of adequate market institutions is crucial: many of the examples of social cost problems turn out on examination to be cases in which demand cannot produce a market response. Consider, for example, Mr J.R. Sargent's discussion of the social costs of road transport in *Lessons of Public Enterprise*:[5]

> '...The social costs of traffic congestion are what they are because the motorist is not generally made to bear the cost of his parking space, and because the traffic congregates in morning and evening peaks. To reduce these costs charges for parking must not only become the general rule but must be made to vary according to the time of day...'

The factual description is accurate. But the problem of public policy arises out of the absence of a satisfactory competitive market in road use or in parking places. Agreed, there are technical difficulties in creating such a market, but it would be more efficient to try to solve them than to conclude (as Mr Sargent does) that there should be a public monopoly of parking space. A monopoly must inhibit the creation of the necessary market conditions rather than encourage them.

PUBLIC OWNERSHIP DOES NOT HELP

This brings me to the final point. Of itself, the substitution of public for private ownership does nothing to make policies to deal with problems of social cost easier to formulate or implement. If the government is not to abdicate its responsibility for policy-making, the public enterprises will have to be subjected to general rules specifying the social costs to be taken into account, and how. Exhortations, for

[5] London: Jonathan Cape, 1963.

example, to cover costs while promoting the (unspecified) 'public interest', are fruitless. They must lead public corporations either to give no more attention to 'costs' they are not required to pay than private enterprise would, or to the use of the 'public interest' injunction to avoid public accountability or to assume social responsibilities for which they are politically and structurally unfitted.

What happens if public corporations are allowed to determine 'social costs'? Suppose the Coal Board decides against closing a high-cost pit because miners would become redundant and the Board cannot move them elsewhere (or is unwilling to bear the cost). Such a policy must raise the cost of coal, so that the 'social cost' is borne by coal users. But the Coal Board cannot know the full implications of its decision: the government itself is concerned about distribution of industry and labour over the country as a whole, and there is no more reason to allow the Coal Board to take such a decision than to allow or expect a private producer to do so. If we must have a nationalised coal industry (I argue below that we would be better without it), it should be required to follow normal economic criteria so far as they can be applied. A proposed closure might be notified to the government (in the same way that one would expect private enterprise to give advance notice of a major redundancy), but the decision on the necessary 'social' adjustments would be for the government alone. Further, if it was desired to keep the pit open, logic would suggest that a specific subsidy from general taxation should be provided for the purpose.

Similar arguments apply to many other common proposals, such as that for the subsidisation of railways to reduce urban congestion. Thus, Messrs Ernest Davies, Austen Albu and Michael Shanks in *Lessons of Public Enterprise*[6] support the view that 'responsibility for defining the public interest and for seeing that the nationalised industries conform to it is the Minister's' (as opposed to the boards of management). But if this is so, the Minister's (i.e. Parliament's) responsibilities in social cost/benefit problems embrace the whole of the community's economic activity and provide no reason for the nationalisation of parts of it.

In practical politics, no serious attempts have ever been made to deal specifically with such social costs as public corporations might be generally agreed to create. We do not compensate those who live near gasworks, or in the houses bordering Mr Sargent's congested roads. Indeed, it is not unfair to say that in its purer forms the social cost/benefit argument has never been reflected in public policies towards nationalised enterprises: on the contrary, the crude assertion that the industries confer social benefits has been used to impede the development of market procedures that might improve their economic efficiency and accountability.

In short, the social cost/benefit arguments do not produce support for nationalisation, but argue rather for the need for constant

---

[6] *Ibid.*

attention by government to definitions of property rights and to the development of market institutions. These are not easy tasks, but they can hardly be lightened by replacing private markets by statutory monopolies.

NATIONALISATION TO CONTROL PRIVATE MONOPOLY?

We now turn to other (economic) arguments in favour of public ownership: first, the need to control or prevent private monopoly.

There are many examples of the willingness of statutory monopolies to raise revenues or to defend their position, protected as it is by law, by measures that would be condemned in private industry. A recent illustration is provided by the violent reaction (including proposals for preventive legislation) to the 'pirate' radio stations which dare to offer pop music in competition with the BBC. On the one hand, prevention of private monopolistic practices by law is feasible given determined government. But by a strange alchemy the competition whose absence is said by some to make nationalisation essential becomes unnecessary and even 'harmful' once a public corporation has been created. On the other hand, other supporters of nationalisation share a belief in the virtues of competition:

> 'It may be regrettable', said Mr Hugh Gaitskell in *Socialism and Nationalisation*, 'but it seems to be a fact that people's enthusiasm about almost any group to which they belong is enhanced by competition.[7]

I would disagree only that it may be regrettable. But this kind of view does not lead to support for denationalisation, only to suggestions for more competition within and between public corporations. For both philosophical and practical reasons such views have had little influence, and cannot be expected to have much in the future. Genuine competition requires that enterprises should be able to go bankrupt. What is the difference between this and denationalisation? Anything less can be only a sham.

Secondly, there is the argument that in some industries nationalisation is the best means of increasing economic efficiency. The notion that a competitive market for some products is 'inefficient' or 'impossible' has been very common, but it is unlikely that there are many industries in which technical factors alone require for efficiency a minimum scale of production so large that competition between efficient units is impossible. The minimum capital investment needed to build a modern strip mill is absolutely large, but the output is a tiny proportion of the world demand for steel. Private capital after all built the railways, yet who can doubt that if such a task were envisaged nowadays there would be a chorus

---

[7] London: Fabian Society, 1956.

of despairing voices saying that it was not a task that private industry was competent to perform? More usually these apparently 'technical' difficulties turn out to have their real roots elsewhere – for example, in monopoly conditions in bordering markets or in the influence of legislation upon the competitive process. The most satisfactory solution for such problems is to take steps to remove the *obstacles* to enterprise and competition, rather than to superimpose a public monopoly upon them.

DISADVANTAGES OF NATIONALISATION

The nationalised industries are statutory monopolies vulnerable to political interference and to the pressure of vested interests, whose resistance to competition and to change is as effective as a set of tariff walls. In the words of the White Paper, *The Financial and Economic Obligations of the Nationalised Industries*,[8] 'economic objectives are blurred by political expediency'. For this reason and others already explained, the public corporations suffer, and must be expected to continue to suffer, from disadvantages of size, unavoidable over-centralisation of management and control, and inability to pursue efficiency by the devolution of authority (e.g. to give local managers effective power to vary pricing policies in response to variations in local market conditions). Among other things the corporations have to solve problems of pricing policy which are inherent in the form of organisation, and particularly in the lack of competition. If the corporations are not to be left to decide what is the 'public interest' when fixing prices (we have argued the case against this), then Parliament must. But what competence have Ministers in such a matter? We should recognise that this problem like many others is largely artificial, created by the existence of the public corporations and most efficiently resolved by their abolition.

An important aspect of these difficulties has recently been exemplified in the attempts to subject the public corporations to more realistic financial discipline. While laudable as an effort to improve earlier confusions, the proposals fail to establish satisfactory criteria for borrowing, investment policy or rates of return. They are not explicit about the social costs and benefits which are held to be relevant, and effectively accept Ministerial (i.e. political) control of pricing policy. These problems cannot be solved by administrative reform, or even by the removal of the statutory monopoly unless this implies a willingness to let corporations that cannot pay their way disappear.

We come finally to stabilisation policy. The influence of Keynes was to encourage the belief that a large public sector might be used as a weapon for promoting economic stability, for instance by increasing nationalised industry investment at times when the level of

[8] Cmnd. 1337, HMSO, 1961.

unemployment showed signs of rising. Actually Keynes' own views were less simple as the following forthright quotation from *The End of Laissez-Faire*[9] shows:

> 'there is for instance no so-called important political question so really unimportant, so irrelevant to the re-organisation of the economic life of Great Britain, as the nationalisation of the railways'.

Post-war history has also refuted this view. The rapid rate of growth of investment by nationalised industries has hardly contributed to stability. This is not surprising: it is not easy to see how large-scale investment of the kind these public corporations require can be geared to the needs of short-term stability. The very existence of these large organisations makes the marginal adjustment of investment more difficult than it need be and interferes with the efficient functioning of the market for capital.

Taken together, these objections to nationalisation seem to me overwhelming. They suggest that public organisations not only create problems in themselves, but frequently have serious repercussions on the economic and social organisation of the community. It is a mistake to regard the issues as unimportant or unworthy of serious discussion, as in the 1963 *Encounter* symposium, or to treat nationalisation as an irrelevance, a sort of coelacanth as Mr P.J.D. Wiles describes it in *The Unservile State*,[10] or to concentrate on administrative and organisational reform like the contributors to *Lessons of Public Enterprise*.[11] The issue of nationalisation is fundamental; the solution is the eventual denationalisation of all activities capable of private operation and the subjection of the rest to all possible competition.

RE-ORGANISATION OF THE NATIONALISED INDUSTRIES

Since the weaknesses of the nationalised industries derive basically from their large size, their statutory monopoly and their susceptibility to misuse for social and political purposes, the cure lies in removing all three. At the least, they should be broken into smaller and competitive units, subjected to outside competition, and required to act as commercial undertakings. If possible they should be returned to private ownership. How?

As a first step, I would propose the appointment of a Select Committee of the House of Commons aided by a permanent secretariat to act not as an instrument for direct control but as a reviewing body for pricing and investment policies. More important, it would decide upon the need, if any, for given nationalised

---

[9] The Hogarth Press, 1926 (the Sidney Ball Lecture, Oxford, 1924); reprinted in *The Collected Writings of John Maynard Keynes*, Vol.IX: *Essays in Persuasion*, London: The Macmillan Press for the Royal Economic Society, 1972, pp.272-94.

[10] London: Allen & Unwin, 1957.

[11] *Op.cit.*

industries to remain in public control.

We might divide the nationalised industries into two groups:

Group 1	*Group 2*
Coal	GPO
Rail Transport	BBC
Gas and Electricity	Bank of England
	Cable and Wireless
	Civil Aviation

Group 2 is the more heterogeneous, the unifying element being that enterprises are all affected by generally accepted social or political factors which influence the most economically satisfactory form of organisation. This is not to say that commercial considerations are not relevant to their operation. Indeed, it is clear that in the GPO and civil aviation, for instance, they are of first importance. Nor does public participation in these services of itself require public monopoly. The need for public access to means of communication, for example, is perfectly compatible with competitive services. The public interest is not less well served because the BBC is in competition with ITV; indeed, more competition, for example by metered services, would improve the situation further. Wherever public enterprise is held to be necessary for this kind of reason, it should be a first principle of public policy to encourage competition in the most equal terms possible with private producers. Furthermore, pricing policies should as far as possible be organised so that payment is related to quantity consumed and is not on a flat-rate basis (as with TV licences). The public subsidy to this form of activity should reflect ideally only its value to government.

DENATIONALISING RAILWAYS AND COAL

In Group 1 it is possible to make more far-reaching proposals for re-organisation. Commercial considerations are here of dominating importance for policy. It should be remembered that the four industries did not come into public ownership as the result of decisions of principle of the kind examined earlier but rather from a combination of intense competition (as in gas and coal) that encouraged the industries themselves to accept controls and of measures of public policy that inhibited competition (such as the Coal Mines Acts and the Road Traffic Acts of the 1930s). These influences contributed far more to the pattern of post-1945 nationalisation measures than doctrinaire insistence on the superiority of nationalisation as a form of economic organisation.

Once created, nationalised industries of this kind can exist for longer than the market would allow them, for absence of the dynamic of competition retards change and inhibits adaptability. The first requirement is therefore that we should get rid of this irreversibility: the prime purpose of the proposed Select Committee would be to keep the possibilities of denationalisation regularly under review.

Let us consider some particular instances. In transport it is clear that the railways enjoy no general monopoly power because of competition from road transport (and airlines). The first requirement is to set about creating the preconditions for 'fair' (efficient) competition between road and rail. This is a difficult task, but the very difficulty is a good reason for us to cease to ignore it: there is clearly much that can be done and some interesting suggestions are contained in John Hibbs' *Hobart Paper, Transport for Passengers.*[12] Dr Beeching's streamlining operations, while welcome as a recognition of a need, must be unsatisfactory in detail pending the creation of such a genuinely competitive background (which would include *inter alia* the elimination of 'common carrier' obligations and of economically unjustified cross-subsidisations). Thereafter, if rail transport still fails to pay its own way, why should the public corporation be allowed to continue? For that matter, if the railways did not prove to have significant monopoly power, why should they remain in public hands even if they can make a profit? It should be the function of the Select Committee to consider such questions, and if appropriate to recommend procedures for orderly denationalisation. There might be local areas in which some monopoly power continued to exist, but these are unlikely to be significant, and would be easily controlled by measures far short of nationalisation. Similarly, if the government itself has a strategic or other interest in particular lines, the appropriate procedure is to furnish specific subsidies where these are needed.

Even more obviously than the railways, the coal industry could and should be returned to a competitive system. The basis of competition was destroyed not by technical factors but by the property laws and the quota legislation of the 1930s. It is time to think about how to recreate a private and competitive market.

LEAVE GAS AND ELECTRICITY NATIONALISED?

Gas and electricity pose more difficult problems since technical factors make the creation of a satisfactory basis for competition difficult. The difficulty of generating a competitive market does not arise out of the size of the production units but rather out of the indivisibility of the distribution network. In practice, in recent years imports of cheap oil have posed problems for the public corporations which have gone some way towards restoring healthy competition and more forward-looking attitudes. (They have also produced successful pressure for heavier taxes on fuel oil.) This new breath of fresh air might be re-inforced by action on the part of the public authorities: the electricity grid, for instance, might be operated independently with individual suppliers selling power to it. But there is perhaps

[12] Hobart Paper No.23, London: IEA, 1963, 2nd Edn. 1971.

more room for debate here than in coal and railways: the costs of creating a market might themselves be high, and it would have to be considered whether unsubsidised public corporations in this field could be left alone once the size of the nationalised sector had been reduced in other directions. Charges for gas and electricity should of course be kept under review by our Parliamentary Select Committee, to prevent misuse of monopoly power.

In recent years, Dr Beeching (in tackling problems of cost) and Lord Robens (in tackling problems of marketing) have shown that the internal organisation of public corporations can be improved in ways that conduce to efficiency. But they are being asked to cure cancers with corn plasters: both the structure of the public corporation and its relations with Parliament and with the rest of the economy place the fundamental problems beyond the reach of internal reform. Even more, they are not to be dealt with by the kind of proposals for administrative reform now proposed by the nationalisers.

The cure for bureaucratic management and political control is not more bureaucratic management or more political control. The only way to ensure that service to the public is put before administrative convenience, spurious social purpose or political party manoeuvring is to press first for competition and second for denationalisation. The solution to the problems of public corporations is to abolish as many of them as possible and to subject the rest to as much outside competition as possible.

2

TEN STEPS TO DENATIONALISATION*

S.C. Littlechild

Professor of Commerce,
University of Birmingham

DEBATE continues apace on the various problems of the nationalised industries and the appropriate measures to deal with them. What can be learned from the experience of the last 40 years to suggest a significantly different approach? What are the achievements of the Conservative Government in its first years of office?

THE LESSONS OF THE PAST

There is broad agreement that the nationalised industries should

(a) attempt to discover the goods and services that consumers want and produce them in the most efficient way, subject to

(b) not exploiting the monopoly power they frequently have, and

(c) acting in the wider public interest (i.e., uncommercially) when called upon to do so.

Yet there are substantial differences of opinion concerning the weight to be attached to these varying objectives and the most appropriate means of achieving them.

The original statutes of nationalisation, embodying the Morrisonian 'arm's length' philosophy (that government did not interfere in day-to-day operations), gave considerable leeway to the managers of the industries. Many economists, however, have always

---

* This chapter was first published in the IEA's *Journal of Economic Affairs*, Vol.2, No.1, October 1981 (Basil Blackwell in association with the IEA).

emphasised the need for explicit guidance on pricing and investment policies. Specifically, they have urged that, in order to achieve an efficient allocation of resources, prices should be set equal to marginal costs and investment projects should be appraised according to a common test discount rate (with appropriate allowance for risk). These rules were eventually incorporated into the 1967 White Paper[1] and re-affirmed, although half-heartedly, in the 1978 White Paper.[2]

Subsequent developments in the economic theory of 'public choice' have cast serious doubt on the adequacy of these rules for achieving efficient allocation of resources. Setting the price of a first-class letter equal to the marginal cost of collecting, sorting and delivering it, for example, does not guarantee that the most efficient methods of collection, sorting and delivery will be adopted. Nor does it ensure that the range of postal services available will be continually updated to meet changing customer requirements. No account is taken of whether the industries have any incentive to adopt the rules, or government any incentive to enforce them. Indeed, the theory of public choice would suggest that the pursuit of abstract economic efficiency is likely to be jeopardised by conflicting political pressures.

And so it has proved. The 1976 National Economic Development Council (NEDO) Report[3] found that the pricing and investment rules had been largely ignored or violated. Despite the initial understanding of an 'arm's length' relationship, governments have repeatedly intervened in the day-to-day business of the industries, either in furtherance of macro-economic policy on demand management or to protect politically powerful groups of employees, customers or suppliers against market forces. The nature, extent and timing of these interventions have been largely unpredictable. In retrospect, it is not surprising that NEDO reported a lack of trust and mutual understanding between government and the nationalised industries, confusion about their respective roles, no systematic framework for making long-term decisions, and no effective system for monitoring performance.

Party Politics Becomes Public Policy

In its 1978 White Paper, the Labour Government re-affirmed its belief in the 'arm's length' relationship and the appropriateness of the 1967 pricing and investment guidelines. But the underlying problems remained. Within a month the Government had to announce a new freeze on electricity prices. Similarly, the incoming 1979 Conservative Government, likewise pledged not to intervene, found it necessary first to peg gas prices then to order a steady rise in domestic tariffs.

---

[1] *Nationalised Industries: A Review of Economic and Financial Objectives*, Cmnd. 3437, London: HMSO, 1967.

[2] *The Nationalised Industries*, Cmnd. 7131, London: HMSO, 1978.

[3] *A Study in UK Nationalised Industries: Their Role in the Economy and Control in the Future*, London: HMSO, 1976.

Investment and finance decisions have been constrained and distorted by external finance limits designed to fight inflation. The allocation of funds has been heavily influenced by political considerations. Thus, National Coal Board (NCB) decisions on pit closures were over-ridden in the face of a threatened strike, whereas nearly 70,000 jobs have been lost at British Steel since January 1980.

It would be wrong to see such policies as the product of ill-advised Ministers or temporarily adverse circumstances. *The problems of the nationalised industries are largely inherent in nationalisation itself*, at least in the form it has taken in Britain. Nationalisation was designed to achieve political ends: to redistribute income and power. *The whole purpose of public ownership is to make the allocation of resources subject to political rather than market forces.* A government which has the power to intervene cannot help but exercise it even despite its better judgement, whenever circumstances seem to require it, that is, as and when it is politically expedient to do so. As the NEDO Report commented:

> 'Ministers do not and cannot in practice keep their involvement restricted within predetermined guidelines'.[4]

The lesson to be learned from the last 40 years of nationalisation is that the real task is not to control the industries but to control government itself. Even welfare economists must now accept the futility of pricing and investment guidelines as a means of ensuring efficiency. And managers must accept that the 'arm's length' relationship is a chimera. The only way to secure substantial and lasting improvements in the industries now nationalised is to restrict the scope for political pressures and to give more weight to the automatic forces of the market. This can be done only by changes in the institutional framework.

CHANGES IN THE INSTITUTIONAL FRAMEWORK

Three aspects must now be considered: the organisational structure, the market environment, and the capital structure.

(a) Organisational Structure

The NEDO proposal of a Policy Council for each nationalised industry, located between the government and the operating Board, received no significant support. It was widely acknowledged that Ministers would not, and could not, delegate their powers to make decisions on matters of major political and public importance. Essentially the same objection applied to the variant proposed by Sir Leslie Murphy (in a lecture to the Institute of Administrative

---

[4] *A Study in UK Nationalised Industries..., ibid.*, p.44.

Management in February 1981), for grouping the nationalised industries into four major sectors (transport, energy, communications and manufacturing) with a state holding company, similar to the National Enterprise Board (NEB), in control of each. A state holding company is unlikely to provide the same spur to efficiency as do private shareholders and the threat of bankruptcy. And there is a danger that competition within each sector will be discouraged in order to facilitate co-ordination and the achievement of plans.

There are, however, other possible changes in organisational structure which would serve a limited but useful purpose. Splitting large organisations into smaller components would make them more manageable and shed valuable light on the performance of the constituent components. Division along regional or municipal lines would facilitate comparison of performance and provide a market (albeit limited) in executive talent. Vulnerability to crippling nationwide strikes would probably be reduced.

(b) Market Environment

The most significant and constructive change in market environment would be the elimination of the statutory monopolies, legal privileges and artificial limitations on entry which still characterise many of the nationalised industries. Competition, whether existing or merely potential, is a vital protection for consumers against such manifestations of monopoly power (or restrictive government policies!) as higher prices, lower quality of service and reluctance to innovate. A competitive market has the added advantage that a government wishing to intervene in pursuit of wider 'social' considerations will have to do so explicitly, making financial provision for the departure from a commercial policy, instead of by 'arm-twisting' and hidden cross-subsidisation. Such an open approach is likely to contribute to more informed public debate.

Valuable though it is, there are limits to what competition can be expected to achieve. Whether or not it is helpful to describe such industries as electricity, gas, railways and telecommunications as 'natural monopolies', it is undoubtedly true that competition there takes a different form. Competing networks are viable only to a limited extent, and competition *for* the market (as with ITV franchises) is not always easy or economic to arrange. There is important competition *between* such industries as electricity and gas, posts and telephones, rail and road transport. Yet the scope for substitution (and hence competition) is wider for some products and services than for others. Coal, gas and oil, for example, are effective competitors with electricity for heating, but not for lighting.

Thus, for many of the nationalised industries, the 'perfect market' beloved by many economists cannot exist. What can and should be done is to ensure that such opportunities for competition as are or might be available are not precluded by artificial restrictions imposed by government.

(c) Capital Structure

Public ownership reduces the incentive to secure profits and removes the threat of bankruptcy. Private ownership would undoubtedly provide a significant spur to managerial efficiency. Capital would be allocated according to market rather than political considerations and intervention would largely cease. To secure these advantages, Mr Enoch Powell and Professor Milton Friedman have advocated immediate and wholesale denationalisation.

There are two main difficulties. First, would the forces of competition, even backed by the Monopolies and Mergers Commission, be sufficient protection against private monopoly power in local electricity and telephone service? (It must be admitted that nationalised industries have not shirked from exercising this power.) Second, would subsidies to private companies (to maintain employment, keep down prices, provide uneconomic services) be adequate and appropriate for furthering the wider public interest?

Joint Ownership is not Enough

Joint ownership is sometimes proposed as a way to deal with such problems by securing the benefits of both private and public ownership. But as long as ultimate control lies with government, one cannot realistically hope to avoid all the problems described at the beginning of this paper. Joint ownership may be useful as a transition measure (as in British Aerospace) but it is not a viable long-term solution. A preferable approach would be to form separate organisations for parts of the industry where considerations of monopoly or the wider public interest loom large, and to defer the introduction of private capital there until progress has been made in the more straightforward areas of the business.

With the external finance limits being tightly enforced, several of the nationalised industries are pressing for access to the private (loan) capital market (as in Telecom bonds), and exploring the possibility of joint ventures with private enterprise (as with rail electrification and the building of gas pipelines). There are significant advantages in such developments, insofar that they may allow worthwhile projects to go ahead which might otherwise be deferred. They should also help to impose tighter financial discipline on the industries, and deter government from excessive intervention. But the rights and responsibilities of the parties may be difficult to define or enforce. If the NCB found difficulty in repaying a private loan, should the government protect the coal buyer, the miners or the private lenders? Loans from the capital market and joint ventures thus cannot be expected to account for more than a minor and well-defined part of a nationalised industry's capital structure.

To summarise, what seems to be required is a policy which

(a) divides the larger nationalised industries with more manageable components,

(b) encourages competition wherever this is feasible, and

(c) transfers to private ownership those parts of the industry where there are no significant problems associated with monopoly or the wider public interest – in short, not complete and immediate denationalisation, but a significant movement *towards* denationalisation.

That Sir William Barlow, former Chairman of the Post Office, has advocated a very similar approach (in a lecture given to the Royal Institute of Public Administration in January 1981) suggests that it could be both practicable and acceptable to the nationalised industries. It is also worth noting that not only Conservatives but also many Liberals and Social Democrats have indicated their sympathy with such kinds of reform.

THE RECORD OF THE GOVERNMENT

The Conservative Government was pledged to a policy on nationalised industries which closely approximates to the one advocated here. How far has it been implemented?

Several substantial achievements have been recorded. Entry into bus and domestic air transport has been liberalised, resulting in new services and lower fares. British Aerospace has been successfully launched on the Stock Exchange with 52.5 per cent of the shares held by the public. BR has sold some Scottish hotels, BL has sold Prestcold and is offering Alvis for sale, and British Gas has been ordered to sell Wytch Farm oil field and its showrooms. British Telecom has been split off from the Post Office, and two organisations are competing for electronic mail. Competition is now possible in the terminal equipment market, and private operators may be licensed to provide courier services and value-added network services. The private digital network proposed by the Cable and Wireless, BP and Barclays consortium has been reported as favourably received, but is still subject to a technical examination, and regrettably there are still substantial limitations on entry into posts and telecommunications.

Powers have been taken to sell shares in British Shipbuilders, BNOC, British Airways, the National Freight Corporation, the non-rail subsidiaries of British Rail, Cable and Wireless and the BT Docks Boards. These are important steps in the right direction, but it is unfortunate that some sales were postponed on the dubious ground that the time was not right. Surely investors are able to look beyond a single year's trading results – if not, ICI would have been out of business by now! – and any remedial action required is more likely to be taken by a private company.

Efficiency at BL and British Steel depends to an uncomfortable degree upon the personalities of the managing directors. In approving the expensive reconstruction and investment plans, opportunities were missed to subdivide the companies and hive off the profitable businesses. Limited progress is now being made in the steel industry, where several joint ventures have been started (Phoenix One and Two), and plans to raise £100 million by privatisation are reported. BL is being divided into four divisions, but piecemeal privatisation has been resisted. Perhaps it would have been desirable explicitly to relate Sir Michael Edwardes' remuneration, like Mr McGregor's, to his achievement in fostering privatisation.

The promise to allow private companies to sell electricity has not been kept. A more significant step *backwards* was the Government's undertaking to limit coal imports, thereby removing an important spur to productivity in the British coal industry and a decisive protection for the coal consumer.

The general picture, then, is of a government mostly moving in the right direction, but by no means as far or as fast as desirable. There is more competition, but the size of the nationalised sector remains virtually unchanged. Considerable scope remains for further imaginative reforms.

THE REMAINING TERM OF OFFICE

The first and most straightforward task is simply to complete the implementation of the Government's existing plans, hence

Suggestion 1: *Sell Cable and Wireless, the NFC, the Docks Board, British Shipbuilders (or part thereof), British Airways (possibly as two companies), a majority shareholding in BNOC, and the remaining half of British Aerospace.*

MANUFACTURING

Progress in the steel industry beyond the privatisation currently envisaged will inevitably depend upon the state of the economy as a whole, but some progress can be made with BL immediately.

Suggestion 2: *Convert the four BL divisions – Cars, Leyland, Land Rover and Unipart – into independent companies. Sell the last two, which are now profitable and the other two if and when they become commercially viable.*

RAIL

British Rail is making urgent requests for capital to electrify its network, yet the evaluation and financing of this proposal are because a substantial part of the rail network is believed to be uneconomic, operated purely for 'social' considerations, while other parts are now or potentially commercially viable. BR is developing separate organisational and accounting structures for its component rail businesses, as has been done for its non-rail businesses. This process should be accelerated and used as the basis for hiving off separate companies, mostly private, which would negotiate with one another commercially. The rights and responsibilities of each would have to be defined with some care, but given the range of alternative modes of transport, monopoly considerations should not be a severe problem.

Suggestion 3:

(a) *Sell BR's non-rail subsidiaries (Sealink, Seaspeed; hotels have begun to be privatised but in a very small way).*

(b) *Form separate subsidiaries for Parcels and Freight, with a view to selling majority shareholdings in each.*

(c) *Divide the rail network (including track, rolling stock and stations, etc.) into two independent subsidiaries: BR (Intercity) and the Social Railway. The former would be a purely commercial organisation, ultimately to be privately owned and free of political constraint. The latter would initially be publicly owned, and partly financed by subsidies for the provision of specified (uneconomic) services. It could well be advantageous further to sub-divide the Social Railway (and perhaps the other companies) on a regional or municipal basis (e.g., Social Rail Scotland, Birmingham Rail Social, London and South East Social Rail, etc.).*

COAL

Several of the NCB mining areas are profitable, even by international standards, but others make heavy losses. Pits in 'politically' sensitive areas such as South Wales are kept open at high cost purely to maintain employment. As with railways, this severely distorts the appraisal of capital projects. The NCB monopoly also gives the miners unparalleled political power.

Suggestion 4:

(a) *Form separate subsidiaries for the 12 mining areas of the NCB and sell the commercially viable ones. Sell shares to miners at reduced prices.*

(b) *Transfer from the NCB (perhaps via the relevant local authority, in order to give some protection to the environment) the rights to mine unexploited reserves, to be auctioned to the highest bidder.*

ELECTRICITY

The electricity industry comprises three distinct businesses: generation, transmission and retailing. By making them more independent, and facilitating competition where possible, it should be possible to intensify the pressure for efficiency throughout the industry and provide better protection for consumers.

Suggestion 5:

(a) *Divide the Central Electricity Generating Board (CEGB) into two (or more) companies, one responsible for generation, the other for bulk transmission.*

(b) *Give the area boards freedom to choose their sources of supply from the CEGB, from private companies or by constructing their own plant. Allow them to buy or lease CEGB power stations located in their areas.*

(c) *Remove the statutory monopolies of the area boards, thereby allowing private companies to offer power for sale.*

(d) *Allow local authorities and major industrial users to negotiate with neighbouring area boards for long-term contracts of supply (as in West Germany).*

Experience in the USA shows that private ownership of electricity utilities tends to raise prices (because they have more incentive, and are protected by local monopoly), but also to lower costs, increase output and stimulate innovation. It seems worth experimenting along these lines in Britain, but avoiding the costs and distortions of the American regulatory procedure.

Suggestion 6: *Sell majority shareholdings in, say, three of the electricity area boards, with preference given to local applicants. Give notice of a reference to the Monopolies and Mergers Commission (MMC) five years after disposal.*

Selling the contracting and appliance activities of the electricity boards, often urged, would not make a very significant contribution to denationalisation, insofar as such activities typically account for much less than one-tenth of turnover. Yet their frequent losses suggest ample scope for improvement in efficiency under private ownership.

Suggestion 7: *Require electricity area boards not privately owned to relinquish their contracting and appliance activities.*

GAS

Like electricity, gas can be seen as three separate businesses (procurement, transmission and retail). It is a much smaller industry than electricity, and how far it is worth separating them or re-introducing separate area boards is not clear. Gas is subject to sufficient competition from other fuels to make its potential monopoly power under private ownership not a major source of concern. The problem lies on the supply side, where the legal monopsony (sole buying) of the Gas Corporation enables it to extract 'rent' from the North Sea oil companies, some of which is transferred to the Treasury by the gas levy. It would seem preferable to allow competition in supply and extract the North Sea 'rents' by auction.

Suggestion 8:

(a) *Sell the Gas Corporation as a single private company. Give notice of a reference to the MMC five years after disposal.*

(b) *Remove its statutory monopsony by allowing oil companies to sell gas direct to major users.*

(c) *With an eye to the future, allow free competition in the manufacture and distribution of synthetic natural gas from coal.*

(d) *Re-negotiate the rights to existing North Sea gas fields and distribute subsequent rights by auction.*

TELECOMMUNICATIONS

Alternative suppliers are already available for customers' equipment, 'value-added' services and international circuits. The private consortium is proposing a domestic business network utilising optical fibres along British Rail track. The 'natural monopoly' of British Telecom is steadily shrinking, and ought not to be artificially preserved where competition is viable.

Suggestion 9:

(a) *Divide British Telecom into five subsidiaries: Terminal Equipment, Network Services, International Circuits, Domestic Network, and Local Distribution, with a view ultimately to selling the first three.*

(b) *Allow unrestricted competition in all areas.*

POST

The Post Office is seriously overmanned and mechanisation is resisted. It also has an extensive portfolio of land and buildings in central city locations which would probably be more valuable in other uses. What is required for the Post Office is an imaginative asset stripper. It is unlikely that this task could be tackled effectively by a public corporation. Under private ownership and stimulated by competition, it is quite conceivable that both price and quality of service could improve throughout the country. Provision should be made, at least initially, for subsidies to outlying and rural areas.

Suggestion 10:

(a) *Identify areas where a 'Social Postal System' might need the support of government and/or local authorities.*

(b) *Sell the remainder of the Post Office, with provision that part of the sale price be available to finance redundancy payments.*

(c) *Exercise the power in the current Telecommunications Act to license all applications to run competing postal services.*

CONCLUSIONS

The existing 'arm's length' framework within which the nationalised industries are supposed to operate is not sustainable in practice. Governments will necessarily intervene in response to short-term political pressures. Creating smaller organisational structures and introducing competition where possible will yield useful benefits, but to ensure that the industries have the incentive and freedom to operate efficiently requires a transfer to private ownership. Accordingly, a move *towards* denationalisation is appropriate for activities where the problems associated with monopoly and the wider social interest are least severe.

The Government has introduced competition in several nationalised industries but has made little progress with the transfer to public ownership. My 10 suggestions for reform could be considered for the remaining term of office. To avoid introducing each suggestion in a separate Bill, it might be possible to introduce a single enabling Bill giving the appropriate Secretary of State power to order the nationalised industry to form and dispose of subsidiary companies for the activities to be denationalised.

If these suggestions were fully implemented, the nationalised sector would be reduced to approximately half its present size. It would still include most of British Steel, half of BL, the 'Social Railway', much of the NCB, the CEGB and most of the electricity area boards, the domestic network of British Telecom, and the 'Social Postal System'. These activities ought not to remain nationalised for evermore but decisions about policy in them can be reserved until experience has been gained with the moves towards denationalisation suggested here.

3

PRIVATISATION: MONOPOLY MONEY OR COMPETITION?

Cento Veljanovski

Research & Editorial Director, Institute of Economic Affairs

The long-term success of the privatisation programme will stand or fall by the extent to which it maximises competition. If competition cannot be achieved, an historic opportunity will have been lost.

JOHN MOORE (1983)[1]

Competition is indisputably the most effective means – perhaps ultimately the only effective means – of protecting the consumers against monopoly power. Regulation is essentially a means of preventing the worst excesses of monopoly; it is not a substitute for competition.

STEPHEN LITTLECHILD (1983)[2]

THE HALLMARK of the Conservative Government's industrial policy has been the transfer of state-owned industries to the private sector. This policy – known as privatisation – has been largely a British innovation which has been 'exported' to many other countries. Despite the economic and political attractions of privatisation there is a widespread view that the Thatcher Government has sacrificed the prospects of more competition in its attempt to withdraw the state from the production of goods and services. This has been particularly true for the privatisation of the basic infrastructure industries –

[1] J. Moore, *Why Privatise?*, HM Treasury, 1983.
[2] S.C. Littlechild, *Regulation of British Telecommunications' Profitability*, London: HMSO, 1983, para. 4.11.

telecommunications, gas, water and electricity. These industries were monopolies before privatisation and have retained significant monopoly privileges after privatisation. The British Government's privatisation programme has raised in the minds of friend and foe alike an unease that whatever the merits of privatisation, it has been driven by short-term goals which have led to 'monopoly mongering'.

The debate now centres on two principal issues. The first surrounds the role of competition in privatisation. The reason why privatisation policy should maximise competition is straightforward. Where feasible it is the surest and most effective means of generating greater efficiency and consumer benefits. Thus future policy must address the question of how to introduce 'effective' competition into the utility industries. The second issue is how the privatised utilities should be regulated so as to protect customers without at the same time creating offsetting inefficiencies and distortions. In this chapter the discussion focusses on the first of these issues. Whatever the specific answers and detailed proposals put forward one factor is clear – government will continue to be involved in the business decisions of these firms.

THE ISSUES BRIEFLY STATED

The decision to sell British Telecom was a watershed in Britain's privatisation programme.[3] It ushered in the Government's commitment to sell all the nationalised industries including the utilities – telecommunications, gas, and the proposed sales of the water and electricity supply industries. These industries raised controversial and complex interrelations between competition, co-ordination, regulation and monopoly. Most of the industries in question have capital intensive co-ordinated networks which many argue are 'natural monopolies'.

Until the 1988 White Papers on the privatisation of the electricity supply industry[4] there was no significant structural reform accompanying the sale of the utilities. Telecommunications, gas, and the proposed sale of water will leave the structures of these industries intact, creating private companies with overblown monopoly privileges.

For several industries, such as the recent privatisation of the British Airports Authority (now BAA plc), a large proportion of revenue derives from a government privilege – duty-free sales of goods. Similarly for the British Airways sale. The commercial value of BA arises not from its ownership of aircraft but from the government allocation of routes and the international cartel

---

[3] For an extensive analysis of the points raised in this section, C.G. Veljanovski, *Selling the State: Privatisation in Britain*, London: Weidenfeld & Nicolson, 1987.

[4] *Privatising Electricity – The Government's Proposals for the Privatisation of the Electricity Supply Industry in England and Wales*, Cm. 322, London: HMSO, 1988; *Privatisation of the Scottish Electricity Industry*, Cm. 327, London: HMSO, 1988.

arrangements which restrict competition.

Many have argued that privatisation has acted to inhibit the introduction of greater competition. This is so for two principal reasons: (a) substantial structural reform of the industry would make the sale more complex, delay it and make it more controversial, and (b) it would reduce the proceeds of the sale. The sale of monopolies by governments has a long pedigree. The entrenching of the private interests of the Monarch and of monopolists dates from the 14th century. Monarchs granted monopoly rights for a large number of industries such gunpowder, saltpeter, salt, pepper, paper, mineral extraction and others[5] as a means of raising revenue.

Yet the scope for greater competition is considerable. If BT had been split up into local telephone companies and functionally into long distance, international and local services, a number of firms could have been created and more direct competition fostered. Yet BT remains a vertically integrated operation which supplies both value-added services (that is, data and information services) and apparatus for connection to the network, and is protected from outright competition by others, except the fledgling telephone company, Mercury Communications Ltd. If British Gas had been restructured as a common carrier without the right to buy and sell gas – that is, operate solely as a transmission company – then it would not be able to wield the power it does now which has already led to a reference to the Monopolies and Mergers Commission.

The failure to break-up these large corporations, either in terms of services and/or regions, has meant that even if competition is permitted they dominate the industry and their size and scope of activities exceeds that justified by the appeal to natural monopoly arguments. It also reduces the effectiveness of regulation and diminishes the capital market and organisational pressures for greater efficiency and customer responsiveness.

Where the Government has attempted to foster direct competition it has mistaken duopoly – competition between two firms – for effective competition and prohibited the entry of new firms willing to provide competitive networks. In telecommunications only two companies are permitted to compete outright in providing basic voice telephony and two-way business and data services. In the electricity supply industry the potentially competitive generation of electricity will be dominated by two large companies formed from the Central Electricity Generating Board (CEGB). Many argue that this is inadequate and that at least eight generating companies should have been formed. Duopoly, especially where it is fostered by government, has the seeds of collusion and hence monopoly abuses. BT and Mercury can collude either tacitly or explicitly not to compete and to charge a higher price. The two new generating companies created in

[5] For an illuminating discussion, R. B. Ekelund and R.D. Tollison, *Mercantilism as a Rent-Seeking Society – Economic Regulation in Historical Perspective*, College Station: Texas A & M University Press, 1981.

the electricity industry can act in the same way.

THE GOVERNMENT'S RECORD

The emphasis given to competition in privatisation has been patchy and variable. In the early privatisations it was not really an issue since the nationalised industries which were sold operated in fairly competitive markets. For the utility industries, privatisation was not the initial policy response – it was the tightening of financial controls, improving management and in some case removing some nationalised industries' exclusive right to provide the service.

Thus, under the British Telecommunications Act 1981, the telephone system was separated from the Post Office, the provision of services by third parties over the telephone network was permitted, and other measures were taken to allow more competition in the supply of equipment such as telephone sets. Mercury Communications Ltd., the second national telephone company, was created to compete with BT. The cable television industry was deregulated, offering the prospect of an alternative telecommunications system which could compete directly with BT's local network monopoly.

Liberalising measures were taken in the gas and electricity industries. British Gas's and the CEGB's statutory monopoly of the supply of gas and electricity respectively was removed. Legislation permitted the private sector to generate and supply electricity and gas to the transmission networks. Both these steps failed to encourage any significant competition for reasons which will be explained later.

In 1983 the then Financial Secretary to the Treasury, John Moore, firmly bolted the success of the government's privatisation programme to the mast of competition. BT was sold in 1984 without any change in its operations and size. In 1986 British Gas was sold as one entity. The latter transferred to the private sector a massive monopoly where the prospects of future competition were remote. There was widespread concern that British Gas could and appeared to be acting as an 'unrepentant monopolist' and that the watchdog, the Office of Gas Supply or Ofgas, did not have sufficient powers to control this giant and to carry out its statutory duty to 'enable competition'.

So far British Gas represents the height of 'monopoly mongering' in the privatisation programme and it, together with the publicity surrounding the bad service which British Telecom has been providing to its customers, has created a consumer and political backlash against monolithic privatisations of the British Gas variety. There is now a greater emphasis on competition.

Is Privatisation the Enemy of Competition?

Privatisation acted as a positive disincentive to introducing more competition and brought a halt to the liberalisation of utility industries.

Telecommunications

Britain probably has the most liberal and competitive telecommunications sector in Western Europe. As a result of the Government's liberalisation policies in the mid-1980s, which followed the Beesley Report,[6] there has been an explosion in the range, number and variety of services provided over the British Telecom network. Nonetheless privatisation, or rather its impact on the Government, has greatly hampered measures to introduce competition in and between telecommunications systems. Yet the scope for *direct* competition is great. Among the utility industries telecommunications is unique because rapid technological progress has made possible direct head-on competition between different telecom networks.

Present telecommunications policy is plagued not by the question 'Is competition possible?' but by whether and when to permit more direct competition between networks and different technologies. The Government, through the Department of Trade and Industry (DTI), has adopted an extremely cautious approach to managing the introduction of more competition, even though the evidence indicates that this would be beneficial. The reluctance to liberalise the telecom sector further is partially explained by the undertaking given to shareholders in the BT prospectus that there would be only two public telecommunications operators allowed to provide basic voice telephony at least until 1990. This is the so-called 'duopoly policy' which carves out for BT and Mercury Communications an exclusive market in the provision of basic voice telephony. It is designed to protect BT from competition and to give Mercury the time to grow into a credible competitor. The only real example of an alternative local telephone company in the UK is the Hull Telephone Department (recently renamed Kingston Communications). In 1986 it made a profit of £4 million on a turnover of £23 million with no equity capital, and is fully financed by a local authority on full market-rate loans. The revenue comes from the sale of its services with no subsidy from BT. Nor apparently has this been achieved by offering customers lower service levels and higher charges. Charges are lower than BT's and much more flexible; the equipment is more modern than BT's and the service quicker. Thus there is evidence that smaller regional telephone companies are more efficient.

The duopoly policy, although applied less restrictively than

[6] M.E. Beesley, *Liberalisation of the Use of British Telecommunications' Network*, London: HMSO, 1981.

originally feared, nonetheless affected other industries. Apart from giving BT and Mercury sole rights to provide voice telephony, the Government decided against permitting the resale of BT capacity. If this were possible people could buy capacity on the BT network and effectively set themselves up in competition with BT by providing dedicated networks to customers. This, in turn, would reduce the ability of BT to cross-subsidise services and to charge monopoly prices. This prohibition was imposed despite the recommendation in the Beesley Report[7] in 1981 that the resale of BT capacity should be permitted.

The duopoly policy also had an impact on the infant cable industry which had hitherto been stifled by broadcasting policy. Prior to 1984 cable networks were permitted only to re-transmit BBC and ITV programmes. In 1984 the Broadcasting and Cable Act liberalised the industry, permitting the new generation of broadband cable systems to compete directly with the BBC/ITV system. It was also the Government's plan that they should compete with BT and Mercury by encouraging cable companies to build systems which could also be telecommunications networks. Even though the underlying reason for deregulating cable was that it offered the prospect of real competition in the one area where BT had a monopoly – the local network – cable operators were prohibited from competing outright with BT. Under current regulation a cable network can provide telecommunications services only if it does so in a joint venture with either BT or Mercury. Thus the new cable networks which were designed to provide both television and telecommunications services found themselves caught in a pincer movement by two sets of government-created duopolies – BT and Mercury on the one hand and the BBC and ITV television cartel on the other. Moreover, the cable sector was disadvantaged by new regulations which required that they cable all their franchise area and place their cables underground.

Privatisation has subverted the original intentions of telecoms policy. Instead of BT being constrained it has expanded its operations into potentially competing telecommunications technology. It has a substantial interest in the new broadband cable systems and under the Intelsat and Eutelsat agreements has the exclusive right to connect with international telecommunications satellites. Privatisation has also been accompanied by an extension of the breadth of operation of the privatised utilities which have diversified into potentially competitive and complementary industries.

The Government remains cautious about injecting more competition. One of the few exceptions to the duopoly policy was that the Secretary of State for Trade and Industry would keep under review the possibility of authorising 'specialised satellite services'. These would use satellites to provide closed telecommunications links between users such as, for example, a major European company

---

[7] Beesley, *ibid.*

linking all its branches with head office. This would pose a competitive threat to BT because its major business customers could use a satellite to by-pass the BT network. In June 1988 the DTI invited applications for *six* licences to provide 'specialised satellite services'. Yet once again the DTI has placed significant restrictions on this competitive threat. They will not, for example, be permitted to impose 'significant economic harm' on BT and only point-to-multi-point services will be authorised. That is, the service will be restricted to, say, transmitting the racing results to all betting shops but the betting shops would not be allowed to communicate with head office or the race track. Again, these restrictions are an attempt to limit the amount of competition in the one area where there is considerable scope for it.

In Professor Carsberg's chapter,[8] he makes plain that his top priority is the promotion of 'effective competition' in the UK telecommunications industry. Yet his ability to do this has been thwarted by the duopoly policy, the DTI and the politicians. If one of the benefits of privatisation is to depoliticise industries and to place regulation at arm's length from the government of the day, then this is a clear breach of the underlying policy. It is also to be noted that under the Telecommunications Act 1984 (sub-section 2(b)) both Professor Carsberg as Director General of Telecommunications *and the Secretary of State* have a duty

> 'to maintain and promote effective competition between persons engaged in commercial activities connected with telecommunications in the United Kingdom'.

The clear evidence from this brief description of telecommunications policy is that the Secretary of State has failed to carry out this duty.

Electricity

The electricity industry will be sold at the beginning of the 1990s. This will be the largest and most complex privatisation. It is the first to involve a major re-structuring of the industry.

The electricity industry can be divided into three components – generation, transmission and distribution. The Central Electricity Generating Board (CEGB) in England and Wales (Scotland and Northern Ireland have their own systems) operates the generation and transmission (the super-grid) sectors of the industry. The local distribution of electricity to customers takes place through 12 more or less autonomous Area Boards (Figure 1). The White Paper proposals will separate the CEGB into three companies – Big-G (responsible for nuclear generation and 70 per cent of its coal-fired generating capacity), Little-G (with the 30 per cent coal-fired fossil fuel generation), and a separate grid company which will run the

---

[8] Director General of Telecommunications.

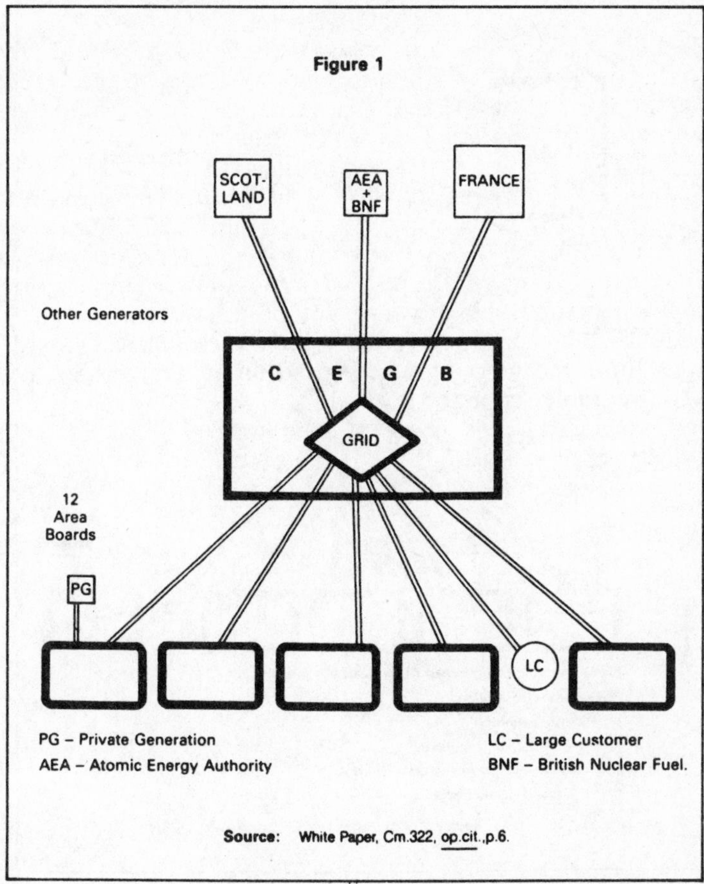

super-grid and will be jointly owned by the 12 Area Boards. The 12 Area Boards will be sold as separate companies and new private sector activity will be encouraged to enter the generation sector (Figure 2).

Whatever one's view about the ideal structure for the electricity supply industry (ESI) it is clear that electricity generation is a potentially competitive industry. All proposals for the introduction of greater competition into generation prior to the White Papers have had two key features:[9]

(i) the break-up of the CEGB's generating capacity into at least eight (broadly) equal generation companies; and

(ii) the creation of a separate 'Nuclear Board' operating nuclear generation directly funded by the taxpayer.

---

[9] A. Sykes & C. Robinson, *Current Choices: Good Ways and Bad to Privatise Electricity*, London: Centre for Policy Studies, 1987; A. Henny, *Privatise Power – Restructuring the Electricity Supply Industry*, London: Centre for Policy Studies, 1987; C. Robinson, *Competition in Electricity?*, IEA Inquiry No. 2, IEA, March 1988.

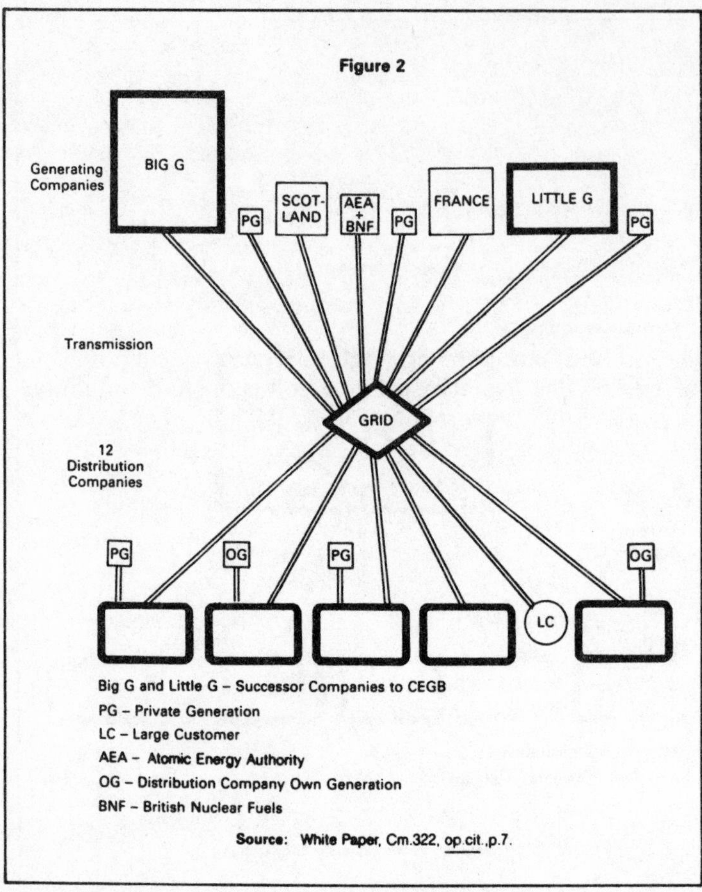

As far as (i) is concerned, the CEGB possesses 38 fossil fuel stations with generation sets in excess of 100 Megawatts. This would enable the creation of around eight generation companies, each with four or five stations of considerable size. Each of the larger stations would have an average capacity of around 6,000 megawatts, which is substantial by, say, American standards. The White Paper proposals simply split the CEGB into two large generating companies which will dominate the industry.

As regards (ii), the Government's commitment to nuclear power is totally at odds with a commercial ESI run on market principles. The plan offered in the White Paper, to place nuclear generation within Big-G, will have profound implications for both electricity tariffs and competition. Recent analysis indicates that in the light of the capital investment and expected financial returns, building new nuclear plants is not a commercially attractive way of generating electricity.[10] The Government supports the nuclear industry because it believes that it is necessary for security of supply and that it will become an

[10]G. Yarrow, 'The Price of Nuclear Power', *Economic Policy*, Vol. 6, 1988, pp.81-127.

economic source of energy in the future. While these reasons carry weight in political minds they must be recognised as yet another example of political second guessing of industrial matters. One of the principal ideas behind privatisation was to de-politicise these industries, leaving commercial decisions to businessmen who are best able to decide how and what to produce. The 20 per cent 'nuclear quota' damages significantly the prospects of fostering new competition in electricity generation. The nuclear sector (run by the largest generating company) will have a guaranteed market protected from effective competition.

The proposed structure for the electricity generating sector in England and Wales has the seeds of collusion and monopoly abuse. The reasons are relatively straightforward:

- the potential gains from collusion are high – electricity has very few close substitutes, so that the market demand curve is highly price inelastic. Therefore the gains from colluding, either explicitly or implicitly, will be correspondingly high;
- competitive forces will probably not be sufficiently strong in a duopolistic market, either to reduce costs dramatically, or to pass on to consumers any gains which did occur;
- the two generating companies will have strong incentives to inhibit new private electricity generating companies by flexing their market power over price and non-price terms to potential consumers of new generating companies.

Regulation will be required to prevent collusion. But competition is by far the surer way.

ECONOMIC CONSIDERATIONS

Adam Smith on Privatisation

It is instructive to start by noting Adam Smith's observation on privatisation.

In the *Wealth of Nations* Smith favoured the privatisation of Crown Lands on efficiency grounds. He believed that

> 'In every great monarchy of Europe the sale of crown lands would produce a very large sum of money, which, if applied to the payment of public debts, would deliver from mortgage much greater revenues than any which those lands have ever afforded the crown'.[11]

According to Smith, private ownership improves productivity and efficiency. He estimated that the productivity of publicly owned land was 25 per cent that of privately owned land. The reason Smith gave is now familiar to economists:

---

[11] A. Smith, *Wealth of Nations* (Glasgow edn., 1776), Oxford: Clarendon Press, 1976.

'The attention of the sovereign can be at best a very general and vague consideration of what is likely to contribute to the better cultivation of the greater part of his dominions. The attention of the landlord is a particular and minute consideration of what is most likely to the most advantageous application of every inch of ground upon his estate.'

Put simply, because private ownership concentrates the costs and benefits of decisions on the owners of capital, they have strong incentives to use resources efficiently.

Some Simple Propositions About Property Rights

For the same reason that Smith gave, privatising a nationalised industry alters its incentive structure. It becomes owned by investors. This is a substantial difference from its position under nationalisation. The idea that the 'people' or the 'taxpayer' owned the nationalised industries was a fiction. The rights could be exercised only through a collective political process which did not recognise any one individual's ownership of these firms. The nationalised industries are better described as 'political firms' which had monopoly privileges, unclear and conflicting objectives, and a myriad of social and regulatory responsibilities. The great influence of politics in the nationalised industries is a matter too often forgotten by economists analysing the difference between public and private enterprise.

One of the major attractions of privatisation is that it takes politics out of the day-to-day operation of these industries. It replaces profits for politics as the dominant factor influencing commercial decisions. But it does not take politics out of the privatisation process or remove it completely from the *regulated* private utilities. The political pressures have altered substantially into more indirect concerns about ownership and through new regulatory agencies set up to control potential monopoly abuses and which function at arm's length from the government-of-the-day. The utility sector still must tread the tricky path between profits and politics.

Private property is the basis of a market economy and of liberty. An essential element in an efficient privatisation policy is that the ownership rights – the equities or shares – can be freely traded amongst individuals. Without the freedom to use and transfer property rights there can be no market and there can be no effective mechanism which ensures that resources are allocated to their highest-valued uses. But while freedom to trade is a necessary condition for an efficient market order, it is not a sufficient condition. There must also be competition.

Monopoly – Natural and Un-Natural

Monopoly as such, whether private or public, is undesirable. If unconstrained it acts to harm consumers and generate losses to the economy. A monopoly operates to restrict output so as to raise prices in order to maximise profits. Thus while a private monopoly may produce goods and services more cheaply and more profitably than a nationalised industry, it does not produce the quantity of goods and services at a price which maximises the welfare of consumers. Monopoly generates other inefficiencies: potential profits are converted into excessive costs, lack of innovation and poor customer service.

There are reasons for believing that a state-owned monopolist behaves differently from a private monopoly. Public ownership is usually accompanied by the goal of universal service which in economic terms implies an output-maximising model of the firm. That is, many nationalised industries may have pushed the provision (rather than the quality and diversity) of output beyond that justified by economic considerations. Yet, as we shall see later, a nationalised industry threatened by the prospect of competition will react in a similar way to a private monopoly – it will attempt to kill off the competitive threat.

In the utility sector the monopoly factor takes on a different hue. The prospect of *direct* competition between different firms in the basic utility industries such as gas, water, electricity and parts of the telecommunications industry is limited by the technology of transmission networks. All these industries have a monopoly element which will not be competed away even in the most permissive market régime, nor would new entry be profitable other than in the short term. This is because the transmission networks of the gas, electricity, water and to a much lesser extent the telecommunications industries are 'natural' monopolies.

A natural monopoly was once defined by economists as an industry where economies of scale existed throughout the range of the demand which was forthcoming at different prices. Recent economic research has redefined the concept as a situation where it is cheaper for one firm to supply the market than production of the same quantity by two or more firms.[12]

In the utility industries this condition is easily derived from the simple technology of transmission. Take the water industry. A water pipe's capacity is roughly proportional to its cross-section, while the cost of a pipe is approximately proportional to the pipe's circumference. If the cross-section area of a pipe is doubled, the circumference is less than doubled; therefore, doubling the volume of water to be transmitted between any two points leads to costs rising by less than 100 per cent. Hence the average costs of transmission

[12] For an excellent introduction to the subject, M. Waterson, *Regulation of the Firm and Natural Monopoly*, Oxford: Basil Blackwell, 1988.

decline as the volume of water transported increases. The electricity industry provides another simple example. The capital and operating costs of the transmission facilities increase in roughly direct proportion to the voltage, whereas transmission capacity increases as the square of the voltage. Thus the larger the transmission lines, the cheaper the transmission costs per unit.

Statutory Monopolies

It is not clear whether these cost conditions were responsible for the historical emergence of monopolies in the provision of gas, water and electricity. The historical record shows that collusive behaviour between competing utilities or government action has played a major role. The claim that competition is not possible in these industries has been greatly over-extended and some argue that many of these industries are not true natural monopolies.[13]

The reality of nationalisation was that it created large monolithic organisations whose size went well beyond any justification in terms of costs. After the Second World War nationalisation went hand in hand with rationalisation whereby hundreds of municipal gas and electricity companies were combined to form national vertically integrated monoliths. British Gas is as a result a unique company since it undertakes everything from the landing of gas to delivery and sale to the final customer.

Moreover, the monopoly position of the nationalised industries was legally protected. Even if cost conditions will only sustain one utility in each locality it leaves open the question of how large that locality should be in the interest of efficiency. Put more technically, when are the economies of scale exhausted? While British Gas's transmission network may have natural monopoly features, it is doubtful that one gas transmission company serving the whole United Kingdom is justified on these grounds.

In many cases the nationalised industry acted as regulator of the industry. It regulated the use of its services, set quality and technical standards and often had the power to license competitors. British Coal is only now losing its right to license private coal-pits. Privatisation has gradually brought an end to many of these exclusive privileges, although this has been a slow and protracted process and has often fallen far short of full competition.

---

[13] J. S. Foreman-Peck, 'Natural Monopoly and Railway Policy in the Nineteenth Century', *Oxford Economic Papers*, Vol. 39, 1987, pp. 699-718; R. Millward & R. Ward, 'The Costs of Public and Private Gas Enterprises in Late 19th Century Britain', *Oxford Economic Papers*, Vol. 39, 1987, pp. 719-737; R. Millward, 'The Emergence of Gas and Water Monopolies in 19th Century Britain: Why Public Ownership?', in J. Foreman-Peck (ed.), *Reinterpreting the 19th Century British Economy*, Cambridge University Press, forthcoming.

FORMS OF COMPETITION

Despite the limited scope for direct competition between different utilities in the same area, considerable scope exists for promoting effective competition in the supply of inputs, equipment, and services to these industries. For some industries the existence of natural monopoly has itself been challenged.[14] Here some of the issues surrounding the introduction of effective competition are discussed.

Technical Change and Direct System Competition

In some utility industries technological change has and does enable the entry of new network providers which have lower costs and which are able to supply a superior service. Technical change can significantly alter the contours of natural monopoly. This is particulary relevant in the telecommunications industry where the extent and rate of technical advance have been phenomenal. Technical change has radically altered other utility industries in the past. In the 19th century the development of iron pipes placed new water companies at a great advantage to the older established ones using wooden pipes. This led to a period of direct competition and falling prices for water consumers.[15]

In telecommunications the development of optic fibre technology, which transmits audio and visual signals as pulses of light, has revolutionalised telecommunications and enabled new networks to offer customers cheaper and better services than the old telephone network. Moreover, this sector can employ a variety of distribution technologies. Thus instead of thinking of a national integrated network, the model of the future is a patchwork of interconnected networks, consisting of telephone networks, broadband cable systems, satellites and other technologies such as microwave systems. The difficulty with present government policy is that it is based on managing the transition. The Government has prohibited some technologies, such as microwave links and satellite master antenna television (SMATV) systems, and protected other new technologies which it believes will eventually succeed. Thus it has vigorously encouraged high-powered satellites (so-called Direct Broadcast by Satellite or DBS) and protected BT from outright competition from other satellite operators. The major issue for pro-competition policy is how to leave as much of this transition to the market.

---

[14] Walter J. Primeaux, Jnr., below, Ch.9: 'Electricity Supply: An End to Natural Monopoly', pp.129-134.

[15] B. Rudden, *The New River Company*, Oxford: Clarendon Press, 1985.

Borderline Competition

Even if direct competition is not possible, one can permit local utilities to compete along their common boundaries for customers. This presupposes that there are a number of utilities operating on a regional basis. In water, electricity and telecoms this is a possibility. To foster this type of competition it is necessary that the local utilities do not have an exclusive territory which is legally protected from encroachment by other operators. The Cable Authority can, if it wishes, grant multiple franchises for each area but has not, as yet, done so. The electricity White Paper[16] contains one brief paragraph which indicates that such competition will be permitted when the industry is privatised.

Inter-Product Competition

Competition can also take place in the product market. British Gas's supply of gas for heating competes with electricity and heating oil. British Telecom could face competition from other types of delivery networks such as broadband cable systems. Other parts of these industries are virtually non-competitive. There is very little inter-product competition in the use of electricity for lighting. Indeed, two-thirds of the electricity supplied is for uses which have no real close or realistic substitutes.

However, apart from the implications for pricing structures and the price controls which have been placed on the privatised utilities, this form of inter-product competition is only indirectly determined by privatisation.

What is important is the way the degree of substitutablity between products and services is reflected in the regulatory framework. A pro-competition policy would attempt to distinguish between the degree of competition faced by the various markets the network industries serve. On this point the regulatory policies which have been devised to control monopoly have been partially sensitive to this. Only the most monopolistic parts of the industry should be price capped and competition should be fostered elsewhere.

Competition for Capital and Control

The capital market provides a number of competitive pressures on a privatised company which do not exist for a nationalised industry. Again the issues are complex and interrelated – involving considerations of structure, ownership restrictions and regulation.

Professor Littlechild has put the point succinctly:

'Competition is possible in the water industry, but it takes place in the

---

[16]Cm.322, *op.cit.*, para. 42.

capital market rather than the product market. The possibility of takeover ensures that each authority is under pressure to run its entire business efficiently and innovatively'.[17]

To the economist the essence of this pressure is captured by viewing the capital market not solely as a source of finance but principally as a 'market for corporate control'.

Private and tradeable shares put pressure on companies for several reasons. First, they lead to specialisation in ownership. Those who own shares in the company do so as an investment and/or because they have knowledge of the industry and particular circumstances in which the firm operates. Secondly, it concentrates the risks and benefits of ownership on those who want to bear them. This has an immediate efficiency effect because shares in a company are allocated to those who can best bear the risks. Thirdly, the ability to trade shares creates a competitive market in ownership which disciplines the management of the firm. In the modern 'public' corporation there is a separation between management and ownership. This has led many to argue that the shareholder-owned company is run for the benefit of its managers rather than for the profit of its owners. But the capital market acts as a discipline on this potential conflict of interests. If the firm performs poorly and has the potential to increase its productivity and profits, then it will find it difficult to raise equity and debt finance. Moreover, those who see the opportunity for improvement will purchase shares with the aim of a hostile takeover which will displace the inefficient management resistant to wealth-increasing changes.

The conceptual link between the capital market and the efficiency of private enterprise, whether monopolistic or not, and regulation designed to foster efficiency has not been fully appreciated in the rhetoric of privatisation and government policy. The capital market is viewed largely as a source of finance for investment at market rates. The impetus for the privatisation of BT arose from the Government's perception at the time that selling BT was the best way of attracting the private capital, on terms which would not be seen as being guaranteed by the Government, which was required to finance BT's modernisation programme. Capital market forces also penalise inefficiency. The privatised firm, whose profits are not sufficient to cover debts and costs goes insolvent. The fear of insolvency acts to encourage prudent profitable investment and sound financial practices. This is often contrasted with the no-fault guarantees of the nationalised industries which saw the taxpayer paying subsidies to cover large losses.

The Conservative Government has, however, remained unwilling to cut all its ties with many of the privatised firms. Of the 13 companies in which assets have been sold to the public only two (Associated British Ports and BP) are entirely free of the reins of

[17] S.C. Littlechild, *Economic Regulation of Privatised Water Authorities*, London: HMSO, 1986, para 1.9.

government. All the rest have restrictions on ownership either in the form of a 'Golden Share' or limits on the shareholding of individuals and foreigners. In 10 of the companies the Government has a Golden Share which can be used to block a hostile takeover bid or one that it finds 'unacceptable'.

These restrictions remained very much in the background until early 1988. The attempt by BP to buy Britoil, both firms being creations of the Government's privatisation policy, led to public concern. The Government has retained the most powerful type of Golden Share in Britoil and Enterprise Oil. It enables the Government to outvote a shareholder with over 50 per cent of the equity and effectively protects the company from a hostile takeover bid. The rationale for this is that oil is vital to the nation. After much speculation over how the Government would use its share and a clear statement by the Chancellor that he would block an unacceptable change in ownership, the bid was allowed to proceed but with conditions imposed by the Government.

The foreign and individual ownership restrictions which have been imposed on many privatised firms are also beginning to bite. Many privatised firms have a 15 per cent limit placed on the proportion of shares which can be owned by any one individual and similar limits exist for foreigners. The latter have already led to the forced sale of Rolls-Royce shares because the 15 per cent limit on foreign ownership had been exceeded. The purchase of BP shares by the Kuwait Investment Office has caused consternation and an official investigation by the Monopolies and Mergers Commission on the grounds that KIO had acquired 22 per cent of the BP equity and that Kuwait is a member of OPEC, the oil price-fixing cartel. Both these examples indicate that there is a frustrated demand for British privatisation equities overseas.

The contradiction inherent in these restrictions is obvious. The major attraction of private ownership is that it subjects a company to the disciplines of the capital market. This operates in two ways: first in the raising of capital which must meet market tests and, secondly, in the prospect of takeover which enables inefficient management to be removed. The Golden Share makes the latter subject to Ministerial approval and thus politicises the issue of ownership and, as we have seen in Britoil's case, commercial judgement. The restrictions on individual and foreign ownership similarly operate to reduce the efficiency of the capital market and the latter in particular ignores the increasing internationalisation of financial markets. Preventing substantial foreign equity to enter some of these industries could restrict their ability to raise funds. Finally, the failure to break-up the utilities and the heavy regulation of these industries weakens the take-over threat and the likelihood that there is a real risk of insolvency. Would a government really let British Gas go out of business because it ran up huge debts?

Competition for Inputs

Competition can also be encouraged in the supply of inputs to the utilities. Most of the utilities are vertically integrated and this process has intensified when privatised. Electricity stands out – the Government proposes that generation be separated from the transmission system.

Yet the energy sector, where most of the industries were nationalised – BP, British Gas, the electricity supply industry and British Coal, has been (and continues because of the Government's commitment to nuclear power) riddled with restrictions on the use of inputs.

Until recently under a government-sponsored 'joint understanding', the CEGB bought 70 per cent of its coal from British Coal at twice the world price. Present policy now faces the absurd situation that an island built on coal must pay more for its own coal than imported coal, and the threat of imported coal must be used to get British Coal to charge a price which reflects its real economic value. Under EC directive, natural gas cannot be burnt to produce electricity. Fortunately both these restrictions have been removed as part of the privatisation proposals for electricity.

As we have seen, the Government, while relaxing a number of important input restrictions, still intervenes. The commitment to nuclear power imposes a high-cost energy source on the electricity industry and has considerable implications for the prospect of private company entry into the electricity generation sector. Under the privatisation proposals for the electricity industry, 20 per cent of electricity will have to be produced from non-fossil fuels. This 'nuclear quota' damages the prospects of competition in the generation sector. While there may be competition to supply nuclear power – the cheapest possibility probably being importing it or the nuclear plants from France – the reality of the scheme is to foster a British nuclear power industry (which in international terms is expensive).

Competition on the Network – Common Carriage

Many of the services provided over utility networks are potentially competitive industries. This is why many economists have advocated that they should become common carriers. The essential feature of the common carrier proposal is that the owners of the transmission network should withdraw totally from the provision of services on the network. The analogy is often made between the operation of the railways and canals during the 19th century – the railways owned both the tracks and the rolling stock; the canal companies only owned the waterways and not the barges. Common carrier status would seek to make the utility companies more like canal companies.

The common carrier solution sees as the major evil of monopoly utilities their ability to deny others access to the system and to extend their monopoly power to the provision of services.[18] By separating carriage from services and requiring the network operators to lease capacity on the network on a first-come-first-served basis, monopoly can be confined and its abuse limited. The service component is thus made competitive.

To implement this solution as part of the privatisation programme would have meant the dismemberment of BT and British Gas into common carrier companies and service providers. Both these companies remain vertically integrated. It is only in the case of the electricity industry that functional separation has been proposed, although the successor companies to the local area boards will be permitted to generate a small fraction of their own electricity.

Common carriage, but not totally separate operation, has been in operation for a number of years. The British Telecommunications Act 1981 liberalised the provision of value-added network services on the BT network, and this has been successful in fostering a significant degree of vigorous competition on the network. However, the story differs in the energy sector. The Oil and Gas (Enterprise) Act 1982, the Energy Act 1983, and the Gas Act 1986 all permit third-parties to supply gas or electricity over the transmission system of the then nationalised industries. These common carriage provisions have all failed to produce competition except in BT's case. The reasons are straightforward – the dominant nationalised utilities thwarted the emergence of competition by predatory practices – namely, by adversely raising the charges for access to the network, and threatening selective discounts to customers that were offered supply from potential entrants.

Oil and Gas (Enterprise) Act 1982

The Oil and Gas (Enterprise) Act 1982, and the Gas Act 1986 failed to encourage competition to the British Gas Corporation (BGC) both when nationalised and as a privatised company. Because BGC is a vertically integrated operation the scope for it to engage in anti-competitive practices has been considerable. The specific problems raised in gas are:

- BGC's access to cheap North Sea gas under long-term contracts signed when it was a nationalised industry with the exclusive right to land gas in the UK. This gives British Gas an artificial cost advantage over new entrants.
- BGC ownership of the gas pipelines enables it to know in advance its potential rivals' intention to supply gas. This gives it time to offer more favourable terms by selective discounting

[18] E. Bailey, 'Contestability and the Design of Regulatory and Antitrust Policy', *American Economic Review*, Vol. 71, 1981, pp. 178-83.

to customers expressing an intention to buy gas from other suppliers. The Director General of Gas Supply has no power to restrict such localised reactive (possibly predatory) pricing practices designed to forestall the entry of competition.

Thus, in the gas 'contract market' (i.e., large users buying in excess of 25,000 therms of gas per annum) British Gas's pricing and common carriage terms and conditions have led to considerable dissatisfaction among industrial users and a Monopolies and Mergers Commission investigation. In addition, industrial customers have also complained that the questionnaire which BGC gives to customers who have expressed an interest in the third-party supply of gas is 'invasive'.

Deficiencies of the Energy Act 1983

The experience in the nationalised electricity industry has been similar. The 1983 Energy Act required two significant things:

- that Area Boards publish the tariffs at which they would be required to purchase electricity offered by private producers; and
- it permitted private producers to use the transmission and distribution networks so that they could supply final customers directly.

Private generators of electricity were paid according to a private purchase tariff (PTT) which was based on the Area Boards' 'avoidable costs'. This in turn was based on the bulk supply tariff (BST) set by the CEGB, which is essentially the wholesale price of electricity. Put simply, if a private generator could supply electricity to an Area Board cheaper than a unit of electricity supplied by the CEGB, it would make a profit.

The immediate effects of the Act are instructive. The CEGB's response to the threat of competition from the private sector was to restructure the BST in a way that made it unprofitable for private generators to supply electricity to the ESI. Essentially it raised the non-avoidable cost component of the BST tariff by the introduction of a new system charge in 1984/85, and in 1987/88 introduced a 'non-marginal energy charge' designed to recoup a fraction of the coal costs attributable to the protection of British Coal under the 'joint understanding' already mentioned (above, p.43). As can be seen from Figure 3, there has been a dramatic increase in the fixed charges in the BST since 1983/84 to 1987/88 from 1 per cent to over 20 per cent of total revenue generated from the BST.

The CEGB, by increasing substantially the fixed (unavoidable) cost component of the BST, effectively reduced the average price paid to private generators well *below* the average cost paid by the Area Boards for CEGB bulk electricity. In 1987 the average price per

Figure 3

The Rise of Fixed Charges in the BST

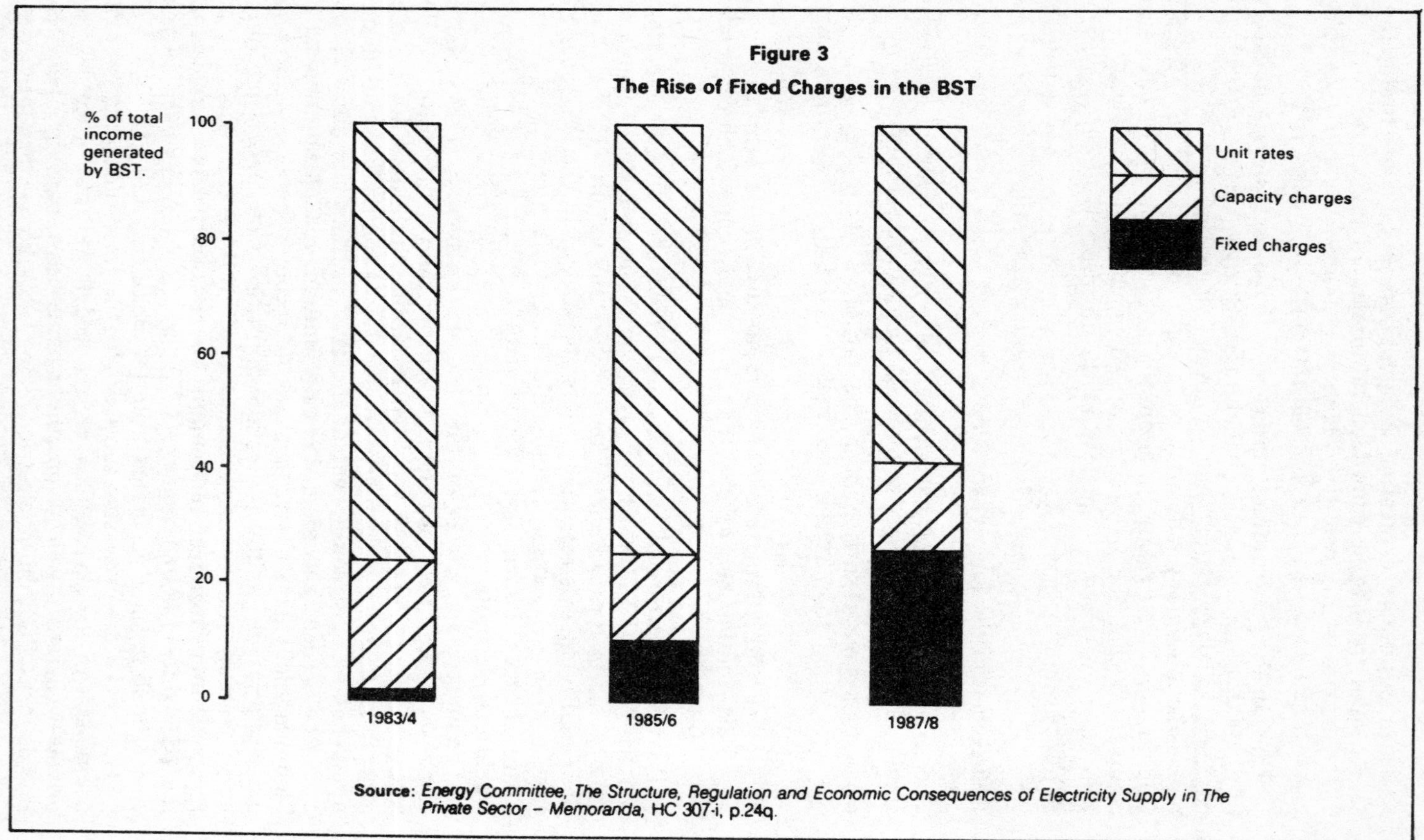

Source: *Energy Committee, The Structure, Regulation and Economic Consequences of Electricity Supply in The Private Sector – Memoranda*, HC 307-i, p.24q.

kilowatt paid by the CEGB to private generators was 2.76 pence compared to 3.66 pence paid for CEGB-generated electricity.

Reasons for Failure

Several lessons for the ESI emerge from this discussion of earlier attempts to foster competition in the generation and transmission of electricity.

First, competition failed to arise because the 1983 Act allowed the dominant competitor to set the terms both of wholesale prices and the PPT for electricity. The CEGB blatantly abused its dominant position and the 1983 Act failed to put in place any effective enforcement which would constrain the CEGB from rebalancing its charges in this way.

The failure of the Act lay not with its principles so much as the belief that the CEGB would act in the interests of its potential competitors. It predictably responded to the removal of its monopoly by raising artificial cost barriers to new competition.

The reaction of the CEGB is empirical evidence that competition is a real possibility in electricity generation. It also reacted in a way that a profit-seeking firm would have been expected to do by engaging in practices which forestalled the entry of new competitors.

The experience of common carriage in the electricity industry confirms Dr Stelzer's view (in Chapter 5) that competition has to be managed by regulation and backed-up by effective enforcement that ensures that it will not be subverted by the vertically integrated transmission operators.

The Scope of Competition

The prospect of competitive supply and sale of electricity arises from a number of sources:

- o through links with the Scottish and French ESIs. These at present have limited capacity but could easily be extended.
- o the ability of the new distribution companies and large industrial consumers to shop around for cheap wholesale electricity.
- o self-generation.
- o common carriage and supply of electricity from Combined Heat and Power Schemes (CHP).
- o new entry into generation.

Some indication of the scope and extent of possible competition in generation can be gleaned from the operation of the US Public Utilities Regulatory Policy Act (PURPA) 1978. PURPA operated in a way similar to the Energy Act 1983. It required electric utilities in the

USA to buy electricity from private generators at a cost below the utilities' avoidable costs whether they needed it or not. For example, if an industrial plant produces surplus electricity, the local electricity distribution company is required to buy it at a price equal to the costs the utility avoids in not having to produce the same amount of electricity. Consequently, those who can generate electricity at a cost cheaper than the utility can make a profit.

Thousands of independent firms have taken advantage of PURPA. In the 10 years of its operation over 24,300 megawatts of capacity has been built. In some regions of the USA, such as California and Texas, independent generators have filled the total demand for new capacity.

In addition, large industrial customers and utilities are permitted to trade electricity over the transmission lines. This 'wheeling' and 'shopping' for bulk electricity supplies has been interpreted in different ways by commentators. There are those who regard it as evidence of the potential for a genuine market in electricity; there are others who argue it has been artificially created by regulatory anomalies, namely rate disparities between States, the temporary excess capacity in generation and Federally subsidised hydro-electricity and other power forms.

Irrespective of these interpretations, the US experience shows that there is considerable scope for competition. The electricity White Papers state that large industrial customers can negotiate freely with generators for bulk electricity, thus raising the prospect of competition. A large user can 'shop' around for the cheapest electricity which will act as a constraint on the ability of the new local electricity distribution companies to behave monopolistically.

COMPETITION FOR THE MARKET – FRANCHISING

Franchising has often been advocated as a method of introducing competition into utility industries. For example, *The Economist* has suggested that:

> 'The Tories ought to think more about franchising ... as a halfway house between state and private ownership for enterprises with an element of natural monopoly. Franchises have worked rather well for independent television stations, though they would have worked better if the levy on profits had been better designed. It is relatively easy to compare the quality of output of the regional networks and to see how well (or badly) they are delivering what they are contracted to produce. Regional franchising might be a more sensible way to supply gas than to sell off the whole corporation'.[19]

The Government has explicitly rejected this form of regulation for the privatised utilities. Yet franchising has been used as a method of regulating utility industries for well over a hundred years both in this

[19] *The Economist*, 12 July 1986, p.18.

and other countries. The first franchise contract for water distribution in France was awarded in 1882 to the Perrier brothers who were given exclusive distribution rights in Paris for a 15-year period. Today about 55 per cent of France's drinking water is supplied by private companies. French water supply franchises take one of two forms. First, the *concession*, where the private company constructs the facilities with its own capital and maintains and operates the system. The contract usually runs for 30 years and prices are set in the contract. The second type of franchise is the *affremage*. Under this arrangement the costs of constructing the water system are borne by local government while the private company manages and maintains it. As with the *concession*, a contractual formula fixes the price at which water can be sold.

In the UK the television, cable television and radio industries are regulated, in part, by franchising.

While there is a range of methods of franchising utilities, one in particular has attracted considerable attention from economists. This is competitive tendering for the right to serve the market at *the lowest price to the customer for a fixed or agreed quality of service.*

This type of auction relies on competition at the licensing stage to eliminate monopoly prices and practices. Applicants are told that the franchise will be awarded on the basis of one criterion – the promise to supply a service of a given quality at the lowest price. Provided there are a sufficient number of applicants and that they do not collude, rivalry between them will ensure that monopoly profits are eliminated.[20]

This method of franchising has several obvious attractions. First, it deals directly with the problem of potential monopoly abuse. Competition for the franchise ensures that monopoly rents are passed on to consumers in the form of lower prices for services they actually want and are not dissipated in complying with regulations and conditions which satisfy the wishes of the regulatory authority but no-one else. Secondly, it is simple and relies almost exclusively on the self-interest of the applicants to define the terms of the franchise and reveal the information necessary to choose the best applicant. All that appears to be required is that the bids are compared in terms of one objective quantitative variable – price. Thirdly, it reduces to a minimum the role played by the regulatory agency, removes its ability to impose onerous terms on the industry which have nothing to do with the control of monopoly and customer protection, and, perhaps most importantly, it minimises the likelihood that the agency will be captured by the industry since it greatly limits the scope for the exercise of discretion.

The initial attraction of franchising is that it relies on competition

[20] This type of auction was first proposed by Chadwick in 1859 based on his observation of water franchises in Paris. (E. Chadwick, 'Results of Different Principles of Legislation & Administration in Europe; of competition for the field, as compared with competition within the field of service', *Journal of the Royal Statistical Society*, Vol. 22, 1859.) It was further analysed in H. Demsetz, 'Why Regulate Public Utilities?', *Journal of Law & Economics*, Vol. 11, 1968, pp. 55-65.

and it is simple. However, the technique has considerable limitations when used to regulate utility companies. It is less likely to be an effective approach where large capital investments have been made since the duration of the franchise will have to be long (15 to 20 years) and hence the spur of competitive re-tendering will be weakened.[21] Moreover, the existing franchise holder will invariably have an advantage over newcomers when the franchise is offered for competitive tender again. A component of the existing owner's costs will be sunk in the sense that they have zero scrap or resale value. The existence of sunk costs enables the existing operator to offer more favourable terms and thereby undercut new applicants for his franchise area who will have to invest in a whole system and must base their bids on the full costs of that investment. This is why some commentators have combined franchising with common carrier schemes.

YARDSTICK COMPETITION

The concept of 'yardstick competition' has gained a certain currency recently. It has been proposed by Professor Littlechild in his report on the economic regulation of privatised water authorities[22] and by Yarrow in this volume.[23]

Yardstick competition is based on a simple and appealing idea. It proposes that the economic performance of each utility be compared either to best practices, or to some weighted average of the performance of all utilities. This information can in turn be used to guide regulatory intervention or assist in setting price controls on the monopoly utilities. Thus the regulator does not have to make guesses at what would be efficient practices but can simply survey the field and make a judgement taking into account inter-firm differences as to which firm requires stronger incentives to improve their performance.

Yardstick competition is not a genuine form of competition but an approach to regulation. It provides the regulator with a number of benchmarks or comparisons useful in making regulatory decisions by using information on the comparative performance of utilities. It can obviously only occur in industries where there are regional utilities.

The relevance of the data generated by the independent activities of separate utility companies depends critically on the extent to which they are similar in other respects. If the range of variables is large which would make one utility different from another, then it is difficult to see how evidence of one utility's performance has any relevance to that of another. In short, the value of this form of

---

[21] For a general discussion of the problems associated with franchising in the context of the UK cable television industry, see my chapter, 'Cable Television – Agency Franchising and Economics', in R. Baldwin & C. McCruddin (eds.), *Regulators and Public Law*, London: Weidenfeld & Nicolson, 1987.

[22] S.C. Littlechild, *op. cit.*

[23] Below, pp.63-64.

regulation (not competition) has been overstated. Unless a reliable technique can be found to strip out the unavoidable differences, yardstick competition does not help.

CONCLUSION

In this Chapter I have attempted to identify the scope for the introduction of greater competition into the privatised utility industries and some of the missed opportunities which have accompanied privatisation. The failure to dismember BT and British Gas and the additional range of restrictions which have been imposed on the ability of new firms to compete either directly with the established utilities or in the provision of services on the network have serious consequences for the efficiency of these industries and the ability to contain their monopoly abuses. It has placed a heavy burden on the regulatory 'watchdogs' which will have the difficult task of controlling monopoly abuses and promoting a range of other objectives. The greater danger is that regulation will grow and its burden will become another source of inefficiency. Perhaps in a decade from now commentators will be talking about the crisis in the regulated industries as they once spoke of the crisis in the nationalised sector.

4

DOES OWNERSHIP MATTER?

George Yarrow

Fellow and Tutor in Economics, Hertford College, Oxford

INTRODUCTION

THE objectives of the British privatisation programme have been many and varied. Among the most important have been the desires to reduce the public sector borrowing requirement, widen share ownership, and effect politically advantageous redistributions of income and wealth. At the micro-economic level, however, the most important of the programme's goals has been the promotion of increased economic efficiency; it is upon this aspect of public policy that I want to focus.

Unfortunately, at the theoretical level, economic analysis has not accorded a high priority to the question of the likely effects of ownership on industrial performance. Despite a number of distinguished contributions from property rights theorists,[1] the literature is much less well developed than in other areas of the subject. Thus, as an examination of economics textbooks will show, it is hard to find convincing *positive* theories of public enterprise behaviour. This may be because of factors such as the complexities arising from international differences in the frameworks of accountability and control for state industries but, whatever the cause, the point is simply that, on this issue, the cupboard is remarkably bare.

[1] A. Alchian, and H. Demsetz, 'Production, Information Costs and Economic Organization', *American Economic Review*, Vol. 62, 1972, pp. 777-795.

The position is rather better on the empirical side. There have been numerous attempts to compare certain dimensions of the relative performance of public and private firms and, although the studies are beset by serious methodological problems, some fairly general lessons have emerged.[2] I would summarise these as follows: where market failures - arising from factors such as monopoly power and externalities - are of minor importance, private ownership tends to have significant efficiency advantages over public ownership, but where market failures are substantial the balance of advantage tends to be small, and may go in either direction. Since public ownership has often been motivated by a desire to correct market failures, this is a not altogether surprising outcome. Nevertheless, it does serve to draw attention to the importance for industrial efficiency of factors such as the degree of competition facing the relevant firms and, in particular, the interactions between ownership, competition, and government regulatory policies in influencing economic performance. The discussion that follows will therefore be focussed upon these links, seeking both to examine the conduct of British privatisation policies to date and to draw lessons for the future.

OWNERSHIP, COMPETITION, AND REGULATION

Ownership 'matters' because the transfer of a firm from the public sector to the private sector (or vice versa) will lead to a change in the incentive structures facing its decision-makers. Viewing this shift from the perspective of agency theory, two effects can be distinguished. First, there will be a change in the *objectives* of the ultimate principals of the firm (shareholders in the case of private enterprise, the voting public in the case of public enterprise). Second, there will be a change in the arrangements for *monitoring* the performance of management: the managers of privately-owned firms will be concerned with meeting the requirements of the capital markets and may be faced with threats of take-over and bankruptcy, whereas public sector managers will concentrate on the satisfaction of ministerial objectives and will not typically be threatened by take-over or bankruptcy.

In private ownership there is a fairly direct link between agents (managers) and principals (shareholders), but the public monitoring hierarchy is more complex, involving *two* major levels of delegation: first to ministers, and then to managers (monitored by ministers). The most fundamental weakness of the latter stems from the interactions between voters and politicians, which occur through a highly imperfect political market-place that is not specifically designed for efficient handling of the types of monitoring issues under

[2] R. Millward, 'The Comparative Performance of Public and Private Ownership', in E. Roll (ed.), *The Mixed Economy*, London: Macmillan, 1982; G. Yarrow, 'Privatisation in Theory and Practice', *Economic Policy*, Vol. 2, 1986, pp.324-377.

discussion here. The public control hierarchy is therefore highly vulnerable to goal displacement, and it this problem that most likely accounts for the observed relative inefficiency of state enterprises operating in competitive product markets.

That ownership matters - in the sense that it affects incentive structures and hence industrial behaviour - is, however, an extremely weak conclusion. Of much greater significance are the issues of how ownership affects incentives and of the magnitudes of the resulting effects. To tackle these latter questions it is necessary to take account of the structures of the relevant markets and of the conduct of regulatory policies, since both these factors will also affect incentives. Moreover, the interactions between the three sets of influences - ownership, competition, and regulation - can be expected to be *non-separable*: the impact of a change in any one will depend upon the other two.

A simple example will serve to clarify this last point. The privatisation of, say, a monopolistic utility can be expected to lead to a greater emphasis on profits. One effect of the shift may be an increase in the internal efficiency of the firm (although it may be noted that this outcome is by no means guaranteed). On the other hand, profit-seeking behaviour may also lead to monopolistic abuses, including higher prices to consumers, and hence to a deterioration in allocative efficiency. The net impact on overall economic efficiency depends upon the relative magnitudes of these two effects, and may go in either direction.[3] In contrast, in competitive markets the allocative efficiency effect either disappears or is of trivial importance: the internal efficiency implications of ownership transfer are dominant and, in the absence of other substantial externalities, privatisation is much more likely to have positive overall effects on economic efficiency. In short, the magnitude (certainly) and the direction (possibly) of the efficiency impact of ownership transfer is affected by market structure and competition.

In the case of monopoly firms, the negative effects of profit-seeking behaviour can be countered, at least in theory, by regulatory policy. Thus, as has happened in Britain, the pricing policies of newly privatised monopolies can be constrained by regulatory interventions. Price controls do, however, have their own difficulties and their impact on economic efficiency is far from being universally benign. For example, in setting allowable prices, regulators will necessarily be influenced by the past performance of the monopolist, including past cost performance. This generates incentives for regulated firms to act strategically so as to influence pricing decisions: firms may pad costs or deliberately bias their investment programmes so as to induce more favourable decisions at the time of regulatory reviews. Moreover, in the absence of long-term contracts - and here it is worth noting that a five-year guarantee on price is a relatively short-term

---

[3] J. Vickers, and G. Yarrow, *Privatisation: An Economic Analysis*, Cambridge, Mass.: MIT Press, 1988.

contract in industries such as telecommunications, gas, electricity, and water - there may be under-investment arising from what is known as the *policy credibility problem*: firms may fear that at some point in the future policy-makers may partially expropriate investors by reneging on the implicit regulatory bargain by, for example, setting prices at a level that does not produce a market return on *sunk* investments.

For monopolies, therefore, regulatory policy has to confront the problem of avoiding the unfavourable incentives generated by cost-plus pricing decisions whilst simultaneously providing adequate long-term profit guarantees to private investors.

INFORMATION AND ASYMMETRIES

Underlying the often unfavourable trade-offs in this area is a fundamental information problem. In reality, *policy-makers have to deal with not one but two monopolies*: monopoly in the supply of the product and monopoly in the supply of information. Most economic analysis has focussed upon the first but in many ways it is the latter that is much the more important. Given perfect information, the formulation of regulatory policy is relatively trivial. Indeed, it is probably for this reason that price controls often appear seductively attractive to those familiar only with elementary economic analysis, which tends to be based upon assumptions of perfect information. It is imperfect information that leads to substantive incentive problems and, from this perspective, monopoly is a particularly unfavourable market structure because of the power it accords to managers in the control of information flows to regulators and shareholders alike.

The information point will immediately be obvious to anyone familiar with recent developments in agency theory, but it is not a new one. In his early critiques of socialist planning Hayek pointed out the difficulties of providing incentives for firms to discover and reveal information in centralised resource allocation systems. With good information, centralised decisions would be relatively straightforward - although there might be difficulties in processing large volumes of data - but to assume that such information is readily available is simply to beg the important question. Unfortunately, as I will argue below (p.60), privatisation policy in Britain appears not to have accorded sufficient weight to this Hayekian message.

REGULATION

As with ownership and competition, the conclusion that 'regulation matters' is a trivial one. What is required is much more detailed analysis of (a) the economic consequences of the various regulatory options that might be available to deal with strategic behaviour, problems concerning the credibility of policy, and the like, and (b) the interactions among regulatory policies, the type of ownership, and market structures. For example, depending upon the accompanying legislation, privatisation of a monopoly utility could easily lead to a diminution of information flows to monitors, rendering control of management more difficult. Similarly, information flows to both capital markets and regulators will be affected by market structure. Thus, competition is important not only because of the direct effects of rivalry amongst firms but also because it tends to improve the information available to monitors and regulators, which in turn facilitates the development and implementation of more efficient managerial incentive structures and regulatory policies.

I conclude by noting that incentive problems in industries such as telecommunications, gas, electricity, and water are inherently difficult to resolve because of the nature of their technologies. These make it harder to establish effective competition than in other sectors of the economy and, in the absence of competition, poor information is likely to impair the emergence of favourable incentive structures. That is, monopolisation of information flows means that there is no quick and easy 'regulatory fix' that can be used to resolve the difficulties. It should be noted, however, that although policies on ownership, competition, and regulation may not have substantial impacts when considered individually, their cumulative effect may be much weightier. If the aim is to improve industrial efficiency, the key to success lies in taking account of the interdependencies among ownership, competition, and regulation and using these links to get each strand of policy working in the same direction.

THE DEVELOPMENT OF GOVERNMENT POLICY

Phase I: Summer 1979 to Summer 1984

In this section I will first describe and then briefly evaluate some of the main policy developments that occurred between 1979 and 1984.

Ownership: The first phase of the privatisation programme involved the transfer to the private sector of firms that operated in reasonably competitive product markets. Some of the sales were clearly motivated by Public Sector Borrowing Requirement (PSBR) objectives. The 1979 disposal of stock in British Petroleum, for example, had virtually no effect on agency relationships and incentives, and can be viewed chiefly as a revenue-raising exercise. In most cases (Cable and Wireless, National Freight, Amersham, British Aerospace, Britoil, Enterprise Oil, etc.), however, whatever the underlying objectives, incentive structures *were* materially changed and, because of the nature of existing market structures, in the majority of these examples a presumption in favour of private ownership could readily be justified on both theoretical and empirical grounds. Despite some unevenness in their subsequent performance records, the post-privatisation evidence broadly supports this judgement.

Competition: In industries retained in the public sector, a number of measures were taken to increase competitive pressures on the incumbent firms. These included the Transport Act 1980; the Telecommunications Act 1981; the Oil and Gas (Enterprise) Act 1982; and the Energy Act 1983. The record has, however, been mixed. Deregulation of express coach services led to a period of intense competition, but the publicly-owned incumbent firm (National Express) was able to retain its dominant position. Nevertheless, deregulation has had durable effects on performance and, among other things, rivalry between coach and rail services has been intensified. Similarly, in telecommunications the 1981 Act led to a significant increase in competition in areas such as apparatus supply.

On the other hand, the liberalising measures designed to foster competition in the gas and electricity industries have had little practical effect. The 1982 and 1983 Acts removed a number of statutory barriers to entry, but significant new competitors to the publicly-owned corporations did not come forward in the subsequent years. The principal reason for this outcome was *not* that the incumbent firms were publicly owned - the transportation and telecommunications legislation was, for example, more effective - but rather that the legislation failed to weaken the considerable market power of British Gas and the Electricity Boards. Statutory entry barriers were removed, but very substantial non-statutory barriers were left intact. What was required was strong pro-competitive regulation of terms of access to transmission and distribution facilities but, while the objectives of the legislation were laudable, the technical implementation was flawed. Unfortunately, this lesson was not learned in time for the subsequent 1986 gas privatisation, which has perpetuated the deficiencies of the 1982 Act (below, p.62).

Regulation: Because the early privatisations were restricted to reasonably competitive industries, the Government correctly did not consider it necessary to establish new regulatory structures for the firms concerned. Developments in regulatory policy were therefore focussed upon the remaining nationalised industries. Here the approach was a more vigorous application of the principles laid down in the 1978 White Paper on the nationalised industries,[4] based upon the steady tightening of the financial constraints imposed upon the public sector. The result was a clear improvement in the productivity performance of those corporations that faced competition in product markets (an improvement that in some cases, of which British Steel is the most notable, was quite dramatic). However, the effect on productivity of tighter financial constraints in the utility industries

---

[4] *The Nationalised Industries*, Cmnd. 7131, London: HMSO, 1978.

was less marked.[5] As might have been expected, it was much easier for public corporations in these sectors to meet the constraints by increasing prices, thereby attenuating the impact of the policy on internal efficiency performance. In principle this adjustment could have been blocked by price controls but, as I argued in the previous section, the monopoly nature of the industries makes it hard for policy-makers to avoid cost-plus pricing decisions.

Evaluation: The 1979-84 experience contains a number of immediate lessons for the conduct of public policy. The first is that market structure is of central importance for incentives and performance. Where markets are reasonably competitive and are free of major externalities, privatisation requires little in the way of accompanying regulatory legislation. The incentive for efficiency and consumer benefits are quickly improved by the transfer of ownership to the private sector. In these conditions, however, performance can also readily be improved by the imposition of tighter financial constraints on publicly-owned firms. Thus, perhaps the most important benefit of privatisation in such cases is, that it raises barriers to the sorts of political intervention in enterprise decision-making that, in the past, have been a major source of sub-optimal monitoring. In other words, privatisation allows more credible longer-term commitments to be made for effective managerial incentive structures.

Second, where incumbent firms have considerable market power, the intensification of competitive pressures in the relevant industries must rely upon strong, pro-competitive, regulatory measures. The removal of statutory entry barriers is, by and of itself, likely to be inadequate. In other words, certain aspects of regulatory policy should be seen as a complement to, and not as a substitute for, other measures to promote competition. In such circumstances the technical detail of regulatory policy is likely to be of considerable importance.

Third, irrespective of whether the firm is publicly or privately owned, the regulation of monopoly is an inherently difficult exercise. The greater the degree of monopoly the greater the difficulty, not least because of the information problem. Thus, and again irrespective of ownership, the most important goal should be to improve the flows of information to monitors. Here privatisation may or may not help. The creation of thousands, perhaps millions, of principals introduces public-good problems in the market for the acquisition of information but also gives some of the new owners much more direct incentives to acquire relevant information (generally, the major participants in capital markets are much more geared up to searching for and processing information than government departments). What is more certain is that greater product market competition will tend to increase information flows and to improve the effectiveness of performance monitoring, whether

[5] R. Molyneux and D. Thompson, 'Nationalied Industry Performance: Still Third Rate?', *Fiscal Studies*, Vol. 8, 1987, pp. 48-82.

by owners or regulators.

Competitive Pressures and Regulatory Structures

I would argue, then, that in the utility industries, the analysis indicates that the path to better performance lies in the simultaneous development of greater competitive pressures and stronger regulatory structures. For the reasons stated, each of these developments is difficult to achieve if the two policies are conducted independently of one another, and if policy is restricted to tinkering with pre-existing structures. Compare, for example, the dismal effects of the 1982 and 1983 legislation on the gas and electricity industries with the effects of tighter financial constraints on publicly-owned monopolies. Rather, somewhat more radical surgery is required in these industries.

The discussion thus far also helps to show up the limitations of some of the measures - such as the introduction of more private debt finance into the balance-sheets of nationalised industries - that were actively considered in the period after 1979. Ultimately, such finance would have been backed by Treasury guarantees and, as a consequence, would have had relatively little impact upon the agency relationships between government and managements and hence upon managerial incentive structures. Nor would it have been more than a single step in a long journey towards increasing competition and improving information flows. For example, the product market position of, and information flows from, British Telecom would not have been materially affected by such measures.

Phase II: Autumn 1984 to Autumn 1987

One of the factors distinguishing the second phase of privatisation policy from the first is the increased importance attached by the Government to share-ownership and distributional objectives. Although of great significance in the wider political and economic contexts, it is not the issue with which I am primarily concerned, and this section will therefore concentrate on the second principal distinguishing characteristic of Phase II, *viz* the transfer to the private sector of public monopolies such as British Telecom and British Gas. What, then, can be said about this bold step, which represented a radical shift in the nature of the privatisation programme?

The first point to re-emphasise is that, in these types of industries, there is little in either economic theory or evidence to indicate that we can proceed on the basis of a presumption that ownership transfer *per se* will lead to significantly improved economic performance. Monitors of a private monopoly confront broadly similar problems of information and incentive to those facing monitors of the performance of public monopolies. While private sector agency relationships may reduce the degree to which managers displace the goals of owners, divergences between the private and public interests can lead to offsetting burdens. In the absence of competition, alignment of the private and public interests depends upon regulatory policy, which likewise suffers from the deficiency of information associated with monopolisation.

In practice, of course, what we have witnessed since 1984 has not been a transfer of ownership *per se* but rather privatisation accompanied by a series of measures on competition and regulation. Changes in competition and in regulatory policies could have been introduced in the absence of privatisation but, as already noted, these would have had to have been somewhat more radical than the measures introduced since the 1978 White Paper to have had significant effects on the performance of the utilities. I do not want to dwell upon these alternative approaches, but simply note that the Oil and Gas (Enterprise) Act and the Energy Act could each have been framed in ways that would have rendered them substantially more effective than they turned out to be, and that the delegation of certain regulatory functions (e.g. in pricing and the promotion of competition) to agencies less dependent upon Ministers would have been an obvious option. It is ironic that such an option for the electricity supply industry was considered by a Conservative Government in the mid-1950s and was rejected on grounds that, among other things, it would reduce Ministerial powers!

Coupling competition and regulatory policy reforms with transfer of ownership, as has been done since 1984, has both advantages and disadvantages. On the plus side, privatisation clearly opens up opportunities to consider other policies afresh, free of many of the encumbrances that arise when more piecemeal changes are considered. Thus, privatisation marks a sharp break with the past and forces *comprehensive* re-evaluation of future possibilities. In practice, substantial strategic re-assessments are often difficult to arrange in the absence of major exogenous events. On the other side of the coin, there is the danger that preoccupation with the transfer of ownership - particularly since it contributes to the Government's objectives other than increased economic efficiency (e.g. fiscal, distributional, and share ownership goals) - will lead either to the neglect of competition and regulatory policies or to the explicit overriding of efficiency-enhancing measures whenever they come into serious conflict with other objectives. Unfortunately, there is evidence that this is precisely what has happened in Britain.

In both the telecommunications and gas privatisations, for example, options based upon restructuring the public corporations were rejected. This decision facilitated flotation and the early realisation of sales proceeds, and placated the existing management of British Telecom and British Gas. In both cases, however, it has reduced competitive pressures and impaired the ability of regulators to establish better incentive systems. Structural changes would not, of course, have offered an easy escape route from all the problems associated with these industries: as noted above, many of the latter are inherent in the technologies concerned, which preclude a swift transition to effectively competitive markets. It would have been possible, however, to introduce competitive pressures more quickly and, perhaps more significantly, to weaken the information monopolies that underly so many of the incentive problems.

As a consequence of past decisions, some of the less desirable economic effects of regulation are now becoming more visible. The situation is rather better in telecommunications than in gas, largely because of the existence of Mercury and the faster pace of technological change. Moreover, the Director General of Telecommunications has been pursuing an active pro-competitive policy, exploiting his formal powers to the maximum extent to ensure movement in the desired direction.[6] Although my own views about the consequences of British Telecom's privatisation are now more optimistic than they were in 1984, current public concerns about the quality of BT's service are drawing attention to the type of question that policy-makers failed adequately to address in the initial stages.

By way of an illustration of the difficulties, it can be noted that a regulated monopolist facing fixed, controlled prices will have incentives to supply levels of service that are sub-optimally low at the given prices. By so doing, the firm can reduce its costs but, unlike in a competitive industry, customers cannot easily switch to competitors offering a better price-performance combination. Hence, the revenue consequences of poor service quality are relatively small. If regulators had perfect information they could enforce the optimal level of service on the firm, taking into account the costs of providing different levels of service. To solve this problem, however, a regulator would need considerable information about consumer preferences and the firm's cost conditions, which will be difficult to obtain in a monopolised market. Hence, in the absence of competition, regulators will be driven to considerable involvement in the detailed decision-making of the firm upon the basis of relatively poor information (which it can be noted was one of the criticisms of the framework of accountability and control for the nationalised industries). The resulting solutions are therefore unlikely to be entirely satisfactory.

British Telecom's Licence: a Problem for the MMC?

A second regulatory issue that will soon be with us concerns the revision of the original British Telecom licence, including amendment of the price-control formula. Possibly a reference will be made to the Monopolies and Mergers Commission (MMC) in 1988, but it is by no means clear what approach the Commission would take in considering the problem. Its public interest guidelines are broadly framed and it is not a body that is specialised in telecommunications or regulatory economics. In effect, the Government has delegated important aspects of policy-making to the MMC, leaving the future direction of regulatory policy in an uncertain state. There are, however, strong incentives for strategic behaviour by profit-seeking

[6] Brian Carsberg, 'Injecting Competition into Telecommunications', below, pp.81-95.

regulated firms and, if there are to be adequate incentives for investment and service quality, it will be difficult to avoid cost-plus pricing decisions, and the prospect that they will weaken the internal efficiency of these private utilities. Moreover, the trade-offs in these areas have been worsened by the failure to restructure these industries and by the limited degree of competition which has occurred.

As already noted above, the position is worse in the gas industry than in telecommunications. British Gas was not required to provide separate accounts for different parts of its business and its dominant position in the product market is buttressed by access to low-priced supplies under the terms of its early southern basin contracts. As a result, even an actively pro-competitive regulator will find it difficult to increase the competitive pressures operating on British Gas. Problems arising from poor information and limited competition in the gas industry were vividly illustrated in the summer of 1987 by the dispute between the Director General of Gas Supply and British Gas over the former's rights to inspect purchase contracts and by the conflict between industrial consumers and British Gas over pricing behaviour in the (unregulated) contract market for industrial users of gas.

Summary

To summarise, in the second phase of the privatisation programme the Government failed to implement sufficiently strong measures to promote stronger competition in the utility industries and to take proper account of the regulatory problems that were and are likely to emerge in the longer run. The latter are, in turn, likely to be exacerbated by lack of competition. Much of the detailed conduct of regulatory policy has been delegated to Oftel, Ofgas, and the MMC, and Oftel's record (e.g. in the Mercury interconnection decision) gives ground for hope that some at least of the initial deficiencies in the regulatory frameworks can be corrected over time. It was by no means inevitable that Oftel would take an actively pro-competitive line but, fortunately, under Professor Carsberg's direction, it has done so.

Nevertheless, much remains to be settled, particularly by the MMC, and my own view is that the existing division of regulatory responsibilities leaves something to be desired. Put bluntly, I do not believe that the existing guidelines, procedures, resources, and organisation of the MMC are adequate for its allotted task. Moreover, in the gas case the initial legislation and authorisation were so anti-competitive that Ofgas and the MMC will find it difficult substantially to improve matters.

THE FUTURE

While the decisions of Oftel, Ofgas, and the MMC (and, in the case of airports, the Civil Aviation Authority) will have a crucial bearing on the performance of existing regulated monopolies, in this section I will focus upon Government policy on the privatisation of monopolies that, at the moment, are still part of the public sector. The two most important of these are the electricity and water industries, although the Post Office should also be borne in mind in the longer term. Other candidates for privatisation include steel, coal, and the railways, but in these latter cases the existing public corporations either already face strong competitive pressures or could readily be exposed to such pressures by straightforward policy measures (eg. liberalisation of the domestic coal market). The problems surrounding the privatisation of steel, coal, and rail are therefore connected more with financial viability than with competition/regulatory issues and, in the interests of brevity, they will be set aside in what follows.

The basic 'transportation' services of both the electricity and water industries are supplied under cost conditions that can reasonably be characterised as naturally monopolistic. Although it is conceptually possible to imagine separation of the provision of transportation services from the activity of supplying electricity and water to final customers - by introducing comprehensive common-carrier systems, for example - the complexity and costs of the resulting contractual arrangements, particularly when set against the likely benefits, are almost certain to rule out this solution, at least for any but very large customers. Most retail purchasers will therefore continue to face a single supplier.

YARDSTICK COMPETITION

The important point to note, however, is that because most final customers face a single supplier does not imply that competition in electricity distribution and water supply is infeasible. The common belief to the contrary arises from an overly restrictive view of competition that focusses only upon the final product market. In practice, however, competitive processes include rivalry in areas such as technological progress and cost reduction - which are frequently of more importance for consumer welfare in the longer term than price/output choices - and it is quite possible to create such rivalry among local monopolists. One means of doing this is via franchise bidding, but an alternative approach, based upon what is known as yardstick competition, is likely to prove more relevant for the industries in question.

Yardstick competition requires that allowable prices for a given distribution company (Area Electricity Board or Water Authority) be set with reference to performance data from *other* distribution companies. Thus, if one company is able to reduce its costs faster than its rivals elsewhere it is allowed to retain part of the profitability benefits, even in the longer term. Yardstick competition replicates the rivalry among firms in competitive product markets and, like competitive markets, can reconcile strong incentives for internal efficiency with prices that do not deviate far from unit costs: cost-plus pricing and its associated difficulties are (at least in part) avoided, yet the benefits of performance improvements are passed through fairly automatically to consumers.

British privatisation policy towards the electricity and water industries offers an excellent opportunity for the introduction of yardstick competition, and hence for Britain to take an imaginative step forward in the development of pro-competitive regulatory policies. Electricity distribution and water supply are regionalised, so that existing organisational structures (unlike in telecommunications and gas) are already well suited to the approach. To develop yardstick competition properly, however, it will be necessary for the Government to be much more explicit than it has been in the past about the principles that will be used when variations in the initial price-control formulae come to be made.

That it is desirable to condition regulatory decisions in one firm on performance information from other firms follows from one of the most basic theorems of agency theory.[7] This states that optimal incentive contracts - and regulation can be viewed as a means of influencing firms' incentives - should link an agent's rewards to all relevant information about potential performance, not just the performance of the agent himself. Put another way, electricity distribution companies and water companies may be monopolists in their own regional product markets but, because of similarities among these markets, information flows are *not* monopolised: the performance of one company contains information signals that throw light on the opportunities available to other companies. It follows that the Government has quite correctly resisted the proposal that has been made from certain quarters that existing Area Electricity Boards should be amalgamated into a single distribution company. This would increase the monopolisation of information and would be about the most anti-competitive measure that could be taken in connection with the privatisation of electricity.

LOCALISED COMPETITION

In the electricity supply industry, I have thus far touched only upon policies towards the distribution side of the industry. In policy debate there has been a tendency to place much more emphasis on the future of the CEGB than on the future of the Area Boards, but in

---

[7] R. Rees, 'The Theory of Principal and Agent', *Bulletin of Economic Research*, Vol. 37, 1985, pp. 3-26 and 75-95.

some ways I believe this is misguided. With the right incentives, independent, privately-owned distribution companies would seek lower-cost sources of supplies, which would increase competitive pressures in wholesale (bulk) markets. Even with a dominant bulk supplier in control of the national transmission system, new competitors would be able to supply directly to the distribution companies by connecting generating sets to area networks - new entry is not entirely dependent on access to the national grid - and such localised competition could have very powerful effects on the CEGB's behaviour in general, and on its investment performance in particular. Nevertheless, the future shape and regulation of electricity generation and of the high-voltage transmission system are matters of some importance for the performance of the industry, and it remains to consider what steps might be taken to increase competition further in bulk markets and enhance regulatory effectiveness.

THE AWKWARD TRADE-OFF BETWEEN COMPETITION AND INTEGRATION

It is frequently argued that electricity transmission is a natural monopoly but that electricity generation is not, and hence that the two activities should be separated, with responsibility for transmission assigned to a single public corporation or regulated private company and generation split among a number of competing private companies. There is, however, a certain amount of question begging in this line of argument and it is appropriate to sound a warning note. First, we should ask for evidence to support the proposition that such a solution is likely to be more efficient or competitive than the alternatives. Where in the world do we observe separation of transmission from generation together with effectively competitive bulk electricity markets? I fear that the answer to this question is a short one. Second, at a more theoretical level, the operation of integrated supply networks involves numerous external effects - the costs of supply of any one firm, for example, are directly dependent on the activities of others - and gives rise to complex contractual problems when large numbers of firms are involved.

In practice, therefore, in systems composed of many firms we typically observe quite a large measure of co-ordination in respect of such matters as station despatch, maintenance scheduling, and investment planning. Taking account of these problems, therefore, it may be the case that, taken together, electricity generation and transmission are indeed naturally monopolistic, or at least naturally oligopolistic. This would certainly explain the limited nature of the competition that is found in supply systems around the world but, whether true or not, the point is simply that the question should not be begged.

I would argue, therefore, that to presume that the separation of generation and transmission, together with the creation of several independent generating companies, would lead easily to effective competition in bulk electricity markets is a dangerously simplistic position. As we know from the study of other industries, many of which have market structures less conducive to collusion than electricity supply, there is no simple link between numbers of firms and economic performance. The outcome could, for example, be an unregulated cartel which, from many perspectives, might be the worst result of all.

None of the above points can be viewed as decisive arguments against some restructuring of generation and transmission. They do indicate, however, that great care should be exercised in evaluating the options. In particular, I would caution against any attempt to deregulate bulk markets quickly based upon the creation of several generating companies of roughly equal size. Indeed, in the early post-privatisation period at least, radical structural remedies are likely to impose a rather more severe regulatory burden than some of the alternatives.

Grounds for Optimism

Despite these problems, there are few grounds for pessimism about the prospects for increasing competition in the event that the Government eschews comprehensive re-structuring of the CEGB, particularly if the lessons from the telecommunications and gas experiences are learned. The pressures from privatised Area Boards have already been mentioned, but other, re-inforcing measures are also possible. In such an event (absence of comprehensive re-structuring), the two aims of policy should be to (a) weaken the CEGB's information monopoly, and (b) reduce barriers to new entry. The first could be achieved by divestiture of some of the Board's generating assets. Even if only a fraction of existing capacity were disposed of in this way, as Mercury has shown in the telecommunications industry, small competitors can have salutary incentive effects on much larger, dominant firms and can provide regulators with extremely valuable information as to what is and is not feasible in economic performance.

Equally significantly, it would be possible to lower barriers to new entry into electricity generation. Unlike British Gas, the CEGB does not have access to its major input on terms that are more favourable than those available to potential competitors. To the contrary, the Board's past dependence upon supplies from British Coal places it at a cost *disadvantage* relative to potential competitors, and even if coal markets are liberalised it would take some time for the differential to disappear. This still leaves entry barriers arising from the CEGB's dominant position in the market and, should it be retained, its ownership and control of the national grid. In the past, and despite the existence of the Energy Act 1983, the Board has impeded new entry by structuring tariffs in such a way as to make the terms available to rival suppliers (from the Area Boards) considerably less favourable than those available to the CEGB. In other words, the

Board increased the spread between its own average wholesale/bulk prices and the prices that could be obtained by its potential rivals. Regulatory policy would therefore have to guard against this type of behaviour and ensure equitable access to transmission facilities where this was desired. How can this be achieved?

RIGHT OF SUPPLY

Clearly, what is required is regulation to limit the differential/spread between CEGB bulk prices and the prices available to rival generating companies. Apart from ensuring access of rivals to the transmission system at regulated rates and preventing the use of 'lock-in' wholesale tariff structures based, for example, on the levying of tariff components unrelated to demand, one simple way forward would be to create a right for new producers to sell *directly* to the CEGB at prices similar to those charged by the CEGB to Area Boards less a regulated allowance for transmission costs. This right to supply electricity to the CEGB would obviate the necessity for a new producer to engage in simultaneous, perhaps complex, contractual arrangements with the CEGB and distribution companies. The contract would be between the supplier and the CEGB only, and the latter would have an obligation to purchase any supplies offered at the designated, market-related rates. This obligation would impose a competitive penalty on the CEGB; this penalty may be viewed as a means of offsetting its strategic advantages deriving from dominance, incumbency, and control of the grid. Another way of looking at the proposal is to think of it as requiring that, in return for its control of the grid, the CEGB would be compelled to act as an electricity broker with a regulated spread between its buying and selling (bid and ask) prices.

Given that the CEGB would be unable to widen the spread between bid and ask prices, the only way of deterring new entry would be for it to lower its own wholesale selling (ask) prices. Thus, whether or not entry actually took place, the threat of potential competition could exert a strong downward influence on bulk prices. If new producers were more efficient than the Board they would find entry profitable; if not they would stay out of the market unless the Board was charging excessive prices. This is exactly the result that is desired.

Creating rights to sell to the CEGB (i.e. establishing a put option) would also involve fewer problems of co-ordination than some of the alternative proposals that are based upon comprehensive re-structuring of the industry. Consider a private producer with marginal operating costs at a particular moment of x per kilowatt hour (kWh) facing a buying price of y per kWh, where y is less than x (if y is less than x, it will be unprofitable for the company to offer supply). Suppose further that, for whatever reason, the CEGB's own marginal operating cost is z (some figure which is less than x). In such circumstances, cost minimisation requires the private producer *not* to supply power to the system, yet the put option implies that supply is profitable. This does not mean, however, that minimum costs will not be achieved since there is clearly scope for mutually beneficial trade (yielding a maximum joint pay-off of x-z).

Thus, if the CEGB pays the producer a sum equal to y - (x+z)/2 not to supply, both will be better off by an amount (x-z)/2 compared with the position where the producer exercises the put option. It should be noted in particular that (a) the CEGB itself has profit incentives to achieve the least cost production pattern, (b) the rival producer is guaranteed a return of at least y - x (regulation provides an effective fallback position in the event of failure to agree), and (c) similar arguments will apply in the cases of scheduled maintenance periods and longer-term investment planning. Thus, co-ordination benefits can be achieved without jeopardising competitive pressures in the industry.

I do not want to suggest that the type of proposal just outlined solves all or most of the regulatory problems on the generating side of the electricity supply industry. Rather, it is intended to illustrate the sorts of steps that could be taken to increase competitive pressures in the absence of major restructuring. Nevertheless, I believe that in current conditions entry threats could have a very powerful influence on prices and performance, and recent experience in California and Massachusetts provides (albeit indirectly) some supporting evidence for this view. There are many ways to skin the cat, and we need not despair of competition even if the more drastic proposals for the future of the industry are not implemented.

CONCLUSIONS

The transfer of ownership to the private sector is most likely to have beneficial effects on managerial incentives and industrial performance where product markets are competitive and reasonably free from other externalities. Most of the early privatisations in Britain satisfied these conditions, and the subsequent records of the companies involved are generally good, with some spectacular successes. In the utility industries, however, the position is much less clear and much depends upon accompanying policy measures to promote competition and improve regulatory processes.

Competition is important not only because of its direct incentive effects on firms in the industry but also because it tends to generate more information which can be used by the owners of a firm to improve performance monitoring. Better information also contributes to the effectiveness of regulation, helping to overcome the incentive problems associated with cost-plus pricing controls. In turn, regulatory measures can be used to strengthen competitive pressures in the utility industries. This is important because, as a result of technology and cost conditions, these pressures will tend otherwise to be relatively weak.

The key to improved performance in utilities, then, is to get competition and regulation working in tandem to provide improved information flows and better incentive structures. If this can be done the benefits of privatisation will be increased. On the other hand, if competition and regulation are neglected, the effects of privatisation on industrial performance are likely to be disappointing. There is little in theory or evidence to suggest that regulated private monopoly is a particularly attractive industrial structure.

To date, Government policy has been distinctly less pro-competitive than would have been desirable, and regulatory policies and structures contain many weaknesses. This is particularly true of the gas privatisation, in which a competitive and regulatory framework was established that might almost have been designed to show private ownership in its least favourable light. There are now encouraging signs that the importance of competition has been more fully recognised, but I am less convinced that as yet both the limitations and potentialities of regulatory policy have properly been understood, despite the availability of a rich experience of regulatory problems in the USA and the unfolding lessons of Oftel's work.

5

PRIVATISATION AND REGULATION: Oft-Necessary Complements

Irwin M. Stelzer

Director,
Energy and Environmental Policy Center,
Harvard University

PRIVATISATION seemed, at first, a beguilingly uncomplicated policy: sell off state-owned enterprises to private investors, then sit back and watch bureaucratic, fossilised institutions become lean, mean competitive machines devoted to serving the consumers. And this formula proved quite workable in the highly competitive oil industry and the more-or-less competitive airlines industry.[1]

But when it came time to put the telephone, gas and electricity industries on the block, the Government found itself with a problem it had not foreseen – or, more precisely, had refused to face. What policies were to be adopted toward industries which, at the time of their privatisation, had monopolies of their markets? Worse still, what policies should it adopt toward industries with strong natural monopoly characteristics?[2] Even if we recognise recent Chicago-school warnings that such monopolies are far rarer than we once thought them to be – technology has destroyed many such monopolies in the past decade or so – some remain. It is simply uneconomic at present, for example, to run two sets of electric wires or gas mains into most consumers' houses, or to build duplicate power grids. And even in industries where competition is emerging – between Mercury Communications Ltd. (the new telephone company) and British Telecom, and between both of these and the new

[1] The presence of the IATA cartel, nationalistic restrictions on competition, and the existence of route awards dilute the force of competition in aviation.

[2] Such monopolies exist not because of legal restrictions or financial power, but because their technical characteristics are such that only one firm can economically render service. (James C. Bonbright, *Principles of Public Utility Rates*, New York: Columbia University Press, 1961, p.11.)

broadband cable systems – substantial elements of monopoly power exist. Companies operating in those industries, freed of the political constraints implicit in state ownership, would be able, in the absence of some other regulatory constraint, to raise prices to levels that would yield supernormal profits.

CAPITAL MARKET DISCIPLINES

Critics of the privatisation programme were quick to argue that, however powerful the case might be for transferring assets from the public to the private sector in industries where competition was workable, there was no point in doing so with monopoly enterprises. This argument is wrong, for two reasons.

First, even monopolies are more likely to operate efficiently in the private than in the public sector. This is not because managers of public enterprises are less able, less efficient or more venal than their private sector counterparts.[3] Rather it is because investor-owned companies must, in the end, subject themselves to the discipline imposed by capital markets. Capital for new plants cannot be conscripted; it must be wooed. Only if investors feel that demand is adequate to produce revenues that yield a fair, competitive return will they make capital available. Compare this with government-owned enterprises. Their managers can often persuade Ministers to make taxpayers' money available to fund unneeded nuclear plants, or uneconomic coal-mines. Conversely, they may fail to obtain funds for economically appropriate modernisation programmes, as the Government permits other, macro-economic goals (tax policy, inflation policy, etc.) to prevail.

In short, decisions about investment in and prices to be charged by state-owned enterprises are often made with little reference to the true economic costs of those decisions. This might result in over-investment (electric) or under-investment (telecoms modernisation); it might result in prices set well above marginal costs in order to avoid more direct tax increases – the Central Electricity Generating Board (CEGB) often resisted Ministerially-imposed price increases as being unnecessary – or below marginal cost to please powerful political constituencies (gas prices were long based on average rather than marginal costs, stimulating wasteful use).

It is true, of course, that similar errors are possible in the private sector. Some of America's electricity utilities, for example, under-estimated the demand-dampening effects of the post-OPEC increases in their prices, and overbuilt generating capacity. But in these cases the perpetrators of the error bore the costs of their mistakes: equity holders suffered large losses, and some managements

---

[3] In the United States, for example, the state-owned Power Authority of the State of New York is generally regarded as being as well-run as any privately-owned electric utility.

were removed.[4] Ministers and public enterprise managers typically pay no such price.

UTILITY REGULATION

A second reason why it made sense to move ahead with the privatisation of state-owned monopolies was that a tool existed for capturing the efficiency-enhancing benefits of private sector reliance on capital markets without conferring monopoly profits on investors. That tool is regulation.

Unfortunately, direct regulation is a tool with which Britain is both uncomfortable and unfamiliar. Uncomfortable, because a 'free-market' government dislikes such direct interference in pricing and other business decisions; because the possibility of effective regulation might reduce the proceeds from the sell-off; and, finally, uncomfortable because the adversarial process associated with such regulation, at least in America, seems too lawyer-dominated for a country accustomed to having its disputes settled by right-thinking gentlemen, out of the view of the public. Unfamiliar, because the long period of state ownership made it unnecessary for British policy-makers and academics to learn the tools of the regulatory trade.

This unfamiliarity was reflected in Britain's first two moves to privatise enterprises with substantial monopoly power. In the case of British Telecom, the Government missed an opportunity to introduce a significant degree of competition into many segments of the telecoms markets. Instead, it chose to create a totally new, smaller, second company, Mercury Communications Ltd., and hoped that the duopoly would perform more like a competitive than a monopoly industry. While the competition between Mercury and BT has indeed produced some economically salutary results – not least the driving of individual prices more closely into line with costs, as BT responded to Mercury's cream-skimming[5] – the duopoly solution surrendered many possible advantages. This is an industry in technological flux, one in which new entrepreneurs can develop services and pricing packages that permit them to threaten incumbents in many markets. It is one in which cable companies could, in the absence of government restrictions, compete with traditional telecoms services. These advantages have been lost to British consumers, at least so far.

British discomfort with 'America-style' regulation was also reflected in the Government's rejection of a regulatory scheme based on the regulation of profits. Here, it had some basis for its actions.

---

[4] The extent to which irresponsible regulators bore some responsibility for these errors is much debated in America. (J.P. Kalt, H. Lee and H.B. Leonard, 'Re-establishing the Regulatory Bargain in the Electric Utility Industry', *Discussion Paper*, Energy and Environmental Policy Center, Harvard University, 1987.)

[5] For a good discussion of cream-skimming, Alfred E. Kahn, *The Economics of Regulation: Principles and Institutions*, New York: John Wiley & Sons, 1971, Vol.II, pp.221-246.

Traditional cost-of-service regulation, as it is known in America, sets prices by adding to operating costs incurred by the utility in some selected ('test') year, an allowance for profit, usually computed as a return on the monies prudently invested in the business.[6]

Such a system has the obvious defect of any administered cost-plus pricing régime: the incentive to keep costs down is weakened by the ability of the firm to pass its costs on to consumers. Indeed, under certain circumstances – when the allowed return on capital exceeds the cost of that capital – a perverse incentive to over-invest is created.[7]

BT AND PRICE REGULATION

Rather than attempting to offset these defects in profit regulation by building in safeguards long-familiar to American regulators,[8] the Government devised its now-famous RPI-3 formula, under which British Telecom could not increase charges for the use and ordinary maintenance of an exchange line, and charges for dialled calls within the UK, by more than the increase in the retail price index, less three percentage points.[9] This use of price rather than profits regulation was seen as a way of providing BT with an incentive to lower its costs, since increased profits resulting from such cost reduction would accrue to the owners of that enterprise.

And so they have. But these increased earnings now appear to have come, in part at least, from costs saved by degrading the quality of service. This outcome is qualified by other factors which may also be responsible for this, such as the recent industrial action and the inevitable problems associated with converting a state-owned monolith into a customer-responsive private enterprise. So price regulation, like profits regulation, contains perverse incentives: price regulation creates pressures to reduce quality of service; profit regulation, which normally allows a reasonable return, somehow defined, on investment, does little to encourage cost reduction. Price regulation, consequently, inevitably involves controlling quality by setting service standards, whilst cost regulation involves the review of the prudence of the regulated entity's expenditure. Neither chore is an easy one.

Indeed, the consumer – and particularly the small residential customer who has little alternative but to rely on BT – has probably been saved from even greater deterioration and higher prices only by the skill and adaptability of Professor Bryan Carsberg, OFTEL's

---

[6] A fuller description is in my 'Britain's Newest Import: America's Regulatory Experience', *Oxford Review of Economic Policy*, Vol. 4, Summer 1988.

[7] Henry Averch and Lelan L. Johnson, 'Behaviour of the Firm Under Regulatory Constraint', *American Economic Review*, Vol. 52, December 1962, pp.1,052-1,064.

[8] These safeguards, which include review of the prudence of the costs incurred and the investments made, are far from perfect instruments. As with many tools, their effectiveness depends on the skill of the user. (Kahn, *op. cit.*, *passim*).

[9] For details, see periodic *Reports* of the Director General of Telecommunications.

Director General. Faced with the problems implicit in the duopoly structure and price, as opposed to profit regulation, he has moved in two directions. First, he has attempted to introduce or encourage competition wherever his remit permits. For example, he has tried to correct the horrendous deterioration of call-box service by allowing competitors to offer alternatives to BT's service. Second, he has begun to supplement price regulation with profit regulation, examining BT's earnings to see if they contain a sufficient monopoly component to warrant revision of the RPI-3 formula (bearing in mind that the –3 was arbitrarily selected).

REGULATION OF BRITISH GAS

The Government's scheme for the regulation of the privatised British Gas Corporation had even greater infirmities than its early telecoms scheme. To understand why, one must understand the political dynamics of this privatisation effort. Most important was the determination of Peter Walker, then Secretary of State for Energy, to achieve two political objectives: maximisation of the financial proceeds from the share offering, and maximisation of the number of people who would become British Gas shareholders. To achieve these goals, and a hoped-for advance in his career (in the event, he ended up in Wales), he had to satisfy the City that Sir Denis Rooke, the Chairman of British Gas, would remain in charge of British Gas, and that the regulatory régime would operate with a light hand.

To keep Rooke he had to agree to privatise BG in one piece: Rooke threatened to resign if 'his company' was vertically dismembered. So Walker missed the opportunity to inject competition into the gas business by hiving off the grid, and permitting producers of gas to compete directly for the patronage of industrial customers and retail distributors, confident that they could move the gas from field to burner tip on reasonable, non-discriminatory terms.

Having eschewed reliance on Adam Smith's invisible hand, Walker and the Government refused to substitute a strong-armed regulator. Instead, they carefully limited the powers of the Office of Gas Supply (Ofgas), the new regulatory agency, even denying it access to vital cost and other accounting information. To BG's gas monopoly they added an information monopoly. This helped the share price, but not the consumer.

ELECTRICITY PRIVATISATION: MAXIMISING COMPETITION

Fortunately, the current Secretary of State for Energy, Cecil Parkinson, has done better for consumers of electricity. Determined not to repeat Walker's error, he has ordered the Central Electricity Generating Board (CEGB) to be broken up into separate generating, transmission and distribution units. And he has created two generating units to compete for the patronage of the 12 area boards. Furthermore, by making the grid an independent unit, he has opened the generating sector to new entrants. If American experience is any guide, there is reason to expect that several new entrepreneurs will enter that business, building plants to meet Britain's rising demands for electrical energy, and competing to sell their output.

Consider, for example, the fact that the managements of area boards will inherit a stock of capital equipment with an extremely long remaining life. No matter how efficient the manager, his range of choice will be limited by the decisions of his predecessors, some of which decisions may seem unwise in light of current circumstances. To use relative current average costs – a figure affected as much by historic as by current decisions – as a measure of the relative efficiencies of current area board managements does not make sense under these circumstances.

Nor would apparently less complicated comparisons of single components of cost necessarily be meaningful. One area board might have seemingly higher power supply costs because its customers demand greater reliability of supply, precluding reliance on lower-priced, interruptible supplies; another may have higher costs than other boards in one year, but lower costs the next, depending on relative prices in fuel markets.

Unfortunately for those who abhor regulation, however, competition cannot be sufficiently workable in all aspects of the electricity supply industry to obviate the necessity of some regulation. The transmission grids remain a monopoly; and each of the area boards will still control most customers' access to supplies of electricity.

So the problem of devising some regulatory plan remains. Because there will be 12 separate area boards, George Yarrow and others have proposed use of 'yardstick competition'.[10] Under this plan, the cost performance of area boards would be compared, one with the other, and high-cost boards forced to become more efficient. Unfortunately, yardstick competition suffers from two serious weaknesses. First, it is simply too weak and remote a goad to performance, especially as compared with more traditional, head-to-head competition. Second, as John Landon has so tellingly demonstrated,[11] the problems of correcting cost data for differences beyond the control of management – it is one thing to dig a trench in the countryside, quite another to do so in London – are sufficiently daunting to make the range of error so wide, the cost comparisons so imperfect, that the authorities would not be able sensibly to order changes in prices or practices on the basis of such shaky evidence alone.

---

[10] Yarrow, in this volume, above, Chap.4, pp.63-64. Also Stephen C. Littlechild, *Economic Regulation of Privatised Water Authorities – A Report Submitted to the Department of the Environment*, London: HMSO, January 1985.

[11] John H. Landon, 'Report to the Iowa State Commerce Commission on Measuring Productivity of Electric Utilities', Washington DC: National Economic Research Associates, Inc., 1983.

STEPS TOWARDS MAXIMISING OPPORTUNITIES FOR COMPETITION

So, if electricity consumers are to be protected adequately, the Government will be forced to take two steps. The first, and the one most congenial to market-loving, monopoly-hating economists, will be to maximise the opportunities for competition. This will necessitate several steps:

- New entry into the generating sector will have to be encouraged by the removal of artificial impediments to such entry. Potential generators will have to be given the right to use the cheapest available fuels – imported coal and natural gas. In the case of the latter, this means access to the monopoly gas grid, so that they can strike the best possible deals with British and foreign gas producers.
- Bidding systems will have to be established to permit generators to bid for the custom of area boards. Because the area boards have been given the option of building their own power stations, and will have sufficient monopoly power to pass their costs on to customers, steps must be taken to prevent them from choosing power they themselves generate over cheaper, more efficient supplies offered by independent power producers. In short, regulatory supervision of bidding systems will be necessary to prevent uneconomic self-dealing.
- Operators of the grid will have to be regulated to assure customers that all potential generators have fair, equal and non-discriminatory access to transmission facilities. And, because it is a monopoly, the prices charged by the grid will have to be reviewed to make certain that they do not yield extortionate monopoly profits.
- The area boards will have to be regulated to make certain that prices of captive, small customers do not subsidise prices charged to larger industrial customers. The latter will have alternatives, ranging from self-generation to 'shopping' outside their areas for supplies. And they are sufficiently vocal and politically potent to supplement their economic power with political power. The area boards will, therefore, be sorely tempted at times to offer these customers uneconomically low prices (below marginal cost), secure in the knowledge that losses can be recouped from customers – residential and small commercial establishments – who have no practical alternative to relying on the area boards.

If the customer is to be protected, in other words, competition will have to be fostered where it is feasible and regulation relied on where it is not. The electricity industry will have to be regulated more thoroughly than British Gas, and with more attention to profit control than was (initially) the case with British Telecom. This will involve blending price control techniques with profit limitations. Fortunately, this is possible: it can be accomplished by initially setting prices on a cost-plus-reasonable return basis, and establishing some RPI-X formula, to prevail for 3-5 years. If the required company can raise its profits by lowering its costs, its shareholders will benefit; if not, they – and not customers – suffer. New price levels can be set every 3-5 years, based on then-prevailing levels of operating and capital costs. This combination of US and British experience can provide both an incentive to efficiency and protection of consumers against long-sustained charges.

Such a solution is, of course, an imperfect substitute for competition. But where competition is unattainable, it ill-behoves policy-makers to avoid tough choices by singing the praises of Smith and Hayek, instead of recognising the need for practical alternatives to non-existent or extraordinarily weak market forces.

PART II

COMMUNICATIONS

6

INJECTING COMPETITION INTO TELECOMMUNICATIONS

Bryan Carsberg

Director General of Telecommunications

THE REGULATORY FRAMEWORK

I WANT to begin by briefly setting the scene with a description of the regulatory framework for telecommunications. In 1984 British Telecommunications plc was effectively privatised with the sale of 51 per cent of its equity. The post of Director General of Telecommunications, which I hold, was established by the Telecommunications Act 1984, and this Act also set down my functions and duties. The Act also provided for the establishment of the Office of Telecommunications (OFTEL) to help me carry out my functions. OFTEL is a non-Ministerial Government Department. This means that it operates independently of Ministers so that it can carry out its activities free from political pressures.

The regulatory framework is embodied in a system of licences. All operators of telecommunications' systems must have licences and the licences contain rules about price control, fair trading, social obligations and other matters. I carry out my job largely through enforcing the rules in the licences and by amending the rules in accordance with the procedure set down in the Act.

I believe that the regulator should aim to develop an appropriate conceptual framework for his activities and to make it explicit. One reason for this is that regulators have to make difficult decisions in which strongly conflicting vested interests are involved. When you have to make decisions in that sort of situation, you have a better chance of making good decisions if you have developed clear concepts to guide you. Another advantage in having clear concepts is evident from the perspective of those firms which are regulated. It helps the regulatee to anticipate the direction of future decisions and this creates confidence in the regulatory arrangements and an ability to plan more effectively for the future.

Competition Highest Priority

The cornerstone of my conceptual framework is given to me by the Telecommunications Act 1984. It says that I have the duty to promote the interests of customers in the price, variety and quality of service. This is an obvious priority and is constantly in my mind as I make decisions. The next step is, perhaps, a less obvious one, though it is extremely important and is also set down in the Act. It is that I should 'promote' the interests of customers, as far as possible, by 'promoting competition'. Whenever I become aware of a problem – some respect in which users are not getting as good treatment as is desirable – I ask first whether the problem can be alleviated by bringing about more competition or better competition. I believe that competition is frequently the best way of securing customers' interests. For example, a regulator can rarely establish with certainty how efficiently – including at how low a cost – a particular service can be provided. Competition will seek out the answer to that question far more effectively than a regulator can. Competition gives firms and individuals the opportunity to succeed by showing that they can operate more effectively than others. Furthermore, telecommunications has a rapidly evolving technology with many opportunities for developing innovative services. Competition is especially important in such a situation: under a monopoly, innovative services may develop slowly but under competition firms develop innovative services slowly at their peril.

Incentive Regulation

The second main leg of the conceptual framework is to use efficient kinds of regulation, regulation with the right incentive properties, for areas of activity where competition has not yet developed. In an industry like telecommunications, competition cannot exist everywhere, and in areas where it can exist it takes time to become fully developed. If competition is not available to protect consumers from the abuse of monopoly power, regulation must do so. I believe that effective regulation to prevent the abuse of monopoly power is regulation that mimics competition: for example, if a firm behaves in a way which would result in losses in a competitive environment, it should experience losses in a regulated environment also. Two main types of regulation are required to prevent the abuse of monopoly power. The first is the enforcement of fair trading rules to prevent the use of monopoly power to drive out competitors in businesses where competition is established; and the second is regulation to prevent the direct abuse of monopoly power by charging excessive prices or denying customers benefits that could be secured in a competitive market.

PROMOTING COMPETITION

The promotion of competition can be particularly difficult in industries like telecommunications which involve networks and therefore very high fixed costs, with the incremental costs of meeting additional requirements of customers low in relation to average costs. In this situation it may be difficult for competition to survive because an established firm can meet an increase in output more cheaply than a new firm and the largest firm can afford to undercut smaller rivals. That question-mark against the viability of competition does not mean that competition should be ruled out altogether. A competitor may believe that it can operate more efficiently than the established dominant company and it should perhaps be given the opportunity to show what it can do: customers are likely to benefit. Furthermore, a network business is often not as monolithic as the first description implies and ways often exist – as, I believe, they do in telecommunications – of enabling competition to be realistically feasible. I shall discuss these issues in more detail below. Before I do so, however, I want to say a little more about competition in some parts of the telecommunications industry where economies of scale are not so dramatic and where competition therefore can flourish more quickly and more freely.

Competition in Apparatus Supply

The apparatus supply business was one of the first parts of the telecommunications industry to be liberalised.[1] Almost no reason exists for limiting competition in that part of the industry. Apparatus supply was a monopoly for many years before the Government developed a policy of liberalisation, mainly because apparatus needed approval for connection to the telephone network, to avoid problems with safety and impairment of the general quality of communication experienced by users; this gave British Telecom control over the market. Even so, British Telecom had abstained from conferring a total monopoly on itself by opting out of supplying very large private branch exchanges and had approved apparatus in this category supplied by others for connection to the network.

The Telecommunications Act 1984 put the arrangements for

[1] Following a report by Professor Michael Beesley, *Liberalisation of the Use of British Telecommunications' Network*, London: HMSO, 1981.

competition in apparatus supply on to a firm basis. However, when I was appointed, also in 1984, this area of business was the subject of great concern. The prospective competitors to British Telecom feared that BT would use its dominance in the basic provision of telecommunications services to give its apparatus supply business an unfair advantage. They feared that competition with BT would simply be impossible.

Fair trading rules were needed to promote competition in apparatus supply and suitable fair trading rules were duly included in BT's licence. The main rules were:

(i) a rule against cross-subsidisation – which prevented BT from making excessive profits on monopoly businesses and using those profits to subsidise prices in the apparatus supply business in order to drive out competitors;

(ii) a rule against undue preference or undue discrimination – which prevents BT from favouring its own businesses over those of competitors by supplying resources at a lower price, and also prevents BT from giving some customers non-financial incentives to deal with it rather than a competitor, for example, by calling on the monopoly business to supply a new service faster on condition that apparatus is purchased from BT;

(iii) a rule against the passing of information from the network business to the competitive business, because that might give some special marketing advantage to BT; and

(iv) rules requiring the attachment of apparatus to the network, provided the apparatus has been properly approved, regardless of the identity of the supplier. Apparatus is now approved by me, under delegated authority from the Secretary of State, after evaluation by an independent valuation authority and testing in approved laboratories.

An area of difficulty, in setting the rules for fair trading, was whether or not BT should be allowed to use resources that are shared between the network business and a business activity where it was in competition with others. Sharing has the advantage of enabling BT to provide a better and more economical service to customers but it might allow BT to enjoy advantages not available to its competitors even to the extent that the business of the competitors would not be viable. The decision was made to allow this sharing of resources. Consequently, for example, an employee can sit at a computer terminal taking orders for a new telephone line at one moment and for the supply of apparatus at the next. The cost has to be apportioned in a reasonable way but the activity is allowed. However, this is an area that I have said I will keep under review. If the joint use of resources were to create a situation where competitors could not survive, I would undertake a review of the situation and consider whether or not a requirement for complete separation of the apparatus supply business from the network business would be in customers' best interests.

Pro-active Regulation

The fair trading rules provide a good measure of assurance about the viability of competition. However, when I became aware of the great concern about the possibility of fair competition in 1984, I realised that *rules alone were not enough.* I had to bring about a situation in which people had enough confidence in my commitment to competition to be willing to enter the market vigorously. I concluded that I needed to undertake a pro-active approach to regulation. It would not be sufficient for me to sit in my office waiting for the complaints to come in. People who were aware of unfair practice might not complain, perhaps because of fear of some retaliation, and cases of unfairness might also fail to come to the attention of people other than the customer and British Telecom.

To meet these problems, I formulated a plan for pro-active regulation published in a document setting out the fair trading rules.[2] I negotiated arrangements with BT under which its top managers would inform BT's own employees about the rules and the intention of top management to observe the rules. I called for information about any breaches of the rules and said that I would use my powers to take legal action that would lead to the imposition of penalties if the rules were broken. Perhaps most importantly, it was made clear that I would search for breaches of the fair trading rules, principally by conducting a survey after a year or so to find out from the experience of purchasers whether or not the fair trading rules had been complied with. If this revealed that things were going wrong, vigorous enforcement action would follow.

Such a survey has now been undertaken.[3] An independent survey organisation interviewed about 800 purchasers of apparatus as well as BT's competitors in the supply of telephone equipment. The survey found, with only minor exceptions attributable to individual excesses, that competition was working effectively. BT's market share had fallen sharply; and a large majority of respondents thought that competition was 'very fair' or at least 'reasonably fair'.

I also needed to take a strong line on enforcing the rule against cross-subsidisation. BT's licence required the production of separate accounts for apparatus supply so that I could check on the cross-subsidisation rule, but it gave BT until April 1987 before this requirement came into effect. The reason for the delay in implementation was that BT did not have good accounting records for its apparatus supply business before privatisation and required

[2] *Effective Competition (Telecommunications Apparatus): A Consultative Document*, London: OFTEL, 1984.

[3] *Competition in Apparatus Supply*, London: OFTEL, 1986.

time to install a system and bring it to satisfactory operation. I heard a number of people advance the astonishing proposition that a state-owned industry did not need to know the detailed results for different parts of its business: the prevalence of this kind of thinking provides substantial evidence of the potential benefits from privatisation. I also thought that I should not wait until April 1987 to check on the absence of cross-subsidisation. I told BT that I thought it must have some numbers for the results of apparatus supply to help top management with its functions and I pressed it to provide that information, accepting that it might not have been audited. As a result of this pressure, I obtained reasonable numbers for the purposes I had in mind.

Competition in Value-added Services

Another promising area for open competition is the supply of services known as 'value-added network services'.[4] These are services provided over the telephone network which involve some additional service over and above the transmission of voice or data. Examples of value-added services include electronic information services, airline or travel agents' booking services, credit card verification, electronic mail, store and forward services, encryption, multi-addressing and many other services that go beyond basic communication. These services are a promising area for liberalisation because, like apparatus supply, they do not involve large economies of scale. To a large extent, the promotion of effective competition in the supply of value-added network services involves the same issues as in apparatus supply. There is a need to have rules against cross-subsidisation and other unfair trading practices, and the regulator must follow pro-active policies to ensure that the rules are complied with.

Simple Resale

In value-added services, however, the interesting additional issue arises of where to draw the boundary between value-added and basic services. If one lists all the services that can be provided over a telephone network, including value-added services, services like store-and-forward, which differ only slightly from basic conveyancing of messages, methods of conveying messages more efficiently, like packet-switching services, and ordinary voice telephony, the dividing line between basic services and value-added services seems by no means clear-cut. An alternative possibility would have been, not to distinguish between value-added and basic services, but rather to distinguish between the provision and the use of facilities. The latter approach would have involved allowing what is called 'simple resale',

[4] Beesley Report, *op. cit.*

the leasing of a line from BT or from Mercury and using it for any purpose without restriction, including a competing switched public telecommunications service.

The Government decided not to allow simple resale initially but to reconsider the position in the middle of 1989. It did this in recognition of its desire to plan an orderly transition to additional competition. A problem existed with the balance of prices. At the date of privatisation, the price of leased lines had been held at a low level in relation to cost. To have allowed simple resale, while prices were low, would have been to allow competitors to set up alternative switched services at prices which would undercut BT at BT's own expense. This would have been a distortion of the market.

This distortion could have been avoided by allowing a sudden increase in prices. However, there were also strong arguments against this course of action because leased lines are used for private networks, developed by large businesses for their own internal purposes. To have increased the prices of leased lines sharply and suddenly would have invalidated the investment decisions on which some firms had based the establishment of their private networks.

These considerations led the Government to decide to impose a five-year transition during which simple resale would not be allowed while prices were rebalanced. I believe that the arguments in favour of allowing simple resale in 1989, or soon afterwards, will seem strong when the time comes. It would be a valuable additional source of competition; and it would avoid the significant difficulties in defining the difference between basic services and value-added services and policing compliance with the regulations. It might create difficulties by bringing further pressures to bear to accept the geographical de-averaging of prices. At present, prices for long-distance telephone calls are the same on many different routes, even though costs vary, partly because of variations in the volume of traffic. If simple resale were allowed, resellers might be able to lease lines and provide competing services over the low-cost routes. They could undercut the prices currently set by BT or perhaps Mercury. BT and Mercury would have to respond by lowering prices on these routes and increasing prices on the more expensive routes to compensate. The alignment of prices with costs is a normal consequence of a competitive market and is acceptable provided it does not have adverse effects such as social disruption resulting from the imposition of very large price increases on remote rural communities. The extent of cost differences in telecommunications is probably such that this would not be too serious a problem. It is, however, an area that needs further consideration before a final decision can be made about the case for simple resale.

COMPETITION IN BASIC TELEPHONY

I turn now to the issues relating to basic network competition which are perhaps the most interesting and controversial. The Government has decided on a duopoly policy for fixed linked telecommunications in the UK. It licensed Mercury Communications in February 1982 to compete with British Telecom and said that it would consider the possibility of licensing others to compete late in 1990 but not sooner. The main idea behind the duopoly policy was that limiting competition could be expected to produce stronger competition. Given the starting position in which BT was dominant, the licensing of two new competitors instead of one might have resulted in a division between the two new competitors of the business of customers who were prepared to move away from British Telecom, with the result that each of the competitors would have been weaker than a single competitor. Indeed, the question of whether increased competition would lead to more or less effective competition will still be the critical one to decide in the 1990 review.

Interconnection

One of the main issues that had to be decided in establishing basic competition in telecommunications concerned the terms on which Mercury's system would be connected to BT's. Connection would be needed, if competition was to take place at all, to ensure that Mercury's customers could telephone BT's customers and that all customers could exercise a choice of routing for their telephone calls, taking advantage of Mercury's network when it was cheaper. The terms on which interconnection took place, therefore, would be important determinants of the effectiveness of competition.

At a crucial time for the development of the Mercury Network it failed to reach agreement with BT on the terms and conditions of interconnection. The licences gave me a kind of arbitrating role in relation to this issue. I carried out this role in a manner I regarded as fulfilling my duty to promote effective competition. In October 1985 I required BT to provide points of connection for Mercury at any exchange at which Mercury requested them, subject only to a few limitations to secure such matters as the technical quality of calls. I also established prices, as required by the licences, which were fair to both parties.[5]

[5] Director General, *Determination of Terms and Conditions for the Purpose of an Agreement on the Interconnection of the BT Telephone System and the Mercury Communication System under Condition 13 of the Licence Granted to BT under Section 7 of the Telecommunications Act 1984*, London: OFTEL, 1985.

Social Obligations

Another important issue that has to be decided in setting the terms on which competition will take place and therefore its scope is the social obligations of each of the competitors. Decisions have to be made about the range of services required from each competitor. Should each operator be allowed to choose whether or not to supply a particular customer – as would happen in a truly competitive market – or should one or both be given the obligation to supply any customer who wishes to have it at a fixed price? Questions also arise on other social obligations. Should there be an obligation to maintain public call boxes in unprofitable areas? Should there be an obligation to provide special services for blind or deaf people or for people who are otherwise disabled?

The Government decided that BT should have a universal service obligation – qualified by the possibility of charging more than the set price for connection of a new telephone service if it required heavy expenditures, for example, because of the remoteness of the location of the customer. BT was also given far-reaching obligations with respect to unprofitable public call boxes and certain aspects of services for blind and deaf people. Mercury was given a limited service obligation. It was not allowed to pick and choose completely. It was required to put down a network of minimum size, particularly a trunk network, and it was given obligations to serve customers on equal terms within a set radius of a point at which it had established a local supply node. It was also given other social obligations, although these were less extensive than those given to BT.

Division of Responsibilities between BT and Mercury

The terms for interconnection and the social and similar obligations will partly determine the extent to which competition is feasible. BT has the advantage of economies of scale. Mercury has the advantage of more freedom to choose where it will operate and lighter social obligations. Possibly the arrangements now established will produce a situation in which a satisfactory amount of competition can take place in a stable manner. Possibly, however, as Mercury's business becomes established, further adjustment will be needed to provide for fair competition into the longer term future. For example, Mercury may have to be given a larger share of social obligations at some time in the future, perhaps by requiring it to pay a contribution towards the maintenance of socially desirable but loss-making public call boxes.

Local Network Competition and Cable

One of the areas in which I most want to see competition is in local telecommunication services. Mercury began, naturally enough, by concentrating on providing competition over long-distance routes. However, the local network is where most of the resources are used in telecommunications; it is where there is direct contact with customers and where there exists considerable room for improvement in performance. Mercury is building local networks to provide competition to those of BT. It has already started competing local operations in London and it is building local networks in other British cities. It will not be able to build competing networks in every part of the country because it is plainly uneconomic to do so in some areas; and it is a long-term job that will take some years to come to fruition. Mercury has, however, brought to the UK the first genuine competition in local switched services in any country in the world and competition appears set to increase, particularly in business districts.

I should like to see firm arrangements in hand for bringing the benefits of local competition to domestic customers as well as business customers. Here the position of cable television companies is of particular interest. These companies are promising candidates for providing competition in local telephony because they can undertake a sharing of costs between television systems and telephone systems and thereby make competition economically feasible. At present, cable television companies are allowed to provide voice telephony only if they do it through an agreement with BT or Mercury. A question for the future is whether or not they should be allowed to provide telephony on their own: this issue will no doubt be the focus of much attention during the 1990 review.

In discussing the case for allowing simple resale of capacity leased from BT or Mercury, I noted that competition had the effect of forcing prices to come into closer alignment with costs. The re-balancing of prices with costs is also important in the promotion of local network competition. The present position is that charges for local telephone calls and for long-distance calls are roughly in balance, though the margin is still probably higher on long-distance than on local calls. However, the standing charge, which pays for the provision of the exchange line from the customer to the local exchange, is still too low as seen through the eyes of a cost accountant. It follows that BT's local exchange business – comprising exchange line rentals and local telephone calls – is less profitable than its trunk business and indeed that long-distance calls are subsidising local operations to some continuing extent. This makes local telephony less attractive than it might be and inhibits the development of competition.

There are sound reasons for not wanting to increase the standing charge very rapidly. It can be disruptive to domestic customers whose overall telephone bills would be likely to increase because the standing charge is a relatively high proportion of the total bill. Those customers would at least have a sense of grievance to the extent that they had assumed standing charges would continue at current levels when they decided to become customers of the telephone network; worse, some customers with low incomes might decide to give up their telephones and this might reduce the value of the telephone network to everyone. In deciding what to do about the imbalance of prices, we find that changes in technology are helpful: technology is bringing down the overall costs of the network so that it may be possible to allow the standing charge to become higher in relative terms without increasing it absolutely; the implication is that call charges would decrease quite sharply. I do not want to make a firm prediction about the future course of exchange line rentals. However, I would emphasise that the issue must be studied carefully and that the decision is likely to have a considerable influence on the prospects for competition in local telephony.

REGULATION OF PRICES

I turn now to my concept of efficient regulation, focussing particularly on the need for incentives to ensure that a satisfactory quality of service is provided, a problem recently much in the news in telecommunications.

RPI minus X Controls

Before discussing quality of service, however, I shall briefly review the basic price control arrangements. British Telecom faces a rule for its main prices – exchange line rentals and direct dialled inland telephone calls – that the average price increase in any year must not exceed RPI-3, that is, 3 percentage points below the rate of inflation as measured by the official Retail Price Index.[6] The rule was set for five years in the first instance and will no doubt be extended for a further period. There are a large number of individual possibilities which could be chosen according to this kind of approach to specify the details of such a price control. The basis for the choice, in my view, is that the rule selected must be expected to produce an acceptable financial performance, including a satisfactory rate of return on capital employed, given reasonable efficiency by BT, over the period during which it applies.

---

[6] S.C. Littlechild, *Regulation of British Telecommunications' Profitability*, London: Department of Trade and Industry, 1983.

Relevance of Rate of Return

The British price control approach cannot therefore be said to ignore the rate of return. But it is often contrasted with the rate of return approach as used in the United States because it is thought to have preferable incentive properties. Because the price control rule is frozen for a period of five years, it gives BT a strong incentive to become more efficient: if BT can reduce its costs it will make more profit and will be allowed to keep it, and if it can reduce costs significantly below the level assumed in the setting of the price control rule, it can make profits above the normal level, whereas under US practice, little incentive exists to make cost savings because such savings have to be passed on to customers as soon as they are made.

Careful consideration has to be given to some of the detailed aspects of the price control rule to ensure that the incentive properties work as well as possible.[7] For example, if prices were to be reduced at the beginning of a period covered by a new price control rule, to bring the rate of return down to the minimum acceptable, after efficiency gains had been made, BT would have little incentive to achieve efficiency gains towards the end of the period covered by the previous price control rule. It would keep the gains for too short a period for them to be worthwhile and it would therefore be tactically preferable to make the gains at the beginning of the following period. Consequently, it may be preferable for the approach to involve a gradual sharing of the benefits of economies with customers. A formula should be chosen which allows the company to keep surplus profits achieved in one period through the first part of the next period but to a decreasing extent.

Basket or Individual Price Caps

The price control rule applies to an average of prices and not to the price for each separate service individually. People have sometimes supposed, therefore, that individual prices are outside the control. That is not the case in practice. I require British Telecom to produce information about its costs for individual services and I use this information to satisfy myself that individual prices are reasonable. Although the licence does not contain a rule dealing with individual prices, I make it clear that I would seek the introduction of a new licence rule if I thought that BT was behaving unreasonably on any aspect of its pricing policy.

---

[7] OFTEL, *The Regulation of British Telecom's Prices: A Consultative Document*, issued by the Director General of Telecommunications, January 1988.

REGULATION OF QUALITY OF SERVICE

1987 was a difficult year for BT. There were numerous complaints about the quality of its service and they centred particularly on arrangements for fault repair and the timely provision of new services.

I have been provided with information from BT's quality of service statistics since privatisation. These indicate that BT's performance showed slight improvement on the whole between the date of privatisation and the end of 1986. The suggestion that BT's quality of service has deteriorated systematically since privatisation is simply wrong. However, a significant deterioration in performance was recorded early in 1987. It took place after the strike of BT's engineering staff and was probably caused mainly by the strike, although I think that teething troubles with the implementation of new technology contributed to the difficulties and also that managers were not focussing on quality of service as strongly as was desirable. Nevertheless, I do not believe, from what I have seen, that managers took a cynical decision to reduce the quality of service in order to gain extra profits.

Even though they were not mainly attributable to the form of the price control rule, the experiences of 1987 with quality of service indicate the need to consider again whether or not the incentive arrangements are as good as they could be. The first step taken by OFTEL was to undertake its own surveys of quality of service and publish the results. The publicity associated with this kind of activity has a strong incentive effect.

Secondly, I pressed British Telecom to accept direct public accountability. I told it that I thought it should publish statistics for quality of service, as it used to do before privatisation. I told it that I thought it should set itself targets for its performance, tell the public what those targets are and explain actual achievements in comparison with the targets. BT agreed to do that under strong pressure from me late in 1986. It published its first report recently.[8] It has undertaken to repeat reports at six-monthly intervals. These improvements in procedures have been obtained by agreement between BT and me although, if I had not succeeded in achieving my aims by agreement, I would have sought a licence amendment requiring a change in procedure.

FINANCIAL INCENTIVES TO IMPROVE BT'S PERFORMANCE?

I am also considering whether BT should have additional financial incentives to improve its performance. There are two possibilities in particular. One concerns contractual liability. At present, BT has excluded its contractual liability to the customer for its failure to

[8] *Quality of Service*, London: British Telecom, 1988.

repair a fault within a reasonable period of time or to provide new service when it says it will. I recognise that it shares this exemption from liability with every other telephone company in the world so far as I have been able to discover. However, the exemption from contractual liability seems to me to have led to some very poor performance in particular cases. I have seen one case where a person living in a London flat had to wait 11 weeks for a fault on the exchange line to be repaired and I am aware of some large businesses which have ordered many new exchange lines over the course of the last year but which have not had a single exchange line connected on the 'date' given by BT in the contract. I find it impossible to avoid the conclusion that these aspects of performance could be improved very significantly if the right kind of financial incentives existed.

I published a discussion document[9] in August 1987 about the case for requiring BT to accept some contractual liability and my staff are now analysing the comments received in response to the document before I decide what further action to take.

A second possible way of improving the financial incentives for BT is to link permitted price increases to quality of service. That would have a similar incentive effect to contractual liability but it would not quite have the same desirable property of directing the financial compensation to the people who have suffered from the poor service. I recognise that setting the level of any financial penalty for poor performance is an extremely difficult matter. However, I am not sure that I need to be able to demonstrate that the amount of any financial penalty is exactly appropriate. Provided it is broadly appropriate, it is likely to have the desired effect on performance and that would be the main purpose of the exercise.

CONCLUSION

In conclusion I want to emphasise my enthusiasm for the new arrangements in telecommunications. I believe that services and products *are* improving. We have had some problems during the past year and we have a long way to go before we can be satisfied with all the arrangements but we can make changes to the regulations to satisfy additional demands that become apparent – and we are on the right track. The range of services now available and the range of apparatus are much wider and much better than in the days before privatisation and liberalisation. Some improvements would no doubt have come about anyway, as a result of improved technology, but I do not believe they would have matched the scale of what has actually happened.

The feature of the new environment that I find most impressive is the way in which people are now thinking more entrepreneurially about the provision of products and services. Economic theory can

[9] *PTO Contract Terms and Conditions: A Consultative Document*, London: OFTEL, 1987.

explain why this should be so and yet I often feel that economic theory fails to capture the excitement of the market-place which depends on psychological attitudes as well as calculations of gains and losses. I recently visited a company that manufactures payphones. At present, BT still has an effective monopoly of supply of such phones because the standard, against which competing apparatus can be approved, has not yet been finalised. However, the standard will be completed soon and the industry is gearing up for the beginning of a truly competitive market in payphones. During my visit, I was shown the kind of products that were under development, including a relatively inexpensive model that will be available for purchase for use in the home – or in shops, offices and similar locations – on a plug-in basis. The product is remarkable for its ingenuity. It can be programmed to apply different rates of charge so that, if you want to use such a telephone at home to discipline your children, you can require them to pay the rate charged by BT – 4.4 pence per unit – or you could charge them less – for example, 1 pence per unit – or you could charge them more. You can programme in a free allowance so that your children can have, say, £5 worth of free calls before they start paying. You can programme in certain numbers that can be telephoned free at any time: the manufacturers called them 'granny numbers' because of the thought that you might wish to allow your children to call granny without paying while they would have to pay to telephone their teenage friends.

My visit to the payphone manufacturer is just one example among many that I could have chosen to show how things are changing in the industry as a result of the introduction of competition. I do not believe that new products and services get developed as quickly in industries that are not competitive: and I regard that as the main benefit that we are deriving from the liberalisation of our telecommunications industry.

7

LIBERATING THE LETTER*

Ian Senior

Managing Director,
Economists Advisory Group Ltd.

THEORETICAL CONSIDERATIONS

The Indefensible Letter Monopoly

In 1970 I argued that the Post Office's letter monopoly was unjustified by economic or any other logic.[1] Since then nothing has occurred to alter the force of the argument. In essence, a letter is nothing more than a thing-to-be-carried, like a newspaper or a parcel. That most letter packets contain information is immaterial since the carrier is paid for carrying and not for analysing the contents of the packet. The concept of a 'letter' is therefore an historical accident, and statutory monopolies world-wide have their roots primarily in commercial exploitation by governments of what was once the sole, and therefore inherently profitable, means of communication. No monopoly has been granted for the carriage of parcels, newspapers or any other thing-to-be-carried, and there is no ground whatever for singling out the 'letter'.

Indeed, nobody in the UK is quite sure what constitutes a 'letter'.

---

* This chapter is an extract from Ian Senior's earlier Research Monograph for the IEA: *Liberating the Letter: A Proposal to Privatise the Post Office*, Research Monograph 38, London: Institute of Economic Affairs, 1983. The text has been revised by the author to take into account developments to 1988.

[1] Ian Senior, *The Postal Service: Competition or Monopoly?*, Background Memorandum No.3, IEA, 1970.

The Post Office Act 1953 did not attempt to define it and instead used a catch-all:

> '...the expression 'letter' includes a packet, so, however, as not to include a newspaper or a parcel unless a communication not forming part of a newspaper is contained therein'[2]

Thus, the Post Office maintained at that time that the contents of the thing-to-be-carried, rather than its dimensions or weight, determined its status as a 'letter'. The absurdity of this position was recognised by Mr Wedgwood Benn who, as noted, abolished special concessions for printed mail and substituted a tariff differential offering the user a choice of speed of service. Mr Benn's logical appreciation of the unimportance of the contents of the thing-to-be-carried did not, however, extend to describing all such things as parcels. To have done so would have eliminated the letter monopoly overnight.

A 'Letter' Defined

The British Telecommunications Act of 1981 defined a 'letter' as:

'any communication in written form which –

(a) is directed to a specific person or address;

(b) relates to the personal, private or business affairs of, or the business affairs of the employer of, either correspondent; and

(c) neither is to be nor has been transmitted by means of a telecommunication system,

and includes a packet containing any such communication'.[3]

Thus the original concept that a 'letter' is defined by its contents survives.

It is surprising that so significant a monopoly should have been sustained over the years by such weak and ill-founded legislation. It explains why, historically, the Post Office has threatened litigation to defend the monopoly more frequently than it has taken entrepreneurs to court.

It is worth noting that, for the following reasons, the 'letter' service does not constitute a natural or technical monopoly in economic terms:

- entry to the market by new suppliers is both cheap and simple, as the upsurge of courier companies in the past few years has demonstrated;
- postal services are labour-intensive and require few skills, so that new ones could quite easily be established from a large pool of unemployed workers;

---

[2] *Post Office Act 1953*, Chapter 36, HMSO, 1953, Section 3 (4).
[3] *British Telecommunications Act 1981*, Chapter 38, HMSO, 1981, Section 66.

- while there are economies of scale in handling postal traffic – a postman can deliver two letters to a house as cheaply as one – it is impossible to argue that a 'letter' monopoly would develop naturally, any more than in the distribution of parcels.

It seems evident, therefore, that the Post Office's 'letter' monopoly has been maintained on grounds of pragmatic self-interest by successive governments which have used it as a source of revenue – as well as by the Post Office itself which has enjoyed the financial comfort it affords.

Cross-subsidisation of Postal Services

All governments since the war have stressed that cross-subsiding of services in public corporations misallocates resources and is therefore undesirable. Yet, it is exactly what the Post Office did. During the 10 years to 1981-82, the domestic letter service and the overseas mail service (again, mainly letters) together made a profit of £101.3 million. As the next in importance, the agency services contributed £74.6 million, while the National Girobank, postal orders and services to telecommunications jointly contributed £18.8 million. All these profits derived from essentially monopoly services. By contrast, the one service run in competition with other carriers, including those in the private sector, performed disastrously: parcels recorded a cumulative loss of £151.2 million.

The arguments against cross-subsidisation are well known and do not need elaboration here. The only points to emphasise are the injustice of permitting the Post Office to provide a subsidised parcel service in competition with private carriers and the likely distortion of demand and misallocation of resources. In recent years the Post Office's report and accounts have combined the profit made on letters and parcels into a single figure. This is surprising because the two services were separated in October 1986 and given separate managements and separate internal accounts. However, the report and accounts for the year to 1 April 1988 state that the letter service made a current cost operating profit of £86.2 million and the parcel service an equivalent profit of £39.1 million. This suggests that the two services are now both paying their way.

The figures for the three years ending 1 April 1988 are shown in the following Table. Letters and parcels combined still account for three-quarters of the Post Office's profit, though the proportion is falling.

Unprofitable Rural Services

Although many public figures pay lip-service to the undesirability of cross-subsidising within nationalised industries, they defend the Post Office's letter monopoly as allowing profitable urban traffic to

Table 1

POST OFFICE: PROFIT ON ORDINARY ACTIVITIES BEFORE TAXATION AND INTEREST PAYABLE ON LONG-TERM LOANS

	Year ending 1 April					
	1986		1987		1988	
	£ m	%	£ m	%	£ m	%
Letters and parcels	122.3	78	131.2	76	151.3	73
Counters	25.8	16	19.1	11	33.6	16
Girobank	9.4	6	23.1	13	23.5	11
Sub-total	157.5	100	173.4	100	208.4	100
Group total	167.0		170.0		212.2	

Source: Post Office reports and accounts.

subsidise unprofitable rural mail. What is mistakenly regarded as the 'Rowland Hill principle' of uniform tariffs is held to be sacrosanct, although Hill never regarded it as such. As the Carter Committee noted,[4] Hill's view was simply that different rates should not be charged where this would overburden the system with administrative costs. If it can be shown that the system would *not* be overburdened by such rates, the argument for differential tariffs becomes overwhelming.

The often-repeated argument known as 'creaming off' is that, if the Post Office did not have a monopoly of the letter, private services would handle only profitable urban traffic, leaving the currently unprofitable rural traffic to the Post Office which would thus be forced into permanent loss.

This argument is circular, as will be demonstrated. The starting point for analysis, however, is that people make a choice where to live. In doing so they take into account an array of differing prices. In choosing to live in the countryside a rational person considers the cost of housing and transport first. He does not expect house prices in the country to be identical with those in town. Nor does he expect to commute 20 miles to work by train for the same price as one stop on the bus. And nor does he expect that prices in his village shop –

[4] *Report of the Post Office Review Committee*, Cmnd. 6850, HMSO, 1977.

on the bus. And nor does he expect that prices in his village shop – even for standard branded products – will be the same as in urban supermarkets. Why then, if he chooses a rural retreat with a long drive, should he expect – apparently as of right – to pay the same postage as another postal user who has opted to live in an accessible urban block of flats? People make decisions about location in the light of a set of price signals. There is no reason why *postal* price signals should be excluded.

A Kind of 'Social Service'?

The argument for the Post Office's retention of the letter monopoly is often supported by the claim that letters constitute a form of 'social service' and that the Post Office has some quasi-moral duty to provide it. This was the approach of a report by the National Consumer Council in 1979 – *Post Office, special agent* – the first chapter of which was devoted to how the Post Office could help to improve the take-up of welfare benefits and services. Most of the report's recommendations could be implemented quite cheaply – for example, the more effective display of DHSS leaflets at post office counters. The initial assumption, however, that the Post Office should be a 'social service' rather than a commercial operation remains tendentious.

A further problem is that determining which services are 'social' depends on a value-judgement. A village post office may arguably provide a 'social' service, but so does the village pub and the village shop. No-one argues that there should be a state monopoly of the sale of beer for social service reasons. Another argument advanced is that letters and other postal services are 'essential' and therefore 'social'. Food, however, is much more essential yet nobody claims that Sainsburys should be compelled to open village stores where they do not exist so that people who have chosen to live in the country need not travel to the next village or town to shop.

Historically, the Post Office has cherished its role as provider of a universal 'social service' because this role has enabled it to retain the profitable letter monopoly. In short, the Post Office has embraced its obligation to serve rural communities as a way of keeping the monopoly.

The argument that dwellers in decaying inner-city areas should, through the postal system, unwittingly subsidise the 'gin and Jag belt' in the Home Counties is obscure. If democratically-elected government, either national or local, decides to subsidise the postal services of certain areas – say, the Western Isles of Scotland – the providers of postal services, including the Post Office, could bid for the contract and the most efficient would win it. It seems logical that the source of funds for a local subsidy should be local since this would enable the costs to be borne by those who benefit from the subsidised service. Local councils wishing to retain deliveries in a particular rural area, for example, could provide a subsidy from the rates to any local contractor bidding to supply the service. If need be, a local referendum could be held to determine whether a subsidy was justified or wanted. Such a method would have the attraction of devolving decisions on 'social service' subsidies to those who would have to pay for them – and it would give them the right to refuse.

Transferring wealth from one group of citizens to another by taxation may be the proper function of democratic government. It is not, however, the function of the Post Office – nor indeed of any other trading concern, whether public or private.

We are therefore led to the following conclusions:

(i) There is no economic or social justification for the Post Office's 'letter' monopoly.

(ii) If the Post Office is deprived of the 'letter' monopoly, it must also be relieved of its obligation to supply all parts of the country at uniform prices (indeed, it would be under no obligation to provide a service anywhere and it would do so only if it expected to make a profit).

(iii) Except perhaps in very remote areas, rural services could be supplied with higher tariffs and without cross-subsidy.

(iv) In extreme cases, national or local government could pay a postal contractor to carry out otherwise unprofitable business in rural areas.

Breaking the Circle?

The circularity of the populist argument for maintaining the letter monopoly can be summed up as follows:

- urban services currently subsidise rural ones;
- the Post Office requires the 'letter' monopoly to continue this cross-subsidisation;
- the 'letter' monopoly enables the Post Office to charge uniform tariffs;
- uniform tariffs enable urban services to subsidise rural ones.

And so on *ad infinitum*. Yet the circularity of the argument can be broken the moment it is demonstrated that there is no justification for urban to subsidise rural services at all.

An economist would phrase the arguments differently but would reach the same conclusions. In this instance, the reasoning would be as follows:

- if there were no statutory monopoly of the 'letter', competition would ensue and the prices charged by all contractors would reflect their costs;

- o people whose value-judgements led them to discern 'social' costs and benefits not captured by the pricing systems of commercial operators should be given the opportunity, through democratic channels, to correct the apparent failure of the market through subventions on 'social' grounds;
- o in order to prevent a misallocation of resources, subventions should be voted by those most closely affected and most willing to pay.

When the argument is expressed thus it becomes clear that the onus for demonstrating the 'social' costs and benefits of postal services falls upon those arguing for subvention. To date, reasoned argument on this issue has been conspicuously lacking.

NEW POSTAL SERVICES

Historical Suppression of Competition

In the UK and elsewhere there have been repeated attempts, some successful and of considerable duration, to operate a postal service in competition with that of the state. The majority have been suppressed in one way or another by government. Among the most successful in the UK were William Dockwra's London Penny Post of 1680 which had 400 receiving points and provided house-to-house service. It was put out of business by the government following a long court case. In 1709 Charles Povey introduced a service at a charge of only one-halfpenny, thereby undercutting the General Post Office. He introduced bellmen who collected post on the street, an idea later taken up by the GPO. In 1887 Richard King launched his company, Boy Messengers Limited, and was able to muster enough support from Parliament and the press to force the GPO to grant him a licence. Indeed, it introduced its own messenger service to compete.[5]

In this century, a number of less ambitious services have been suppressed – such as those run by some of the Oxford colleges – which could hardly have been considered a serious threat to the Post Office.

At various times private postal services have been started in the USA, Australia and Holland by entrepreneurs who found loopholes in the law; they have proved successful, particularly when account is taken of the precarious nature of their existence.

That there should be determined efforts to provide competing postal services indicates that entrepreneurs believe they could do better than the state monopoly. They have inevitably begun with the most profitable inter-urban traffic, thus re-inforcing the 'creaming off'

[5] For a fuller account, Robert Carnaghan, 'Free enterprise in the postal services', *Freedom First*, No. 71, June 1972.

argument. Yet it is precisely because state postal administrations make excess profits on the urban traffic that competitors enter that part of the market. If the administrations made profits over the whole network by differential pricing, competition would also be spread over the network.

Private Letter Services During the 1971 Strike

On 20 January 1971, the postmen went on strike. Two days previously Mr Christopher Chataway, then Minister of Posts and Telecommunications, announced that private postal services would be allowed to operate *under licence* for the duration of the strike. This momentous decision meant that, for the first time since 1591, a government had voluntarily relinquished its monopoly over letters. The result was quite remarkable. Within a matter of days no fewer than 562 services had been licensed up and down the country, and others were doubtless operating without a licence.

Many of these operations were intended more to print what philatelists call 'Cinderella' stamps than to carry mail, but some were unquestionably serious operations. One of them, Randall's Mail Service, charged substantially more than the Post Office's letter rate of 3p, yet at the end of the six-week strike claimed to have handled about half a million items.[6]

Perhaps even more remarkable was the speed with which some of these *ad hoc* services linked up during the strike into a network called the Association of Mail Services. In very little time, local services were finding ways to expand their areas of operation.

A further interesting aspect was the attitude of the public which, assuming the claims of the operators were reasonably accurate, was prepared to entrust quite large quantities of mail to completely unknown firms, makeshift in the extreme and with no possible future beyond the end of the strike. How much more would it have been willing to entrust to established firms entering the market-place with genuine prospects of staying there!

Private Parcel Services

The public carriers of parcels are the Post Office, British Rail and the road services. The latter have at times been partly nationalised. For many years the Post Office's parcel service made losses, frequently large. Nevertheless, numerous private services, such as security companies, have entered the market in the past decade, a sure sign that profits can be made by new entrants.

For the security services, it was by no means an obvious move. Their system of armoured vans was developed to move small

---

[6] *Daily Telegraph*, 12 March 1971.

numbers of high-value units between a limited number of points. By contrast, a parcel service requires cheaper (non-armoured-plated) vans to move large numbers of low-value items flexibly between very many points. It might have seemed, therefore, that the security services would start with the wrong structure of vehicles and staff and would compete only at the margin by using unnecessarily expensive equipment at times when it would otherwise be idle. Yet, in practice, these and other new services offer nationwide coverage.

The Courier Service

A remarkable phenomenon over the past decade has been the emergence of a large number of courier services in London and the main cities. It was at one time thought that such services would infringe the Post Office's 'letter' monopoly. In February 1972, for example, a courier service was launched in London by an enterprising Australian, Richard King, who presumably had been impressed by operations which had started during the postal strike the preceding year. King's 'Post-Haste' service offered delivery in four hours within an area of London covering the law courts, Parliament and the Strand using a team of 10 motor-cyclists constituted as a co-operative of self-employed. The Post Office immediately threatened King with legal proceedings. Customers were doubtless afraid they might be accused of abetting King if they used an illegal service, and it was thus short-lived.

Public frustration with the Post Office's service increased during the early 1970s, particularly concerning the unreliability of delivery within the big cities. It became common for urgent letters or packages to be sent by taxi – an extremely inefficient use of resources. Quite soon after the demise of 'Post-Haste', other courier services were launched using motor-bikes controlled from a central point by radio. The Post Office threatened legal proceedings but took none of the operators to court. In a matter of months their number had mushroomed and by 1975 there were probably 30-50 such services in London alone. Since then their number and scope have increased. A recent development has been the advent of pedal cyclist couriers who ride through red lights and up one-way streets with joyous abandon.

The courier services exploited the loop-hole in the law discovered by Richard King. The law permitted people to employ agents (couriers) to collect and deliver individual letters, though not to collect them on a generalised basis. Thus, the couriers could collect items from individual addresses on request but could not install public collection boxes.

It was to meet this new competition that, in March 1976, the Post Office launched its own variant called 'Expresspost'. In many respects the service was an imitation of the couriers and its price was a little lower. Since then it has been widely extended using a special fleet of vans, inter-city rail links, the Post Office's underground railway in

London and a fleet of radio-controlled motor-cycles. 'Expresspost' has been heavily promoted in the media, including prime television time, with resources far beyond the means of individual private couriers whose marketing is very limited.

Yet, despite the Post Office's overwhelming strength – compared even with the combined total of *all* the private couriers – the latter have survived and, it would seem, prospered. More importantly, their legitimacy has now been recognised in law. On 16 October 1981, the then Secretary of State for Industry, Mr Patrick Jenkin, laid before Parliament an order suspending the Post Office's letter monopoly to permit time-sensitive mail to be delivered by private carriers provided they charge a minimum fee, set at £1 per letter. This was the first real relaxation of the monopoly, other than during the postal strike, for a century or more.

The significance of the couriers is two-fold. First, they are a classic example of private enterprise recognising a demand overlooked by a state monopoly and satisfying it to the benefit of the community. Secondly, it demonstrates that the private sector can compete successfully with the Post Office in the provision of postal services. It is remarkable that the private couriers have not been eliminated by 'Expresspost'. No financial details about the service are given in the Post Office's reports and accounts. The private courier services have had to function as profitable enterprises or else they would have gone bankrupt. 'Expresspost' may be profitable, *but it does not have to show a profit*. It could well be subsidised by other services, not least by the letter monopoly, and this cross-subsidy would not appear in the accounts.

Conclusion

From all the evidence reviewed in this section it is clear that the private sector wishes to compete with the Post Office and, when permitted to do so, successfully introduces new or specialised services which satisfy particular users' wants. Historically, the Post Office has tried to eliminate competition by legal or other devices. When it has failed, it has on occasions resorted to imitating the private sector. It is evident that competition in the postal service, limited though it has been to date, has benefited society and should therefore be extended.

IMPLEMENTATION

Removal of the Letter Monopoly

In my 1970 IEA paper I put the case for removing the Post Office's letter monopoly. *The Economist* supported this view, saying that '...it is absurd that the Post Office should have a monopoly to carry letters in Britain...'[7] but few others did.

Mrs Thatcher's first administration took power in 1979 dedicated to returning some nationalised industries to private enterprise. Yet, despite occasional hints that the Post Office's monopoly might be abolished, the legitimising of courier services has been complemented by only one modest reform permitting charitable organisations, such as the Scouts, to deliver Christmas cards. The Government has apparently put its plans to break the Post Office's letter monopoly onto the back-burner, scared off by the Post Office's claim that differential letter charges would be in the range 10p-£1.[8]

It is difficult to think of a cogent reason why any government should not remove the monopoly, other than short-term expediency. Better still, the Post Office should be sold to the public.

The Post Office plc

There has been a succession of reforms over the past 20 years intended to make the Post Office more commercial, more free from political interference, and more responsive to its users' wants. This process, which began in 1964 when Mr Wedgwood Benn was Postmaster General, resulted in the Post Office becoming a public corporation in 1969 and losing its ministerial head. The residual sponsor, the Ministry of Posts and Telecommunications, was short-lived and its main responsibility passed to the Department of Industry. During the 1970s, the postal functions were increasingly separated from telecommunications at local, regional and headquarters levels. The complete separation of the two services was achieved in 1981. The time is now ripe to take the next logical step of selling the Post Office to the public.

The prime reason for this final step is that it would be in the interest of both users and the Post Office itself. At present, users – who comprise virtually every member of the public as well as institutions like mail order houses – have no effective say in the Post Office's operations. The Post Office Users' National Council is a toothless watchdog[9] set up to look after users' interests when the Post Office became a corporation. It has the right to be *consulted* about proposed changes in services, and its 25 or so members are appointed by the government. The intention is that they should have a wide variety of backgrounds and be able to give a good spread of users' views. In addition, there are equivalent councils for Scotland, Wales and Northern Ireland and about 200 Post Office advisory committees throughout the country. Members of the latter are drawn from local authorities, commercial organisations and local voluntary bodies.

It is not to be expected that this elaborate structure of advice can

---

[7] *Economist*, 5 December 1970.
[8] *Daily Telegraph*, 10 May 1988.
[9] The POUNC's annual report for 1981-82 contains a cartoon of POUNC, smiling and benign, with no teeth visible, but bearing the title 'watchdog'.

achieve the same results as competition. We have already seen, for example, that the Post Office launched its 'Expresspost' service in 1976 under the spur of competition from the private courier services – and not as a consequence of pressure from the advisory councils and committees.

Nor is it clear that the POUNC's reports on proposed tariff changes genuinely achieve what users want – not least because different users may have differing and even contradictory requirements. It is even likely that Post Office managers, knowing that whatever they recommend will be whittled down by the Council, ask for more than they want in order to be able to make concessions. Moreover, the success of the new parcel and courier services proves that in some cases there is significant public demand for better service at *higher* prices, whereas the users' representative bodies have invariably fought for the continuation of the same service at similar or lower prices. The prognostication of Mr Ian Mikardo, MP, in 1968 when the users' councils were being set up has been fulfilled:

> 'I doubt very much whether all this great apparatus will be worthwhile – whether the game will be worth the candle and whether it will justify the benefit to the consumer'.[10]

The hallmark of ownership is control and the only people who have control over the Post Office are the responsible Ministers and officials at the Department of Trade and Industry. This stands in stark contrast to my proposal that individuals should be given the opportunity of true ownership of the Post Office through privatisation.

The Post Office is currently profitable and has good prospects of remaining so even without the 'letter' monopoly because it has a national network, specialised equipment, trained staff and experience accumulated over a century or more. If shares in it were offered to the public we would expect them to be taken up. In particular, major users such as the mail order houses would have the opportunity to buy enough shares to gain seats on the board of directors. Individual users with axes to grind could also buy shares and have the forum of annual general meetings to voice their views.

Post Office executives and other staff would be encouraged to hold shares in the company. To judge by several successful 'management buy-outs', we may hope that they would welcome the opportunity to share in the profits and capital value created by their efforts.

Counter Services

As has been noted, postal services have already been fully separated from telecommunications on the ground that they were two heterogeneous operations. The same logic applies with equal force to

[10] *Hansard*, 11 November 1968, col. 64.

the difference between counter services and the mail. The mail service consists of carrying physical objects, while the counter service is concerned with money transactions. Both services will change beyond recognition in the coming decade. Letters written on paper will be replaced by the 'electronic letter', and the Post Office's paper-based banking, money transfer and agency services will be transformed by automated teller machines, point-of-sale registers, home banking, and a variety of electronic systems for transferring funds based on plastic cards.

Although the electronic revolution will lie behind the development of both services, its application will be so different to each that they will require freedom to progress independently. In particular, since the counter services will increasingly compete with other financial institutions and the mail service with private operators, it will be desirable to prevent any form of cross-subsidisation between the services – as there was between posts and telecommunications when they were combined. Since my 1983 paper the Post Office has accepted this logic and separated counters, letters, parcels and girobank into separate services.

For many years the Post Office's counter services have enjoyed a *de facto* monopoly over a wide range of government agency services. An example is the payment of pensions and social security. This monopoly, which has always provided the Post Office with a guaranteed margin of profit, is, however, also being eroded since many forms of benefit are now paid directly into individual bank accounts at lower cost to the government and more convenience to the recipients. The next logical step must be for banks and building societies to be invited to tender in competition with the Post Office to provide other services, such as the issue of vehicle and other licences.

Conclusion

In the past five years Mrs Thatcher's Government has privatised a number of major nationalised industries, notably buses, British Telecom, British Gas, British Petroleum and the Rover Group. Other giants are in the queue, specifically electricity, water and steel. The Post Office's Girobank, much smaller fry, is at the head of the queue. With such a programme in prospect, it might seem churlish to ask yet again why the Post Office's separated services should not also be included.

The time for privatising them is ripe for the following reasons:

- Counter services and parcels compete directly with the private sector and are doing so profitably. Therefore, there is no case for the state to provide services which the private sector can and does perform.
- The letter service is also profitable, as it always has been. The

volume of traffic is growing fast, thanks largely to the increase in direct-mail advertising, which so far has been more than enough to counteract the inroads which facsimile has made to traditional mail traffic.

o The British Post Office's services are probably the most profitable in the world. This is in sharp contrast to many others in industrialised countries which require massive public subsidies despite their monopolies. In addition to being profitable, the British Post Office should be *seen* to be profitable.

Even the argument that the Government's busy agenda for privatisation leaves no room to privatise the Post Office is spurious. The main step could be done overnight by the Secretary of State for Trade and Industry. Only one of two simple actions would suffice. Under his existing powers he has the choice, and could:

(a) either remove the £1 price minimum for the carriage of 'letters', or

(b) announce an open general licence for anyone to carry 'letters'.

The examples cited above of the postmen's strike of 1971 and the rapid growth of couriers are compelling. Within days of either action by the Secretary of State new postal services will begin. Their share of the total market will initially be small, but they will put the Post Office on notice where its services require improvement. As the new services grow this will constitute a form of gradual privatisation.

In one or two years from now, the Post Office will still be the dominant provider of letter services, but by then the Government will have the time to privatise the Post Office in whatever way seems best. The argument for making an immediate start by abolishing the monopoly of the 'letter' is irrefutable.

PART III

ENERGY

8

PRIVATISING THE ENERGY INDUSTRIES

Colin Robinson

Professor of Economics, University of Surrey

THIS PAPER is concerned primarily with matters of principle which arise in schemes to privatise the energy industries. It refers, where necessary, to more detailed analyses of coal and electricity privatisation.[1]

(1) THE STATE OF THE PRIVATISATION PROGRAMME

The present Government's privatisation programme has reached a critical phase. In its early stages, the programme seemed designed to inject competition and entrepreneurial spirit into markets where both had been noticeably lacking. More recently, it has degenerated into an exercise in raising funds for government and spreading share ownership by selling shares cheaply with little regard for the liberalisation of product and factor markets. The nadir of the programme (so far) was the privatisation of British Gas; large numbers of people were tempted into becoming shareholders (or reaping short-term profits from investment) in an organisation which, if anything, had a more powerful monopoly position than its nationalised predecessor, since it had the ability to diversify. Given the recently demonstrated volatility of stock markets, it will for some time be much more difficult to tempt potential investors into subscribing for privatisation issues; the Government's approach to privatisation may have to change for that reason, if for no other.

---

[1] Colin Robinson and Allen Sykes, *Privatise Coal*, London: Centre for Policy Studies, 1987, and Allen Sykes and Colin Robinson, *Current Choices*, London: Centre for Policy Studies, 1987.

My principal concern, however, is with the illiberal track onto which the privatisation programme has shifted. Gas privatisation was unfortunate, not only because it missed an opportunity to liberalise the British gas market, but because of the precedent it set for other privatisation schemes.[2] Naturally enough, the management of the electricity supply industry would also like its industry to be privatised in a way which permits a big increase in salaries and a reduction in political interference whilst retaining its monopolistic structure.

(2) THE POLITICAL ECONOMY OF PRIVATISATION

A serious problem in privatisation programmes, as in other economic policy matters, is that society must use as its agent a government, which is a highly imperfect instrument, for carrying out its wishes even if those wishes are well-formed and obvious (which generally they are not). It is possible that the privatisation programme of the last few years demonstrates the inevitability of illiberal schemes for major industries. One might argue, from the standpoint of public choice theory, that there will always be an irresistible combination of powerful forces in favour of retaining existing big monopolies when corporations are transferred from the state to the private sector. There may well be token gestures in the direction of competition, as with British Gas, but pressure groups will successfully resist genuine competition. The management of the corporation will want to retain its market power, so will its unions which can conclude much cosier arrangements with monopolies than with firms in competitive markets, and so will the City which finds it easier and more profitable to bring monopolies to market. Not least, politicians will want to raise large sums quickly, without management obstruction, from the sale of corporations which face little competition and therefore appear to have good earnings prospects. The social benefits from increased competition appear rather intangible and, in any case, most of them will not be realised within the normal political time-scale. As principals, we must rely heavily on agents with inherently short time-horizons.

Such arguments have considerable force. Nevertheless, there is some hope – also founded on the economic theory of political action in a democracy – that they represent too pessimistic a view. The principal cause for optimism lies in rising consumer discontent with such recently privatised organisations as British Telecom and British Gas, which suggests that the most potent force known to governments (fear of losing votes) may be coming to the rescue. Most people are used to poor service from nationalised industries; we are distinctly less tolerant of poor service from private companies especially if,

[2] Colin Robinson and Eileen Marshall, 'Regulation of the Gas Industry', Memorandum 13, in House of Commons Energy Committee, Session 1985-86, *Memoranda on Regulation of the Gas Industry*, 1985.

according to our elected representatives, they became private in the interests of making them more efficient and responsive to consumers' wishes. It is also possible that a government which professes to believe in competition will, now that it has observed the effects of transferring state monopolies intact into the private sector, give liberalisation much higher priority in the rest of its privatisation programme.

(3) THE SIGNIFICANCE OF ELECTRICITY PRIVATISATION

Electricity privatisation will be an important test of what the Government's objectives now are in pursuing privatisation schemes. We shall be able to judge whether it is concerned primarily with raising revenues for the public purse, or with widening share ownership or with injecting competition into the industry. Moreover, since the electricity supply industry (ESI) has been the focus for most of the protective barriers governments have erected around the British energy market and around particular industries within that market, those barriers will necessarily be re-examined. Privatising the ESI is complicated not only in itself (principally because the industry contains elements of natural monopoly) but because it raises questions of energy and industrial policy which are, no doubt, very awkward in political terms.

For example, the ESI has been used by governments as an instrument of support for the British coal industry[3] and for British generating plant manufacturers, it has been permitted by governments to use only token amounts of natural gas, and it has indulged in a government-backed programme of building British-designed nuclear plants. How one can apportion responsibility for the British nuclear programme as between the Central Electricity Generating Board (CEGB) and governments is not at all clear, though it is plain that governments have intervened extensively. More generally, officially-imposed discount rates for the nationalised industries[4] have been well below those which private sector companies would have taken. The use of such low rates has clearly had significant effects on the nature and size of investment programmes in electricity supply which is a capital-intensive industry but where some types of plant (such as nuclear) are much more capital intensive than others. Low discount rates have favoured nuclear power in comparison with less capital-intensive fossil fuel stations. All manner of side-effects have followed from such government policies. For instance, the virtual prohibition on burning natural gas has forced the ESI into unnecessarily expensive ways of reducing environmental emissions

---

[3] Colin Robinson and Eileen Marshall, *Can Coal be Saved?*, Hobart Paper 105, Institute of Economic Affairs, 1985, and Colin Robinson, 'Liberalising the Coal Market', *Lloyds Bank Review*, April 1987.

[4] *The Nationalised Industries*, Cmnd. 7131, HMSO, 1978. Also David Heald, 'The Economic and Financial Control of UK Nationalised Industries', *Economic Journal*, Vol. 90, June 1980.

from fossil fuel power stations. And, because of the industry's low required and achieved rates of return, the market value of its assets is almost certainly far below their current cost value (about £45 billion for the English and Scottish Boards together).

The Government's commitment to privatise the ESI will thus inevitably lead it to face up to a range of difficult issues. Or, looking at the matter more positively, a rare opportunity now presents itself to reconsider the *ad hoc* collection of measures which is sometimes labelled 'British energy policy', as well as some wider questions of industrial policy. The rarity of such opportunities is because governments, like most other organisations, prefer not to consider policies *ab initio* (from a zero base, as the jargon now has it): changes are generally rather marginal adjustments to policies already in operation. But, on this occasion, privatisation of the ESI virtually forces a radical policy review on the government – unless some apparently easy option is chosen, as it was with British Gas.

If the opportunity is to be seized, genuine competition must be introduced into the two closely-linked industries of coal and electricity supply, in the process sweeping away the bulk of the protection and subsidisation which has characterised the British energy market for so many years. Simply turning the two industries into private monopolies, perhaps with fringe competition, will not do. That will merely replace big, unresponsive state monopolies with big, unresponsive private monopolies. One can sympathise with those managers in the ESI who feel that they deserve a British Gas-style privatisation. There is, indeed, much in their view that similar styles of privatisation are appropriate for gas and electricity. But the proper conclusion to draw is that the Government should take the earliest possible opportunity to liberalise the gas market. That will not be easy given the illiberal form in which the industry was privatised. However, it is extremely important not to compound the error of gas privatisation by some monopoly form of privatisation of the ESI which will then set yet another precedent for transferring big corporations whole from public to private sector.

In the rest of this paper, ways in which the ESI and coal could be liberalised are considered. The discussion of coal is mainly in the context of the ESI because the latter is the industry the Government has decided to privatise first. It might well have been better for the Government to have started with coal.[5] But that issue is now decided.

(4) THE NATURE OF MONOPOLY IN THE ESI

Many schemes for privatising the ESI have evidently been proposed, though the details are not always clear since they are mainly ideas from within the industry or from government which are leaked in sketchy form to the newspapers. Most of these proposals claim to

---

[5] *Can Coal be Saved?*, *op. cit.*

have the objective of injecting competition, but in my view none of them has much hope of doing so because they fail to address the nature of monopoly in the ESI – which is much more widespread and complex than product market monopoly.

There appear to be at least five aspects to monopoly power in the existing ESI:

- o There is power in the product market in the traditional sense, since almost two-thirds of electricity is sold into uses (such as motive power and lighting) where other fuels are not close substitutes. Although companies can generate their own electricity, thus circumventing the public supply system, the lack of an outlet for surplus electricity other than that public system, is a serious disincentive. Because of its strong market position, the ESI can pass on to consumers virtually any costs it incurs. The market therefore fails to exert efficiency pressures and to set performance standards. Regulation by government has, by common consent, been unsuccessful in promoting efficiency and safeguarding consumers.
- o As George Yarrow points out in another chapter in this volume,[6] information monopolies are often as important as product market monopolies. The ESI's information monopoly is particularly significant. Almost all the information which anyone can acquire about generation, transmission and distribution of electricity in Britain must be obtained from, and relates to, the existing nationalised industry. There are no competitors from whose activities one can derive information on alternative ways in which electricity supply might be organised and managed and whose costs one could use for comparison purposes. The information monopoly places the ESI – and particularly the CEGB, which dominates the existing industry – in an extremely powerful position, tempting it to rely on 'blinding with science' outside commentators and indeed the Government itself. The dispute over whether or not there are serious technical difficulties in separating generation and transmission into two organisations is an obvious and topical example.
- o The cost-plus nature of the industry, which minimises efficiency pressures, encourages monopolistic practices in the labour market. It is hardly surprising, therefore, that there appear to be very cosy arrangements between the existing ESI and its unions. Those unions have become a major pressure group which supports continuation of a monopoly post-privatisation.[7]
- o There are also monopolistic practices in the markets for other

---

[6] George Yarrow, 'Does Ownership Matter?', above, pp.52-69.

[7] For example, John Lyons, 'Power shocks in store for Parkinson', *The Times*, 29 July 1987.

inputs, partly as a consequence of government policy but also because of the minimal efficiency pressures. The series of 'Joint Understandings' which the CEGB has had with British Coal since 1979 severely limit the competition which the nationalised coal industry would otherwise have to face from imported coal and from the small private mining sector in Britain. Since about three-quarters of British Coal's sales are to the CEGB, and because of the cost-plus nature of electricity pricing, this competition-restricting agreement is a way of forcing on to British electricity consumers much of the cost of protecting the nationalised coal industry. The price is high since purchases of coal at over £3 billion a year constitute around half the CEGB's annual operating costs of just over £6 billion. Similarly, 'Buy British' policies for plant and equipment, which aim to support British manufacturers, inflate the costs of the CEGB's capital programme which has recently been running at towards £800 million a year.

o As a consequence of its other monopoly attributes the ESI, and particularly the CEGB, has very considerable power in the political market-place. The information monopoly gives it substantial lobbying leverage which is augmented by arrangements with the unions, with British Coal and with the plant manufacturers.

Freeing Entry not the Answer

Taken together, these monopolistic elements constitute formidable barriers to entry which will not easily be removed. Sometimes it is possible to introduce competition simply by freeing entry, taking no positive action to alter the structure of the industry concerned. The incumbent can be left intact whilst the entry of newcomers undermines its market power, reducing costs and prices to the benefit of consumers. In the ESI, however, it is very unlikely that freeing entry would be sufficient to introduce genuine competition. The economic and political power of the existing industry is so widespread that a necessary condition for the introduction of real competition seems to be a break-up of the CEGB which incorporates both generation and transmission and dominates the rest of the industry. About 80 per cent of the existing industry's costs arise in the CEGB; Area Boards have no alternative but to accept these costs in the price the Generating Board charges them and then pass them on to consumers.

A break-up of the CEGB into a number of competing generators would disturb all the elements of the existing industry's monopoly power. Product market power would be reduced, the information monopoly would disappear, restrictive practices in markets for coal, capital equipment and labour would be hard to sustain, and the industry would become a much less cohesive pressure group on government. The Government has said that it wishes to introduce competition into generation, so presumably it would welcome such diminutions of monopoly power.

(5) OPPOSITION TO COMPETITION

It is hardly surprising that the ESI, and especially the CEGB, should oppose the introduction of competition or rather grudgingly propose fringe competition. Those commentators who blame the CEGB for its attitude are disingenuous. They would probably act in the same way if they were in the Board's place. One should expect those who have been placed in a monopolistic position by government to behave like monopolists. Furthermore, it is true that introducing competition into industries which have been monopolised for many years is not straightforward and cannot be accomplished overnight. The transition needs to be handled with care ((9) to (11) below).

Equally, however, one should not dignify the objections to competition too much. Some of those who see all manner of complications imply that the industry is already being run satisfactorily. In practice, it is operated essentially on a cost-plus basis with none of the performance standards which are set by the activities of close competitors. Regulation, instead of being open, is by the backdoor, exercised by politicians and civil servants who do not have to account for specific actions. There have been serious mismatches between demand and capacity and the nuclear building programme appears to have produced power stations in England and Wales which are unsaleable to the private sector. Furthermore, there is a tendency to project demand and then match those projections with capacity additions (since the costs can be passed on) rather than to refurbish existing plant or to use price policy to economise on new construction.

Other apologists for the present régime argue that the 'merit order' (which ranks power stations in order of short-run avoidable cost and assigns the highest load factors to the stations with the lowest costs) already assures efficiency because it minimises system operating costs. Such arguments confuse technical with economic efficiency. As explained in (4) above, capital costs and fuel costs of the ESI are inflated by 'Buy British' policies and labour costs are inflated by agreements between a state industry with power in the product market and its unions. Consequently, although the merit order approximately minimises system operating costs, given individual power station operating costs, the latter are products of monopolistic conditions. So are the capital costs which are irrelevant to merit order operation (because they are sunk and so unavoidable) but which are important determinants of the total costs of the ESI.

(6) GAINS FROM LIBERALISATION

After 40 years of monopoly (and many years of state supervision before that), it would be astonishing if there were not very big gains to be realised from liberalising the electricity supply and coal industries. Competition should bring increased productive efficiency and pass the gains on to consumers, thus improving allocative efficiency; the presence of choice for consumers should lead to better service; security of supply would most probably increase since competing private producers would have every incentive to diversify sources of inputs; and reduced politicisation of decision-making would lead management to concentrate their time and energies on operating efficiently rather than trying to stay on the right side of politicians and civil servants. Possibly more important than the 'static' gains which economists so often think about would be dynamic benefits from the stimulus to innovation and entrepreneurship which signals from a competitive market give to producers.

Quantifying the gains is extremely difficult. In two recent papers,[8] Allen Sykes and I have given some very approximate estimates of the benefits which might be obtained from liberal forms of privatisation of the ESI and coal; we concluded that they might be in the region of £1.5 billion a year for the two industries together. Almost certainly those are under-estimates, simply because after so many years of monopoly none of us really has the imagination to foresee all the changes which would occur once such industries are liberalised and enterprise begins to flourish. The dynamic gains are particularly difficult to estimate.

(7) GAINS FROM CONTINUING THE MONOPOLY?

One argument used by the CEGB[9] is that it might as well be left as a monopoly because most of the gains which will come from electricity privatisation derive from allowing the Board freedom to purchase its inputs from the cheapest sources. Although the Generating Board evidently makes this case in the context of privatisation, it might equally well lead to the conclusion that the Board should remain nationalised but be given greater freedom to operate commercially.

If the CEGB were to be left intact after privatisation, it would emerge with its monopoly power enhanced. Product market power would be unaltered, as would be its information monopoly; arrangements with the unions could stay as they are and the Board would retain its existing power to act as a pressure group. But its monopsony power *vis-`a-vis* the coal industry and the generating plant manufacturers would increase. Although existing restrictive practices

---

[8] Robinson and Sykes and Sykes and Robinson, *op. cit.*

[9] John Baker, 'How best to give power to the people', *Financial Times*, 25 November 1987.

in coal and plant purchasing are undesirable ((4) above), there is not much point in replacing them with another undesirable market situation (private monopsony). If the CEGB remained intact, the consequence might be continued collusion to exclude privately mined coal, overseas coal and foreign generating plant. Even if the CEGB did reduce its costs, there would, in the absence of competition, be no mechanism for passing those benefits on to consumers: regulation of such a complex industry is hardly capable of doing so. There is already one example in the British energy market of the unfortunate consequences of vesting monopsony power in a large state or ex-state corporation: the stop-go exploration and development cycles which British Gas has generated by exploiting its monopsony power relative to North Sea producers set a very discouraging precedent.

(8) THE SCOPE FOR COMPETITION

Competition in Coal?

Before considering the transition to a competitive market, it is best to discuss the scope for competition in coal and the ESI so that we can see what eventual states might be desirable.

In the case of coal, there appears to be no economic reason why a single corporation should run the industry. Coal is a naturally competitive market. The coal monopoly is a political creation (though the reasons for its creation in the mid-1940s are understandable) which has been politically maintained.[10] Until very recently, the political climate has been such that coal privatisation was regarded as virtually unthinkable. But it is now firmly on the political agenda.

Entry to the coal industry has been very tightly regulated by a curious system which permits the nationalised coal industry to decide which small competitors it will allow in and then forces those competitors to pay a royalty to British Coal. The very small private sector which has been tolerated by British Coal is subject to extremely severe restrictions on the size of both underground and opencast operations and is also constrained by the collusive Joint Understanding between British Coal and the CEGB. In the circumstances, it is surprising that so much private mining manages to exist, producing 4-5 million tonnes a year (including coal recovery activities) and making profits. That it has done so says something about the scope there would be for relatively small private operations if the market were liberalised.

A first step in liberalising the market would be to free entry, taking reserves ownership and licensing out of the hands of British Coal. Licence issue and royalty collection (from British Coal whilst it exists, as well as the private miners) would more appropriately be left to the Department of Energy so as to encourage private companies to bid

---

[10] *Can Coal be Saved?*, *op. cit.*

for coal deposits which are not already being mined, for those mines which British Coal has abandoned and for coal tips and other residues from past mining operations. A cash-bidding procedure would probably be best, since it would collect rent as well as allocating licences, but, if that is considered too radical a notion for now, there could be a 'discretionary' régime such as there is for North Sea licences. As well as freeing entry, however, British Coal's existing pits and opencast operations should be sold to the private sector, under a procedure such as that suggested in (9) below.

In a liberalised market, with easy entry and competition to supply consumers from a number of coal companies, instead of the concentration on 'superpits' which appears to be British Coal's policy, one would expect to see a wide diversity of mining operations in which now neglected small pockets of coal would be worked profitably (and, incidentally, to the benefit of employment in some of the regions where unemployment is high). A competitive coal industry would probably consist of large mining companies, somewhat smaller operations run by managers who had 'bought out', small mining companies and worker co-operatives. In other words, the diversity of mining conditions in Britain would be reflected in a diversity of ownership structures and scales of operation. In some cases, pits and nearby power stations might be owned by the same company.

Towards Competition in Electricity Supply

Electricity supply is a more complex industry than coal, primarily because of its natural monopoly elements. But the industry as a whole is not a natural monopoly. Moreover, those parts which appear to be naturally monopolistic need not be so forever as technology advances. The present industry ought to be split vertically into generation, transmission and distribution. Generation, which as already explained is by far the largest sector in terms of costs, appears to have no natural monopoly characteristics and should be transformed into a competitive industry ((11) below). Price regulation would be unnecessary since consumers would be safeguarded by competition, though the government (via general or specific anti-monopoly legislation) would have to be vigilant to ensure that competition was maintained. Regulation is always such an unsatisfactory business that to be able to avoid it for the bulk of the industry is an enormous advantage compared with the present régime.

The main transmission network would no longer be owned by a monopoly generator. Instead, it would act as a common carrier in electricity, providing much freer entry into power generation than there is today. Power station owners, including industrial companies with electricity surplus to their requirements and owners of combined heat and power systems, would use the network to compete in supplying electricity to area distributors or direct to large consumers. There would also be competition from imported electricity.

Transmission would probably have to be regulated – either by remaining in the public sector or as a private regulated company – though franchising is another possibility.

Supplies to smaller consumers would be via area distributors. It is generally assumed that regulation would be necessary for such consumers because of the natural monopolies which the distributors would enjoy. Readers of *Economic Affairs*[11] will, however, be aware that in certain parts of the United States there is competition in local distribution of electricity. It is worth exploring whether some form of competition in distribution would be possible in Britain[12] - for instance, by contracts between individual consumers and local retailers of electricity (who would all use the same network). The idea would be to treat the whole of the transportation system for electricity, from power station to consumer, as a common carrier network via which local retailers would obtain their supplies.

(9) TRANSITIONAL ARRANGEMENTS FOR COAL

In order to move to competition from the highly monopolised and politicised structures which have characterised coal and electricity supply for so many years, transitional arrangements are needed, though it will have to be made clear that they are only transitional.

In the case of coal, a problem which would arise in moving to a competitive market is that of formulating large numbers of prospectuses and trying to deal with the sale of many parcels of assets. Such a process could take a long time and provide many opportunites for obstruction. One way of proceeding would be to privatise the Area Boards initially,[13] probably including in the sale of each Board the opencast operations which lie in its region as well as deep mines. At present, except in Scotland, opencast coal activities are supervised by British Coal's Opencast Executive. The initial investors in Area Boards, which would presumably be large companies in the main, would probably subsequently decide of their own accord that they wished to sell off some of the assets they had acquired. At this second sell-off stage, there would be management buy-outs, sales to smaller mining companies and the formation of worker co-operatives to produce the diversified industry which, as suggested above, should be the eventual aim of coal privatisation. If the initial investors were not divesting themselves of assets in this way, there would be a clear case for the government – in its often-neglected competition-promoting role – to insist that they did so.

---

[11] Walter J. Primeaux, Jnr., 'An End to Natural Monopoly', *Economic Affairs*, January/March 1985. (A revised and expanded version of this article is reproduced in Ch. 9, below, pp. 129-134.)

[12] Ray Evans, 'Property Rights, Markets, and Competition in Electricity Supply', below, Ch. 10, pp.135-143.

[13] Robinson and Sykes, *op. cit.*

(10) ELECTRICITY SUPPLY – EASY OPTIONS FOR THE TRANSITION?

The debate about electricity privatisation has produced a number of suggestions for a transition to competition in generation which seem seductively simple since they involve minimal immediate structural change in the ESI. None of these 'solutions' is likely to work since they do not deal effectively with the sources of monopoly power in the industry ((4) above).

One idea is evidently to free entry by permitting private sector companies to build, own and operate new power stations. The CEGB, however, would be privatised intact. In the form in which this proposal has appeared in the press,[14] it is unclear whether the CEGB would be allowed to join in the bidding for new power plant. If it were permitted to do so, potential entrants would obviously be deterred by the presence of such a strong incumbent generator; their willingness to invest would be diminished by the perceived riskiness of such investment. They would realise that they would have to attempt to compete, probably with a single power station, against an existing system run by an established operator with a large proportion of its costs sunk and able to cross-subsidise. Regulatory checks against 'unfair' competition would be virtually impossible because bidding for new stations would be in terms of estimated future costs. The network of established relationships between the CEGB and the organisations supplying its main inputs (for example, coal and generating plant) would also constitute a formidable barrier to entry so long as the CEGB existed. The Board has dominated the network for many years and that dominance will not easily be undermined. Indeed, some of the organisations which seem to be in the best position to compete for new power stations, such as the generating plant manufacturers, might well be deterred because of their continuing dependence on the privatised CEGB for business.

To circumvent such problems, the CEGB could be prohibited from joining in the bidding, so that it withered away over a period of years. Plainly, the Board would fight hard against such a proposal and, if it were implemented, the fight would probably still continue. Since the CEGB's information monopoly would remain largely intact, it would continue to be a powerful pressure group always urging the government of the day to relent and overturn the legislation which banned it from competing. Some government, some day would probably bow to the pressure. Even if all governments to the end of the century did keep the ban, competition would be very slow in coming despite the relatively large amount of capacity which may be replaced in the 1990s. Thus, in the early years of the next century, probably no more than 10 per cent of installed ESI capacity in Britain would be in the hands of non-CEGB private owners.

---

[14] 'On the starting grid but in need of a boost', *Financial Times*, 7 August 1987.

Another proposal which has apparently been made[15] is to establish a single competitor for the CEGB, presumably by separating-off part of the existing generating system and placing it under new management. This 'Mercury-type' solution might seem rather odd, given the amount of dissatisfaction which has arisen over the activities of British Telecom. Although it is not clear whether or not the Government is taking it seriously in view of the consumer discontent which might arise, it is worth brief discussion.

Disadvantages of a Duopoly

Duopoly is usually a very unsatisfactory market structure. There are strong incentives to collude, especially where, as in electricity, there is a close substitute (gas) only in a limited part of the market so that the market demand curve is highly inelastic with respect to price. The inelasticity of market demand for electricity can be exploited if the 'competitors', either explicitly or (more likely) implicitly, decide not to compete on price. In electricity, competitive forces would probably not be sufficiently strong in a duopolistic market either to reduce costs significantly or to pass on to consumers any gains which did occur. Furthermore, fears of collusion would almost certainly lead to price regulation of a duopolistic generation industry. Duopoly would thus fail to realise one of the great advantages of introducing competition – that competition automatically safeguards consumers and thus avoids the need for regulation. The problems which would face any regulatory body set up to supervise pricing and other matters for the whole ESI – whether a monopoly or a duopoly – would be enormous. Indeed, its task would probably be quite impossible. It would either be captured or so overwhelmed that regulatory paralysis of decision-making would ensue.

A final point which is evidently not always appreciated about these apparently easy options for introducing competition – whether they are supposed to bring in competitors only for new power stations or to institute a single competitor – is that they are incompatible with any liberal form of coal privatisation. So long as the CEGB remains effectively intact, it will be extremely hard to persuade any companies to invest in British coal-mining since potential entrants will know that they will be faced with a dominant buyer for most of their output. Only if there is an early and assured break-up of the CEGB into a number of competing generating companies can competition also be established in British coal-mining.

For anyone who wishes to see a generally liberalised British energy market, this last point is extremely important. The end-result of privatising the remaining British energy industries which are in state hands should surely be to establish a generation industry and a coal industry within each of which there is competitive rivalry and between which there is bargaining among a number of suppliers and

[15] 'Whitehall favours break-up of CEGB into three parts', *Financial Times*, 2 November 1987.

customers. There would also be actual and potential competition from imports of both coal and electricity. Neither industry would dominate the other, there would be downward pressure on costs, consumers' interests would be safeguarded by the force of competition and producers would, in their own interests, act to ensure secure supplies. The result would be far from perfect; there would be an important role for government to maintain competition and to deal with failures in the market (for instance, in safety and environmental protection). But it would be a very significant advance on the present cost-plus régime.

(11) BREAKING UP THE CEGB

For the reasons outlined above, it is improbable that the very strong and widespread monopoly power of the present ESI, which is concentrated mainly in the CEGB, can be undermined without breaking up the Generating Board. Yet an overnight break-up seems impractical. Consequently some transitional process is needed, provided the break-up is assured and does not take too long.

A scheme for the transition which has the characteristics of being early and assured has been devised by Tony Merrett and developed mainly by him and Allen Sykes.[16] The idea (the Privatised Transition to Competition (PTC) scheme) is as follows.

The dominance of the generator would be overcome by placing area distributors (a smaller number than now) in charge of the former CEGB though the latter would still, during an interim period, have its debt held by the Treasury. Area distributors would be private companies in each of which there would be a large shareholding (say, 25 per cent) by one or more corporate investors. Thus new management would be introduced into electricity distribution. The transmission network would be an independent private, regulated company and area distributors would also be regulated.

Distributors would be given both a charter duty and a financial incentive to sell off power stations in, say, five or six blocks over a period of two to five years. Competition in generation would thus be established and the debt held by the Treasury would be redeemed by the proceeds of the sales. The area distributors would award contracts to the new generating companies which would be chosen on the basis of their bids to supply power, at first via the former CEGB, but eventually direct to area distributors and larger consumers. An Electricity Standards and Regulatory Commission would be the regulatory body and would be charged with maintaining competition in the ESI.

There may, of course, be other forms of transitional arrangements which would lead to competition in generation. The advantage of the PTC scheme is that it strikes at all the sources of monopoly power

[16] Sykes and Robinson, *op. cit.*

which at present exist in the ESI. In the early stages of privatisation a number of substantial, competing generators would be established between whom collusion would be very difficult. There would be no need for regulation of generation, except to preserve competition. Coal privatisation – to establish competing sources of British coal supply – would follow naturally. Because transmission would be separated from generation and distribution, any generator would have access to distributors and larger consumers. Thus an extremely significant element of competition from smaller generators would be promoted – for instance, from entrepreneurs who would refurbish 'mothballed' generating plant (in some cases, no doubt, as combined heat and power schemes). It would also be possible for distributors and larger consumers to contract for imports of electricity thereby increasing competitive pressures on British generators.

(12) THE 'PROBLEM' OF NUCLEAR POWER

Another advantage of the PTC scheme is that it can accommodate the nuclear sector which would be placed under the joint ownership of the area distributors. No really satisfactory form of privatisation is possible for nuclear power stations given the present state of public opinion, but that has more to do with past decisions about nuclear power than with privatisation *per se.* Privatising the ESI brings out into the open a number of problems which already exist but which have been concealed by public ownership – the probable unsaleability of some or all of the existing nuclear stations in England and Wales, the probable unwillingness of the private sector to build any more nuclear stations in the present climate of public opinion, and the devaluation of fossil fuel power stations which has already occurred because the low avoidable costs of nuclear stations mean that they pre-empt base-load power. The privatisation debate has also revealed a curious feature of government thinking: although, in general, it wants private decision-making in the electricity supply industry, it certainly does not want the private sector to make decisions about new nuclear capacity, presumably because it thinks it would not like those decisions.

(13) CONCLUSIONS

It is not possible in a brief paper to deal with all the issues involved in coal and electricity privatisation. My principal message is the need to privatise the industries with the deliberate aim of injecting as much competition as is practicable. To realise the benefits which are achievable, both of these closely-linked industries should be privatised in liberal fashion. If it is not possible to privatise coal at the same time as electricity supply, the Government ought at least to declare its intentions towards coal so that potential investors in the ESI are well-informed. Just as a liberal form of coal privatisation will be extremely difficult if a generating monopoly or near-monopoly remains, so there will be problems in selling shares in the ESI if investors believe there will be only one British company from which they can buy coal. Past experience will anyway tell them that a future government might decide to protect such a company from foreign competition.

In electricity supply, very powerful anti-competition lobbies have appeared. One should not blame the industry's management, its unions, electrical plant manufacturers, the nuclear industries and others for trying to protect what they see as their interests by persuading government to retain a monopolistic structure. But it would be a disaster for the community as a whole if there were another British Gas-style privatisation. Still worse would be privatisation of both coal and the ESI as monopolies. The way would then be open for collusion between the two industries and, quite probably, continued government manipulation of the corporations. The new constituency of private shareholders need not stand in the way of government interference if action were channelled primarily through electricity supply since, as we have seen in recent years, a monopoly in that industry has sufficient market power to pass on to the consumer increased costs forced on it by government.

The Government evidently embarked on electricity privatisation without first considering all the complicated issues which would arise, some related to the complexities of the industry itself and some connected with energy and industrial policies. It would be well advised to take its time in planning, rather than rushing into some scheme which may seem superficially attractive but which is incapable of introducing more than token competition in electricity supply and is likely to result in a continued coal monopoly.

9

ELECTRICITY SUPPLY: AN END TO NATURAL MONOPOLY

Walter J. Primeaux, Jr.

Associate Professor of Economics, University of Illinois

CONSUMERS OF most goods and services throughout the Western world can choose between many competing products. They weigh the characteristics of each one against its competitors and buy the item which best serves their tastes and requirements. But these consumers have absolutely no choice in selecting a supplier of electricity among several competitors, from which to purchase their requirements. The average consumer never really understands why not. He never questions the justifications for this monopoly and he accepts it as if it were governed by an immutable law of nature.

But recent research refutes the traditional justification for monopoly – government or private – in the supply of electricity. So why is more competition not allowed between electricity suppliers so that consumers could enjoy the additional benefits monopoly takes from them?

THEORY OF NATURAL MONOPOLY

The argument for not allowing direct competition in businesses supplying 'utilities', such as electricity, gas and sewage disposal, is based on a concept called 'the theory of natural monopoly'. Although it is somewhat complex, the theory states in essence that operating costs and prices to the consumer would be higher if competition in the supply of electricity were permitted, and that, moreover, utility firms cannot compete because they are monopolistic by nature – that is, even if they were allowed to compete, only one firm would survive because operating conditions would permit one firm to drive the other(s) out of business.

This idea appealed to the makers of policy in the USA, the UK and elsewhere, and when the industry was very young, a public policy was developed which essentially prevented direct electric utility competition from taking place; this monopoly became the natural state of affairs in the electricity business. In the USA, for example, competition, although legal in most states, is not very common.

I first became aware that competition existed in the electric utility industry in 1968. After presenting the traditional natural monopoly theory to a graduate class, a student commented, '...that isn't the way it is in Lubbock, Texas', and then explained the nature of direct competition there. I first assumed he was confusing competition with nothing more than a divided city where each of two monopoly firms served a designated territory without directly competing. I investigated and found the student to be correct. Direct competition does exist in Lubbock: two firms sell electricity, and customers can choose between one or the other.

COMPETITION IN SUPPLY OF ELECTRICITY

Questions Raised by the Case of Lubbock

This discovery opened a vast new topic of research for me. I wanted to learn why competition should exist in Lubbock in the teeth of the predictions of the theory of natural monopoly. The mere existence of utility competition in this one city raised several important questions.

- How many other cities also permitted direct electric utility competition?
- Were the fundamental propositions of the theory correct?
- Why did the theory fail to hold up in this case?
- Is direct electric competition a practicable alternative policy to electric utility regulation?

These are all important questions. Economists believed that they knew the answers, but doubt and scepticism replaced the faith and confidence I formerly had in natural monopoly. The discovery that direct competition did actually exist in the electric utility business opened to me for the first time the possibility that the theory of natural monopoly could be invalid. At that point (1968), I began an extensive research programme to discover as much as possible about these unusual situations and how they could exist in spite of the theory of natural monopoly saying that they could not. Since no central source of information existed at that time, I began to put together piece by piece the bits and pieces I gathered in this research programme. Some of the research results are summarised in the following paragraphs and a more thorough treatment is presented in my book, *Direct Electric Utility Competition: The Natural Monopoly*

Myth.[1]

In 1966, only 49 cities in the USA were served by two electric companies, and the number is now even smaller.

One basic argument of the natural monopoly theory is that costs would be higher if competition existed between two utility firms. This argument is an important proposition of the theory. If it does not hold, several other predictions would fail, and so this idea is the cornerstone of the theory of natural monopoly.

COMPETITION REDUCES UNIT COSTS

Cost data collected from cities with two electricity suppliers fail to support the natural monopoly theory. Instead of competition resulting in higher operating costs, they were found to be lower, since competition reduces or eliminates the tendency for monopolists to become lazy and inefficient. This beneficial effect on costs more than offsets the economies of scale which tend to cause an electric firm's costs per unit of output to fall as more units are produced. The net effect is that competing firms produce electricity at lower rather than higher costs per unit because of competitive pressure. This result shows a fundamental weakness in natural monopoly theory: once it fails to withstand the empirical evidence, several companion arguments used to grant monopoly status to utility firms also fail.

For example, the theory of natural monopoly states that consumers would suffer because of the higher production costs by having to pay higher prices for the electricity they used whenever competition existed. If *lower costs* occur with competition, however, the expectation for consumers suffering from higher prices from competition is unfounded. Indeed, my later research confirmed this result: direct electric utility competition causes *lower* consumer prices instead of higher prices. So consumers do not suffer from the rivalry, they actually benefit from it. Consequently, public policy measures restricting competition for the purpose of 'protecting' consumers actually harms consumer interests instead of helping them.

Moreover, even though it may be *technically* possible for a single electric company to operate at lower costs than if two firms served a single city, the research results mentioned above reveal that natural inefficiencies which emerge whenever monopoly exists prevent this outcome from being realised in practice. Consequently, restricting entry in this business merely because the natural monopoly theory states that one firm *could* operate at lower costs than if two firms exist is not only making a public policy decision on the basis of a flawed theory but reflects unrealistic expectations. Monopoly breeds inefficiency in any enterprise; this fact cannot be ignored.

These favourable cost effects from competition help explain why direct competition in the supply of electricity could exist over a long

[1] New York: Praeger, 1986.

period contrary to the predictions of the theory of natural monopoly. They also explain the benefits to consumers in lower prices and better services from direct competition despite the predictions of the natural monopoly theory (below).

Since competitive firms operate at lower costs, they are able to charge consumers lower prices for the electricity they sell. Moreover, my research results reveal that electricity consumers in markets with competition received a better quality of service and the competitive firms were more concerned about consumer welfare than firms operating as monopolists. Upon reflection, this is consistent with the expected outcome whenever competition exists instead of monopoly in any business. The efficiency generated by competition will have a favourable impact on production costs. In addition, it has a beneficial impact on all other firm costs. Consequently, services are provided more promptly to the consumers, giving greater satisfaction because service quality is better. In contrast, the lack of a competitive spur to efficiency causes monopolies to be inefficient. Inefficient firms take longer to perform a service and turn out work of a lower quality; this inefficiency dissatisfies consumers, ironically at higher costs to the business than if service was better.

As mentioned above, prices and price flexibility in competitive markets in electricity supply were examined to discover if higher prices to consumers resulted, as the theory of natural monopoly predicts. But consumer prices for electricity are lower with competition, and the price differences are substantial. The percentage decrease in prices caused by competition varies depending upon the rate category of the individual consumer; for the rate categories examined, the price reductions ranged from 16 to 19 per cent. Competition lowered the average price per kilowatt-hour by 33 per cent. These differences represent substantial gains to consumers from competition in the supply of electricity.

BENEFITS OF PRICE FLEXIBILITY

Consumers were found to benefit also when price *flexibility* was examined. Firms involved in direct competition for the sale of electricity changed prices more often than monopoly firms. Yet price wars, expected by natural monopoly theory, never occurred in practice.

Larger amounts of excess capacity did not develop whenever the electricity firms examined faced direct competition. This discovery, too, is contrary to the theory of natural monopoly. The increased price flexibility and the lower prices of competitive firms probably reduced any tendency for this problem to occur. By allowing firms to react to market forces, it is likely these forces reduced excess capacity.

Case studies of cities with competition in electricity supply show that customers also seem to gain substantial additional benefit from it. The theory of natural monopoly failed totally when it was compared with the reality of competition. The conclusions of a direct comparison of monopoly and competition were:

1. effective competition can and does exist;
2. price wars do not seem to be a serious problem;
3. better consumer service occurs with competition;
4. competition in electricity supply can endure over a long period;
5. a consumer preference for competition.

My later research involved interviews with managers of competing electricity firms. Some said they benefited from direct competition but others said it caused them problems. The benefit came from the stronger incentive to efficiency while the problems were no different from the competitive difficulties of any industry faced with a rival. Monopoly is obviously much easier than competition; firms must work harder when they compete.

In the USA state laws generally provide for competition in electricity supply whenever conditions justify it. Court records show very clearly that monopoly electricity firms are not guaranteed protected markets. The state Public Utility Commission usually has power to decide whether conditions justify admitting competition into an existing monopoly market. The real power of a public utility commission rests in its authority to interpret and relate existing market conditions to 'the public welfare' and to decide finally whether monopoly is justified or competition should be admitted.

US STATE REGULATORS TEND TO OPPOSE COMPETITION

Even though some state regulatory commissions have the authority to admit a rival firm, the majority of commissions questioned in a survey expressed a policy of *preventing* competition. They seem generally to accept the concept of natural monopoly and consider duplication of facilities to result in economic waste. Essentially, they accept the theory of natural monopoly, even though it is no longer valid *and probably never was*. Perhaps their unwillingness to accept competition is because, if it is tolerated, it constitutes an admission by a utility regulatory commission that it is unable or unwilling to fulfil its regulatory function, since, if the regulators were effective, competition would not be considered to improve market effectiveness.

One worry of the opponents of electricity competition, that two firms cannot co-exist in the business, is derived from the belief that a competing firm would strive to eliminate its rival. But anti-trust laws are applicable to other utility firms and seem to do a reasonably good job of curbing anti-competitive practices in other industries. Why should they not be effective in the public utility industries?

Furthermore, in markets where competition exists between electric utility firms the behaviour predicted by the theory of natural monopoly does *not* seem to occur. Evidence shows that anti-competitive practices did exist during the early days of the industry. But the institutions which exist today to control businesses did not exist when anti-competitive practices were common, and I doubt that very many economists, business or others, would support the abolition of the most fundamental anti-trust laws which prohibit anti-competitive practices.

CONCLUSION

My conclusion must be that *there is nothing basic in the electricity supply industry which makes active competition impossible between two firms serving the same customers in the same market.* It is 'public', that is, government policy, not economic conditions, which has restricted entry and prevented the direct competition from which consumers would have benefited. The theory of natural monopoly was developed without the benefit of statistical data during the early days of the industry – the early 1890s – when technology was very different. This is the time to reconsider the 'public' (or perhaps I should say 'anti-public') policy which grants monopoly status to electricity firms, public or private.

10

PROPERTY RIGHTS, MARKETS AND COMPETITION IN ELECTRICITY SUPPLY

Ray Evans

Western Mining Corporation Limited, Melbourne, Australia

In 1831 Michael Faraday discovered the laws of electromagnetic induction which describe the physical relationships between mechanical and electromagnetic energy. It took another fifty years for inventors, enthusiasts and entrepreneurs, such as Edison, to begin laying the foundations of the electricity supply industry which is based on Faraday's discoveries. One such enthusiast was the Third Marquess of Salisbury who first installed arc lights at Hatfield House (1880), and then incandescent lamps, often to the alarm and consternation of his family and guests.

Although Faraday, in 1853, had told Gladstone, recently appointed Chancellor of the Exchequer, that one day the Minister might tax electricity, it is doubtful whether he could have conceived of the gargantuan state monopolies which now dominate this fundamental industry. So dramatic was the improvement in the amenities of domestic, industrial and commercial life which electricity brought that, at the beginning of this century, electricity came to symbolise modernity. For Lenin, communism was socialism plus electricity, and politicians throughout the Western world sought to capture this industry in order to be associated with the benefits it brought. As a consequence of the Great War (amongst other reasons), the prestige of the state had increased, and it was politically easy for the state to take over and operate, allegedly for the benefit of all, this beneficent and symbolic industry.

So, although the electricity supply industry in Britain, the USA and in Australia started out, in the 1880s, as privately-owned industries, after the Great War it was nationalised in the UK and Australia, and heavily regulated as a set of private and public monopolies in the

USA. As a consequence direct competition between electricity utilities has not developed, except in some US cities; it has been an industry in which property rights have been non-existent (UK and Australia); or so heavily regulated as to lose most of the essential characteristics of property rights (the USA).

THE IMPORTANCE OF CAPITAL MARKETS

The absence of tradeable property rights in the electricity supply industry is of the utmost significance. The effectiveness with which the capital stock of a society is used is one of the most significant determinants of economic progress. The only effective mechanisms for monitoring and improving the efficiency of usage of the capital stock of a nation are the capital markets, where price movements of commodities, of company shares, and now of national currencies, are continuously and intensely scrutinised. The capital market is the most important market in the economy. It is in that market where management opportunities are traded and where the success or otherwise of management is monitored. It is in that market where information concerning the effective use of capital is most valuable and is most diligently sought after.

The fundamental doctrine of socialism is that politicians are much more able to direct and supervise the use of capital than are private citizens seeking to improve their individual and family circumstances. In the 1920s socialism was so influential that many conservative politicians in the English-speaking world were at the forefront of the state take-overs of the electricity supply industry.

The Soviet Experience

The quarantining of the electricity industry from the information-gathering and judgement-passing activities of the capital markets for the last 70 years has had an effect on that industry which is impossible to calculate. We can speculate upon what might have happened if it had been otherwise by looking at Lenin's legacy of socialism plus electricity, the Soviet Union.

The Soviet experience since 1917 demonstrates that centrally-directed industries (or national economies) only work to the extent that prices and work practices in the centrally-planned industry are set, by example, from market-based industries or economies which have some influence on them. The Soviet economy – a command economy – improves or declines in accordance with the growth or diminution of the black market, and with the expansion or contraction of private production in agriculture.

The electricity supply industries of the USA, the UK, and Australia have worked as well as they have because they have operated in economies in which most of the prices of their input factors, particularly labour and capital, are set by an outside market. Nonetheless, the lack of open markets within the industry, particularly a market for forward contracts, has led to an alleged extraordinary degree of over-investment and over-capacity in the USA, and to a somewhat lesser degree in Western Europe and Australia. I say allegedly because no-one can be sure that in a market-based, competitively-structured industry, prices would not have been much lower, and consumption correspondingly much higher, than is currently the case.

In Australia the electricity supply industry accounts for approximately 10 per cent of the nation's capital stock. In the UK the figure may be higher. There is no other single industry, not even telecommunications, which uses such a large proportion of society's capital. For over 70 years there has been no market mechanism at work, monitoring and directing the efficient employment of this capital. This must mean that the restoration of tradeable property rights to this industry, thus reviving the possibility of bankruptcy and take-over, together with the establishment of a competitive industrial structure, will lead to massive economic gains.

IS ELECTRICITY DISTRIBUTION A NATURAL MONOPOLY?

One reason for the lack of resistance after the First World War to nationalisation proposals for the electricity supply industry was because its output is produced and consumed simultaneously and instantaneously, and that it has, at least in its distribution sector, the outward appearances of a natural monopoly. Because electricity cannot be stored it was then thought to be different from other commodities, such as wheat or mutton, and, consequently, that electricity could not be bought and sold in a market as these more traditional commodities have been bought and sold since the beginning of civilisation.

Whilst electricity that has been produced cannot be traded, electricity that is yet to be produced is bought and sold frequently. In the USA, as a result of the development of large 'power pools' with substantial inter-connection capacity, particularly on the Atlantic coast, competing power utilities buy and sell electricity forward contracts from each other on markets that they operate, for themselves, around the clock. The price of electricity varies from hour to hour, day to day, season to season, and the forward contracts markets (although they are not called that) allow the utilities that have combined to form the pools to make substantial savings.

It has long been argued that to have more than one set of distribution conductors running down a suburban street was both economically and environmentally ridiculous, and that the resulting natural monopoly had either to be state-owned or heavily regulated by the state. These arguments were never contested to my knowledge in the UK or Australia, but there are, to this day, some 20 cities in the USA where two companies operate duplicate distribution systems and compete for market share.

Walter Primeaux, an American teacher in business management, has performed a great public service by focussing attention on these US cities where competition, however constrained, is the norm.[1] He has been the object of much condescension by economists who entirely miss the significance of his argument and evidence. The issue is not whether or not electricity distribution is a natural monopoly, according to the textbook definitions, but whether the industry, operating under different régimes, can perform much more efficiently because of different rules and incentive structures under which the participants work.

Electricity Distribution *not* a Monopoly

Whether electricity distribution (as opposed to generation or bulk transmission) must always be a monopoly is the crucial question. If competition at the retail end of the industry can be legislated into existence, and the political foundation of continuing widespread support for competition established, then almost all of the debate about the efficacy of this or that regulatory arrangement becomes irrelevant. Primeaux has demonstrated that competition has been brought into being by legislation, and sanctioned by public approval, for many years. In Lubbock, Texas, a city of some 150,000 people, two distribution companies, each operating their own reticulation network (wasteful duplication), vie for market share, under a fairly rerstrictive regulatory régime. Visitors to Lubbock will quickly find that competition, even limited competition, produces lower electricity prices and better service.

In the UK it has always been assumed that monopoly in distribution and transmission was inevitable and that state ownership was the best way of overcoming the problems of private monopoly. If competition can be established as the norm; if it can be shown that competition in electricity supply will not lead to any greater instability than occurs in, say, the oil industry; if markets for electricity forward contracts can operate successfully; then the arguments, not only for state monopoly, vanish; so do the arguments for industry-specific regulation. Given the ink that has been spilled in working up the most desirable modes of regulation, and given the employment prospects of economists in the new regulatory bodies, it is not surprising that arguments about the existence of competition, and the possibility of its extension, do not get much support in the economic literature.

All regulatory bodies are captured, ultimately, by politicians or more usually by the industry being regulated. Economists who dream

[1] Walter J. Primeaux, *Direct Electric Utility Competition: The Natural Monopoly Myth*, New York: Praeger, 1986 (see his Chapter 9 in this volume, pp.129-134). Also Robert W. Poole, Jr., *Unnatural Monopolies: The Case for Deregulating Public Utilities*, Lexington, Mass.: Lexington Books, 1983.

of becoming regulators should study the history of the regulation profession more closely.

The electricity supply industry has traditionally been broken up for analytical purposes into generation, high-voltage transmission, and distribution sectors – the so-called horizontal de-segregation. Let us consider competition and markets in these sectors in turn.

REGULATION BY PRIVATE FORWARD CONTRACTING

It has been argued (but much less strongly in recent times) by the engineers who run state electricity monopolies that generation cannot be broken up into independent and competing power stations because the load-scheduling operations which the electricity authorities carry out on a daily, weekly and monthly basis would be impossible. The latter part of this argument is true but it does not follow that the industry would consequently collapse. Instead of load scheduling being carried out by a central planning department, load scheduling would occur as the result of the operation of a forward contracts market. The most significant consequence would be the introduction of time-of-day pricing. Peak-hour electricity is typically two to five times as expensive to produce as 4 a.m. electricity, and because there is no market this price differential is masked by gargantuan cross-subsidies.

Once a forward contracts market was operating, individual generating companies, placed in a competitive situation, would seek to maximise the returns on their assets. They would have to solve all of the complex problems of deciding what to offer and at what price in the market and, given the operation of competitive forces and an open electricity futures market, it would not take long for a major transformation of the industry to take place. In particular, any cross-subsidisation from, say, power stations to the coal-winning operations would not survive the scrutiny of the market. Those British power stations close to seaports, and capable of using imported coal from Australia or South Africa, would have a clear economic advantage over power stations dependent upon, and dedicated to, a particular coal-mine, unless that coal-mine could compete with imported coal.

Such power station/coal-mine complexes, having a monopsony-monopoly relationship, should be incorporated as integrated operating entities. The market value of the coal-mine/power station complex would be determined by the cost performance of the coal-mine. Power stations with access to the sea, or access to a number of domestic suppliers, would best be incorporated as stand-alone entities. Individual incorporation of scores of power stations, the consequent obligation of the board and management of each corporation to shareholders, an open forward contracts market, a competitive supply position, would quickly create a dynamic coal-winning and electricity-generating industry which would give the UK an enormous economic advantage within the EEC.

ELECTRICITY DISTRIBUTION

A Comparison with Water Supply

The assumed natural monopoly qualities of electricity retailing have led to much debate about optimal regulatory arrangements. Joskow and Schmalensee, in their *Markets for Power*, are typical exegetes of such arguments:

> 'Water supply is a classic and important example [of natural monopoly]; competitive water companies clearly would produce wasteful duplication of facilities.'

The example of water supply is useful in that the physical phenomena are easily understood by non-engineers. Applying Vernon Smith's arguments (private discussion, University of Arizona, January 1986) concerning the fungibility of electricity and the ability of competing businessmen to contract for joint ownership of common facilities, I consider how competition would be established in water reticulation without duplication of the pipe network.

In practice, water from different dams or rivers is not identical, and water quality will vary from season to season. Assume, however, the fungibility of water in this network, which is jointly owned, say, by three competing firms, which are signatories to a contract specifying property rights and obligations arising as a consequence of changes in market share within the market area serviced by the network.

These firms would contract with bulk suppliers of water to obtain agreed quantities at agreed prices. They would then retail the water to domestic and commercial consumers and compete in price and service. There would be opportunity to offer bundled or unbundled services. Each competitor would have a common interest in maintaining the quality of performance of the distribution network of pipes and storage basins. In order to forestall one competitor either through predatory pricing, or through take-over, from becoming a monopolist, a rule requiring automatic bifurcation whenever one firm obtains, say, 80 per cent of the market, would have to have high legal standing. The fact that it is impossible for a customer to determine whether the particular molecules of water he consumes are the molecules which his supplier obtained from the wholesaler, is irrelevant.

What is important is that the retailer has bought so much water, during a given period of time, from a wholesaler or wholesalers and has sold (perhaps) a different amount to his customers. His incentive structure is similar to that of the local greengrocer or butcher, and no specific regulatory apparatus is required to ensure that people are not poisoned through neglect, by suppliers, of water quality.

Now let us move from a network of water pipes and storage basins to a network of overhead wires, underground cables, transformers and switches. There can be no argument concerning the fungibility of electricity. Competing retailers can buy electricity with forward contracts; have it delivered on the high voltage transmission network to their retailing network; and sell it instantaneously to their domestic and commercial customers.

Is Electricity Different?

At this point technically-minded critics may argue that electricity is different from water. Electricity has to be consumed at the instant of production; storage of electricity is not possible; and problems of measurement will make joint operation of a commonly-owned network by competing retailers impossible.

It will be maintained by such critics that it will be impossible to measure who is buying how much electricity, at the supply points of the distribution network, at any moment. Only the combined consumption of the three competitors can be measured. This problem can be overcome by statistical sampling, using online measuring techniques, by each competitor, of its customers' consumptions. Large industrial customers would be online. A representative sample of domestic and commercial customers would be monitored by telephone lines and the instantaneous demand, for each of the competing suppliers, would be calculated at the supply points.

If the City of Hull, for example, were serviced by, say, three competing electricity retailing companies, which each started out, through prescription, with one-third of the market, and which, through a set of contractual arrangements jointly owned and operated the distribution hardware comprising transformers, conductors, cables, poles, and cable ducts, these companies would be able to compete in price, in service to consumers, and would be able to compete without regulatory oversight.

The contracts governing the joint ownership and operation of the distribution network would be complex. If one company increased market share at the expense of its competitors it would have to be obliged to buy the extra portion of the distribution capacity that it was not using from the company which had lost market share. Once again, some authors complain that the complexity of the contractual situation is so great that it is unrealistic to expect ordinary businessmen to be able to manage. However, if competing electricity companies in America can jointly own and operate very large power stations, to their mutual advantage, I cannot see why competing retailers cannot jointly contract to own and operate a distribution network. The incentives are identical in each case.

I use the City of Hull as an example because it is in such a location, given the political traditions of that city, and the success of its telephone company, that the contractual problems of setting up this new situation would best be worked out.

The attraction of this proposal is that it obviates the need for regulation. It allows entrepreneurial ingenuity to reduce prices and improve services, and to specialise in market segmentation. It gives the ordinary consumer a choice of supplier – and the political benefits of this cannot be overstated. It allows local participation in the capital structure of the local distribution companies, thus fostering a Burkeian sense of community.

TRANSMISSION

Electricity has to be transported from generating centres to the distribution areas. This is done over the High Voltage Transmission Grid (HVTG), just as other commodities are transported over road and rail networks. The difference between electricity and other commodities is one of instantaneity and technological complexity.

Most authors who have discussed the future of the HVTG in a deregulated and competitive industry have suggested that it should be retained as a government authority, obliged to operate as a common carrier, with the duty of maintaining voltage and frequency levels throughout the system. Maintaining frequency requires operating spinning reserve with the ability to take up load variations, and maintaining voltage levels requires capacity to generate reactive power. The authority would contract with private power stations or synchronous condenser operators to provide both spinning reserves and reactive power capacity. Whilst the companies which make up the generating sector of the industry could own and operate the HVTG on a contractual joint-venture arrangement, it may be, in the British context, that at present a state-owned and operated HVTG is the best proposal.

However, the HVTG Authority must not have monopoly rights. If a generating company wishes to build a transmission line to a new large customer, it must be able to do so without submitting its proposals to the HVTG Authority. In other words, whatever environmental or other approvals might be necessary, the HVTG Authority must have no role in adjudication.

THE BRITISH COAL INDUSTRY

It would be intolerable for a large number of competing generating companies to be faced with a monopoly supplier of coal. Whilst those generating companies with sea access and port facilities would be able to buy coal on the world market, those without sea access, and not having their own internationally competitive, dedicated suppliers, would be at a distinct disadvantage. In an industry where property rights had been traded for a long time, the most economic structure of the industry, ignoring tax-driven arrangements, would have evolved.

In the UK the introduction of tradeable property rights and competition into the electricity supply industry would make similar developments necessary in the UK coal industry. Those coal-mines which are dedicated suppliers to particular power stations should be incorporated with those power stations. The rest of the industry should be desegregated as much as possible and the capital markets be allowed to work out the most efficient and effective form of the industry. Once a competitive environment was established, a market in coal and coal futures, strongly influenced by world prices, would quickly develop. Who knows what future the British coal industry would have in such an environment?

The British coal industry has been dominated by trade union and party politics for so long that most observers assume that British coal cannot compete with the rest of the world. This assumption may be totally wrong.

For each separate company, whether distribution, generating, or coal-producing, a board of directors, and senior company management, will have to be appointed. Initially the UK Government will own 100 per cent of the shares of each company, and the method and extent of selling this stock will largely be governed by political considerations. For example, shares in the local distribution companies should be offered to local citizens on favourable terms. Management buy-outs would be an easy and effective method of transferring property rights.

Senior management in the large generating companies should have the opportunity to buy options which give them considerable incentives to increase the value of the share price of the company they work for.

The market value of the various components of the industry can be established, and that approximately, only after competition has been established as the norm, and property rights created and secured. Those property rights should not be subject to the whims of regulators. The motto of the electricity supply industry, at this fateful juncture in its history, should be 'Competition "yes", Regulation "no".'

11

LIBERALISING COAL: WAYS AND MEANS *

Colin Robinson

University of Surrey

and

Eileen Marshall

University of Birmingham

PRIVATISATION AND LIBERALISATION

MRS THATCHER'S Government is now in the midst of a 'privatisation' programme in which state-owned industries and other assets (such as local authority dwellings) are being transferred to the private sector. Some contracting-out of services is also taking place (as in local government and hospitals). Such a programme can have a variety of objectives. For the nationalised industries, for instance, it can be a_ means of spreading private share ownership to a wider public, reducing the politicisation of decision-making, and raising revenue for the Exchequer. Another principal objective of privatisation can be to liberalise - that is, to increase the amount of competition in the product, labour and capital markets[1] so as to exert a discipline on management and union leaderships to keep down costs and prices and widen consumer choice. It is, however, important to distinguish between privatisation and liberalisation. A degree of liberalisation can usually be achieved without privatisation. Thus, the freeing of coal imports would increase competition and so

* This chapter first appeared as Section IV in the authors' earlier work, *Can Coal be Saved: A Radical Proposal to Reverse the Decline of a Major Industry,* Hobart Paper 105, London: IEA, 1985.

1 The objectives of privatisation are discussed in Michael Beesley and Stephen Littlechild, 'Privatisation: Principles, Problems and Priorities', *Lloyds Bank Review*, July 1983; J.R. Shackleton, 'Privatisation: The Case Examined', *National Westminster Bank Review*, May 1984; and Alan Peacock, 'Privatisation in Perspective', *Three Banks Review*, December 1984.

liberalise the industry, but it would neither introduce the discipline of the private capital market nor increase the number of British suppliers. Similarly, privatisation does not necessarily imply liberalisation. Indeed, a government mainly concerned with raising revenue by means of a privatisation programme has an incentive *not* to liberalise since the proceeds would be maximised by selling the industries to private shareholders as monopolies. Following privatisation, shareholders in such a monopoly would have an incentive to minimise costs but not to keep down prices charged to consumers.

Ostensibly, the present Government believes in liberalisation. Some of its recent decisions, however, suggest that it is more concerned with raising revenue than with other objectives of privatisation. The proposal to privatise the British Gas Corporation (BGC) as a whole (instead of splitting it) is, in our view, symptomatic of this approach.[2] Transforming a big nationalised monopoly into a big private monopoly guarantees an eager reception in the City, a quick sale, and large proceeds. It is also likely to be enthusiastically received by the monopoly itself, just as the chairman of British Gas has welcomed the Government's proposals. But the Government's proposed method of privatisation would do very little to put shareholder pressure on management (there is, for instance, not much likelihood of a serious takeover threat for the BGC because of the Corporation's size and because the Government will retain a veto in the shape of a 'golden share'), and it does nothing whatsoever to liberalise the market. Instead, the Government proposes to establish cumbersome regulatory procedures aimed at preventing exploitation of the gas monopoly, even though there is a retreat from this kind of regulation in the United States.

The usual argument for privatising whole and then regulating the private corporation is that the activity in question is a natural monopoly. If unfettered market forces would lead to monopoly, because one firm could produce more efficiently than several firms, it can be argued that competition would be wasteful and inefficient, so that the industry in question is naturally monopolistic. British coal is, however, a very unnatural monopoly created by government. Coal deposits are dispersed by nature around the country. There will be economies of scale (reductions in average cost as the scale of output increases) in production from individual deposits. Some managerial, marketing and distribution economies may also be achievable by grouping a number of pits under the same management. It is, however, highly unlikely that, to exhaust economies of scale, the whole of the British coal industry has to be placed under one central management. On the contrary, experience with the nationalised coal

---

[2] Colin Robinson and Eileen Marshall, 'Privatising British Gas: Why Ministers have lost sight of their ideals', *The Financial Times*, 10 July 1985; Colin Robinson, *Liberalising the British Gas Market*, Proceedings of the Conference of the Benelux Association of Energy Economists, September 1985; and Robinson and Marshall, *The Privatisation of British Gas*, Memorandum to the House of Commons Select Committee on Energy, October 1985.

industry suggests that the more likely outcome of such centralisation is severe managerial diseconomies: that is, the organisation becomes much larger than can be efficiently managed and quite probably its costs become higher than they would be if there were a number of competing suppliers. Thus the disadvantages of monopoly - such as manipulation of the prices charged to consumers and the pressurising of government into protectionism and subsidisation - are very unlikely to be offset by cost reductions associated with larger size.

In our opinion, there would be few social gains from privatising coal unless there was a genuine effort to liberalise the industry by introducing competition into coal supply and the associated labour markets. Since coal is *not* a natural monopoly, there is no economic argument for privatising without liberalising. Indeed, it would merely convert an unnatural public monopoly into an unnatural private monopoly. For practical purposes, we can probably rule out attempts to sell the NCB whole as the Government plans to do with British Gas. Unless there is a remarkable and rapid change in the NCB's fortunes and in union attitudes, such a sale would be likely to attract few bidders and would not raise any significant sum. However, it is possible that a government might decide to sell the profitable parts of the NCB as one entity in the interests of revenue maximisation.

In the rest of this section we consider some ways and means of liberalising coal, mentioning in passing some of the benefits.

FREEING IMPORTS

An essential step in a liberalisation programme for the British coal market would be to remove the controls on coal imports which have been applied on and off for the last 30 years. For a short time, government intervened to *increase* imports: during 1955 and 1956, when there was a shortage of home production, the NCB was forced to import coal and sell it at a loss. However, during the period of renewed decline in the British coal industry from 1957 onwards, controls were used intermittently - along with various other devices - to protect the NCB from foreign competition. Controls have generally taken the form of 'arm twisting' of big consumers such as the Central Electricity Generating Board (CEGB) and the British Steel Corporation (BSC) who, despite their initial unwillingness to restrict imports, have been persuaded to do so by Ministers.

It has not been easy to suppress consumption of foreign coal. At times when government's restrictive attitude to imports appeared to change, imports have tended to increase. In 1979-80, for example, after the newly-elected Conservative Government had announced it would reduce subsidies for coal and when the appreciation of sterling had made overseas coal more competitive, imports rose sharply from 4.5 million tonnes in 1979 to 7.5 millions in 1980. The upsurge was short-lived. Early in 1981, a threatened miners' strike made the

Government draw back from confrontation.[3] Among other measures (such as approximately trebling the subsidies given to the coal industry in the early 1980s), the Government put pressure on the CEGB to limit its coal imports to about three-quarters of a million tonnes a year, and imports then fell back to some 4 million tonnes a year. The remaining imports were mainly coking coal for steel making and would have been larger had not the Government subsidised NCB coking coal to allow it to meet foreign competition.[4] Annual imports remained at about 4 million tonnes before rising to about 9 million tonnes in 1984 during the most recent strike. In the three years before the 1984-85 strike there were no formal restrictions on imports - indeed, it would have been difficult to impose any without contravening international trading obligations. But, as is so often the case in Britain, informal agreements with nationalised industries, at the expense of the taxpayer, proved an effective backdoor means of restricting competition.

Imports are a sensitive subject in all industries which have become accustomed over many years to extensive government protection. Yet freeing imports is an essential component of any policy for liberalising the coal market. There are good prospects for growth in the world steam-coal trade, based on exports from countries with production costs much lower than Britain's.[5] In Australia (now the world's largest coal exporter), South Africa and the United States, coal which is exported costs at the mine roughly $20-25 per tonne at mid-1985 exchange rates, which is about a third of the average pithead cost of British coal.[6] Coal from the new El Cerrejon mines in Colombia, which have recently begun to export, may cost rather more than in the USA and Australia, but it seems to be reaching world markets at prices competitive with those from the other major exporters. There is no good reason why British consumers should be prevented from buying coal from abroad when the state of the market and exchange rates make it advantageous for them to do so.

Imports are never likely to be large relative to British production, despite the higher costs of mining in this country. Coal is bulky and expensive to transport so that, by the time imported coal has reached Europe, its cost has approximately doubled (to around $40-45 per tonne c.i.f. Rotterdam in mid-1985).[7] Moreover, the absence at

---

[3] Robinson and Marshall, *What Future for British Coal?*, *op. cit.*, Prologue, and 'The Coal Industry and Coal Policy in Britain', in *European Community Coal Policy*, House of Lords Select Committee on the European Communities, Session 1983-84, 10th Report, 1983.

[4] *National Coal Board: A report on the efficiency and costs in the development, production and supply of coal by the NCB*, The Monopolies and Mergers Commission, Cmnd.8920, London: HMSO, 1983 (two volumes), para. 4.54.

[5] There have been numerous forecasts by international organisations of very big increases in world steam-coal exports. Many of these forecasts are probably on the optimistic side; nevertheless, considerable growth is likely to occur. (For example, International Energy Agency, *Coal Prospects and Policies in IEA Countries; 1983 Review*, Paris: OECD, 1984.)

[6] Information about production costs is given in International Energy Agency, *Coal Information 1985*, Paris: OECD, 1985, Chapter 3.

[7] Regular information about the price of coal imported into Western Europe is given in the monthly *FT Energy Economist*, FT Business Information.

present of deep-water terminals for importing steam-coal into Britain adds trans-shipment costs of about £5 per tonne from the large European ports such as Rotterdam. Imported coal would therefore most likely displace some British coal now sold in areas close to the coast. But the lowest-cost British coalfields in the central areas have considerable natural protection from imports because of the extra costs of transporting coal from the coast. Only in exceptional circumstances in the coal and foreign-exchange markets is it likely that imported coal would undercut British coal in the Midlands.

Although in the next 10 years imports would probably not be larger than 10 to 20 million tonnes a year, they would be important in giving British fuel consumers a choice of supplier. A free-trade policy in coal, with imports always a possibility, would stimulate efficiency in the production and sale of British coal. Even if no other change were made to the structure of the coal market, a free-trade policy would put competitive pressure on the NCB and give it an incentive to reduce its costs. Moreover, once consumers found it worthwhile to expand coal-importing facilities and substantial imports became an established feature of the British market, the resulting diversification of sources would enhance the security of supplies compared with the present dependence on the NCB.[8]

The CEGB in particular, which is one of the world's biggest coal users (over 76 million tonnes in the pre-strike year of 1983), requires access to imports to keep down the price of the coal it consumes and to improve its security of supply. In the late 1970s it formulated plans to raise its coal import capacity from 5 to 15 million tonnes a year,[9] but that was before the restrictions of early 1981 (above, pp.146-47). During the last few years of restricted imports, the CEGB has had to resort to an agreement with the Coal Board which attempts to incorporate import prices even though it is unable to use more than very small quantities of foreign coal. The original agreement ('Joint Understanding') covered the five-year period up to March 1985 and provided that the CEGB would use its best endeavours to take from the Coal Board 'all suitable coal up to a total of 75 million tonnes a year' provided the NCB's prices rose by no more than the rate of retail price inflation.[10] The South of Scotland Electricity Board was already being supplied at a 5 per cent discount on the list price for Scottish coals. According to the CEGB's latest report, the Joint Understanding now runs from 1983 to 1987 with similar provisions about keeping price increases below the general rate of inflation.[11]

Under the present version of the Joint Understanding, the CEGB agrees to take 95 per cent of its coal from the NCB (provided price

---

[8] Eileen Marshall and Colin Robinson, *The Economics of Energy Self-Sufficiency*, London: Heinemann, 1984, which argues the case for diversifying sources of energy supply by importing from a number of countries to avoid undue dependence on any one supplier (home or foreign).

[9] Robinson and Marshall, *What Future for British Coal?*, Hobart Paper 89, London: IEA, 1981, p.76.

[10] Cmnd.8920, *op. cit.*, para. 4.11.

[11] Central Electricity Generating Board, *Annual Report and Accounts, 1984-85*.

increases are below the rate of inflation), but an element of indirect import competition is introduced through a two-tier price structure. The arrangement is that 87 per cent of CEGB coal supplies are paid for at an agreed pithead price of £44 per tonne plus delivery, while the other 8 per cent (about 6 million tonnes) is priced at £36 per tonne at the pithead plus a delivery charge of about £7 per tonne, the intention being to make it competitive with expected import prices. It is significant that 6 million tonnes is approximately the amount of coal consumed by the Thames power stations which are the only major coastal coal-fired power stations.[12] One can see why, with imports restricted by government, the CEGB found such an agreement necessary. But attempts to simulate the effects of competition by agreements between large nationalised corporations are unlikely to be as satisfactory for the consumer as open price competition itself because they are based on guessing a necessarily uncertain competitive outcome.

PRIVATISING COAL PRODUCTION

For the foreseeable future, the bulk of coal demand in this country is likely to be supplied from British reserves rather than from abroad. As well as lifting restrictions on imports, liberalisation therefore requires competition in the supply of British coal and competition for the use of the relevant resources, both labour and capital. In considering privatisation, we must first discuss the ownership of coal reserves.

Ownership of Coal Reserves

Before 1938, coal reserves in Great Britain were privately owned (by the owners of the surface).[13] There was considerable controversy in the 1920s and 1930s over whether coal ought to be privately owned and whether royalties should be received by those owners: in particular, it was argued that mining could not take place efficiently because of the fragmentation of the ownership of reserves. There were proposals that Britain should adopt the same system as in most other coal-producing countries (except the USA) of state ownership of reserves.[14] Eventually, the 1938 Coal Act nationalised coal reserves, setting up a Coal Commission to act, in effect, as resource owner and royalty collector, though not as a producer. The system was scarcely tested, however, because the war intervened and, immediately

---

[12] The latest version of the Joint Understanding is reported in 'Power station coal price agreed', *The Financial Times*, 25 February 1985.

[13] W.W. Haynes, *Nationalisation in Practice: The British Coal Industry*, Folkestone: Bailey Bros. and Swinfen, 1953, Chapter II.

[14] For example, Political and Economic Planning, *Report on the British Coal Industry*, London: PEP, 1936.

afterwards, the NCB was established by the Coal Industry Nationalisation Act to take over unworked coal reserves and to have the duty of '...working and getting the coal in Great Britain, to the exclusion (save as in this Act provided) of any other person'. Thus private deep mines and opencast sites have to be licensed by the NCB and pay royalties to the Board.

Leaving aside the controversy over the apparently high royalties set by the Board, we would argue that licensing of private operations and collecting royalties are functions of the state, not of a corporate body. Giving such powers to a nationalised corporation seems to be based on an assumption which, when made explicit, appears quite unrealistic - that because the NCB is a 'public' corporation it will always pursue the 'public interest' and can therefore be entrusted with holding reserves and receiving royalties on behalf of the nation. Such an assumption, which might have seemed reasonable in the mid-1940s when there was little experience of how 'public' corporations would operate, is no longer tenable. The Coal Board, to say nothing of the National Union of Mineworkers (NUM), clearly has strong incentives to avoid a significant expansion of private sector activities, whatever the 'national interest' might demand. Furthermore, if we accept that rent is available from the exploitation of a natural resource, and that it should accrue to the community as a whole, then it should be channelled directly to the state (not via an intermediary with its own corporate objectives), with some mechanism for distributing it to society. It seems to us quite wrong that an organisation which has been given a dominant market position by the state should also be given a regulatory role which enables it to control the entry of the private sector into the market and collect substantial royalties from such small private operators as it allows to exist. Another important failing in the present system is that the community as a whole derives no natural resource rent whatsoever from the mining activities of the NCB itself.

Experience with natural gas provides a good illustration of the problems that arise when a nationalised industry is used as a rent collection instrument. In the mid-1960s, the Gas Council was designated *de facto* monopsonist for North Sea gas, with the objective of depressing the prices paid to the oil-company suppliers and collecting the rent. The policy failed because it proved to be a cumbersome device which merely shifted the problem. Thus, instead of extracting the rent directly from the oil companies, governments had to extract it from the Gas Council (later the British Gas Corporation). Since it did not emerge automatically, a special gas levy had eventually to be imposed to obtain the rent from the BGC.[15] Although the royalty payments received by the Coal Board from licensed operations (and the hidden rent arising from the Board's own

---

[15]The experience with collecting royalties on natural gas is analysed in Colin Robinson, 'The Errors of North Sea Policy', *Lloyds Bank Review*, July 1981, and Robinson, *Liberalising the British Gas Market*, *op. cit.*

activities) are small compared to those received by the BGC, the principle is the same. Nationalised corporations have no interest in acting as passive rent-collectors for central government. Royalty and rent payments are all too likely to become 'lost' in their accounts; at best, part of the proceeds may be passed on to consumers of their products rather than to the community as a whole.

It would seem more logical and inherently more satisfactory for the ownership of unworked coal and the right to receive royalties to be removed from the NCB and for the property rights to coal to be placed either in the hands of private land-owners or in a revived Coal Commission or in the Crown. The last is the system which operates for oil and gas reserves; they are owned by the state which lays down the terms and conditions (including taxes, royalties, working obligations and environmental constraints) on which private firms or public corporations may exploit them.[16] In the British North Sea, for example, rights to explore for oil and gas reserves and to exploit finds are allocated primarily by a 'discretionary' régime (under which civil servants decide which applicants are worthy to receive such rights), though with occasional limited cash auctions. A discretionary system is also used for awarding licences for onshore oil exploration and production.

In our view, a cash auction (or variants, such as bidding different rates of royalty) has advantages over the discretionary system.[17] In a competitive system, companies will bid what they believe blocks to be worth: licences are allocated and rent is removed without the need for a cumbersome taxation system such as has grown up for North Sea oil. The discretionary system also has the disadvantage that it generally lacks openness: selection of applicants for North Sea blocks is made by civil servants acting under rather vague and general criteria with no requirement to explain their actions in public. Nevertheless, we would regard even a discretionary award system for rights to exploit coal as an improvement on a system in which one corporation, which happens to be nationalised, pays no royalties on its own activities but vets applications from private companies to work coal and, if it grants permission, collects royalties from those companies.

OPENCAST COAL

Opencast coal mining seems an obvious candidate for privatisation in the interests of liberalisation. It originated in Britain in 1942 as part of the wartime effort to maximise indigenous coal production, and was at one time expected to disappear with a return to 'normality'.

---

[16] The British system of licensing is explained in Colin Robinson and Jon Morgan, *North Sea Oil in the Future*, London: Macmillan, 1978, especially Chapter 9.

[17] George Polanyi, *What Price North Sea Gas?*, Hobart Paper 38, IEA, 1967; K.W. Dam, *Oil Resources: Who Gets What How?*, Chicago: Chicago University Press, 1976; and Robinson, 'The Errors of North Sea Policy', *op. cit.*

Control was at first exercised by the Ministry of Works and then, from 1945 to 1952, by the Ministry of Fuel and Power.[18] The NCB's Opencast Executive took over responsibility in 1952. However, opencast operations are carried out by private contractors working for the Executive, or, on the smaller sites, as licensees of the Board. Thus private companies extract coal, carry out associated civil engineering works, transport coal and restore the sites. In the words of the Monopolies and Mergers Commission, the Opencast Executive is

> '...essentially a development and management organisation, its tasks being to find and evaluate workable sites, plan their development and secure the necessary statutory approvals, let contracts, and supervise the subsequent opencast mining on behalf of the NCB'.[19]

The size of the private sector could be substantially increased if the upper limit on reserves which can be worked privately were to be raised. The limit was originally established in the Opencast Coal Act of 1958 at 25,000 tonnes, and then raised in 1981 to 35,000 tonnes (or 50,000 tonnes for adjacent sites). So far, the present Government has shown no signs of accepting the Monopolies Commission recommendation in 1983 that the limit should be raised to 100,000 tonnes. Legislation to implement such an increase would permit more companies to extract and sell opencast coal themselves rather than working under the NCB's supervision. However, the royalty of £16 per tonne now payable to the Board on private opencast operations would probably have to be reduced if private activities were to expand significantly.

A more radical move would be to place all opencast operations in the private sector. As explained above, a precondition would be to alter the legislation which vests in the NCB the sole rights to mine all unworked coal in Britain. Privatising opencast activities in this way would take from the Board the regulatory and rent-collection roles which we have already argued are more properly functions of government. The NCB would no longer be the judge of whether private companies should be allowed to develop smaller opencast sites as licensed operators, paying the Board a royalty. Nor would the Board act as an intermediary, supervising companies working as contractors on the larger sites. It is difficult to belive that experienced civil engineering companies really require such supervision. Companies wishing to work opencast sites would apply to the Department of Energy under a procedure which would have to be laid down (as it already is for oil and gas) and which would incorporate safeguards to protect the environment.

The present Government has already moved a small way towards equalising the terms of competition between the NCB and private opencast operators and towards freeing opencast production from

---

[18] The early history of opencast mining is described in Cmnd. 8920, *op. cit.*, paras. 11.1-11.6. Also N.K. Buxton, *The Economic Development of the British Coal Industry*, London: Batsford Academic, 1978, p.235.

[19] Cmnd. 8920, *op. cit.*, para. 11.7.

some of the constraints imposed on it in the past. In a Department of the Environment/Welsh Office Joint Circular to local authorities dated February 1984,[20] the Government announced its intention to bring planning procedures for NCB opencast coal applications into line with those for licensed (private) opencast working and for other minerals. Under 'transitional arrangements' (apparently still in force), from 1 March 1984 the Board has had to apply to local authorities for planning permission and, should permission be granted, to the Environment Secretary for authorisation to work the site (under the 1958 Opencast Coal Act). The transitional arrangements operate until repeal of the relevant provisions of the 1958 Opencast Coal Act, which the Government promised in the Circular.

Before the 1983 White Paper[21] which preceded the Circular, the Government had endorsed a target of about 15 million tonnes a year for opencast output; output has been around that rate in recent years. The Commission on Energy and the Environment had also recommended in 1981[22] that, on environmental grounds, opencast output should not exceed 15 million tonnes a year. However, the present Government

> '...see no case for continuing to endorse a target for opencast output. Each project should therefore be considered in terms of the market requirement for its planned output...The overall level of opencast output will in practice be determined by the market subject to the acceptability of individual projects as determined by the planning system'.[23]

This move away from a centrally-determined target for opencast output to a more decentralised system seems to us entirely appropriate for a liberalised coal market. Relatively low-cost, high-quality opencast production should not be held down - as it evidently has been on occasions - in order to avoid cuts in deep-mined output. In a liberalised market, opencast coal would be allowed to compete with deep-mined coal - though in a densely-populated country such as Britain the environmental costs of both forms of production need to be estimated and imposed on the producing companies. Privatisation would make no difference to the environmental problem since there is no reason to believe nationalised industries are better guardians of the environment than private companies.

Subject to such environmental regulations (covering, for example, noise, dumping of waste, and land restoration), there seems no reason why opencast coal production should not be fully privatised. A

---

[20] Joint Circular from the Department of the Environment (3/84) and the Welsh Office (13/84) to local authority and local Planning Board Chief Executives, dated 27 February 1984. Previously, the NCB had not been required to apply separately for planning permission for proposed opencast sites because permission was deemed to have been granted under the 1971 Town and Country Planning Act for operations authorised by the Secretary of State for Energy.

[21] *Coal and the Environment*, Cmnd.8877, HMSO, May 1983.

[22] Commission on Energy and the Environment, *Coal and the Environment* (the Flowers Report), September 1981.

[23] Joint Circular, *op. cit.*, para. 15.

government wanting to liberalise the British coal market would not merely repeal the planning application procedures for opencast mining contained in the 1958 Opencast Coal Act (as the 1984 Circular promised), but would also take the opportunity provided by the need to change the Act to remove the NCB's virtual monopoly of opencast coal production. Thereby, it would introduce a significant element of competition into the British coal market without imposing any additional costs on society.

DEEP-MINED COAL

Privatising deep mines raises more difficult issues. Many pits at present make losses, even without taking into account interest payments. Some losses are so large that keeping the pits in question open is more a means of disguising unemployment than of producing coal for the consumer. Since the NCB's deep-mining operation is not the profitable activity which opencast production is, privatisation would inevitably be more difficult. The probable opposition of the National Union of Mineworkers and other mining unions would also reduce the attractiveness of mines to potential private owners. It is true that the NUM has declined in political and social importance as coal's share of the energy market in Britain has declined. There are now only about 160,000 miners compared with over 700,000 in 1947, and the ability of the mining unions to exercise their power at the expense of the rest of the community has diminished. Moreover, the NUM is seriously split because of the divergent interests of different coalfields and differences over the conduct of the 1984-85 strike. Nevertheless, it obviously remains a powerful force which must be taken into account.

Despite such problems, privatisation offers benefits not only to the community at large but particularly to miners.

Relaxing Existing Restrictions on Licensed Deep Mining

In the same way that restrictions on licensed opencast mining could be relaxed, so they could be on licensed deep mining. The present limit of 30 men working underground in a licensed deep mine was set in 1946, since when there has been a major advance in the technologies of mining and of controlling and monitoring underground operations. Even though it is interpreted with more flexibility by the Coal Board, the limit remains a serious impediment to private activity. If it were raised, there would be some expansion of licensed mining which would provide more competition for the NCB. But continuing a system which allows the Board to vet potential competitors and to collect royalties from them is not at all desirable. Of course, it would be possible for applications to be considered and royalties to be collected by the Department of Energy and the Treasury. But that leads on to more fundamental proposals for changing the structure of coal supply in Britain.

Private and Joint Ventures for New Pits

One way of introducing more private capital into British deep mining which falls short of complete privatisation would be for private companies to invest in the 'superpits' which are likely to be developed in the next 20 years. Despite early technical problems, the Board's big new mining complex at Selby (10 million tonnes a year) is already in production, and Asfordby in Leicestershire (about 2 million tonnes a year) is due to begin producing coal in the mid-1990s. But several other big prospects have already been identified - for example, Witham in Lincolnshire and South Warwickshire (near Coventry). Such projects might well be attractive to private investors and would bring wider advantages. In the first place, some new ideas about production, distribution and marketing would penetrate the British market from companies with mining experience abroad. Secondly, the presence of private shareholders would help to keep down costs. Thirdly, keener competition would be introduced into the market. Some of these benefits could be obtained from a less thorough-going privatisation scheme under which the Coal Board and private investors undertook joint ventures in new pits. However, to ensure that the benefits were passed on to consumers, the private companies would have to market their share of output separately without collusion with the Board. If the provision of private capital for joint ventures resulted in all the coal being sold by an unreconstructed NCB, the benefits would mainly accrue to the new private owners in the form of monopoly profits. Joint ventures might be a starting point for a new pit privatisation scheme, but we would not envisage them as more than a transitional solution. Private investment in British mining is likely to be inhibited by the continued existence of a nationalised organisation which would be seen both as a possibly subsidised competitor and also as a joint-venture partner subject to government interference.

Selling Existing Pits

A more fundamental approach to coal privatisation would be to offer not only future but existing pits to private investors with the aim of establishing a variety of suppliers competing both with each other and with imported coal. Private investors could include existing companies with expertise in mining, groups of Coal Board managers interested in 'management buy-outs', or miners wishing to run pits as worker co-operatives.

At first sight, much of the British deep-mining industry as it stands is an unappealing prospect to potential investors. It is, in aggregate, a heavy loss-maker and many of its pits are very old. However, many pits in the central coalfields are profitable at present and, because of their transport cost advantages, are likely to remain so even if imports are freely allowed. It is also significant that the very small private sector which has been tolerated by the Coal Board seems to have been able to operate profitably despite the extremely restrictive condition imposed on it. The NCB's concentration on 'superpits' may have led it to neglect smaller mines[24] which could be more profitable if they were run by private companies prepared to invest in technologies appropriate to such mines.

More generally, potential investors might calculate that the present condition of the industry gives little indication of its future potential under private ownership. After all, it has been run for 40 years by a centralised state corporation and subjected to constant government interference and the attentions of a powerful union. Centralisation would disappear and government interference would be much diminished in a liberalised coal market, but the union problem might remain since the industry has suffered from monopoly in the labour as well as the product market. Even with present union arrangements (especially given the recent breakaway tendencies in the NUM), we think there would be reasonable bids for *some* existing pits. However, a further diminution in union monopoly power or a significant change in union behaviour would probably be necessary before the industry became a really attractive proposition to private investors.

Selling Existing Pits Jointly with Power Stations

The most far-reaching and probably most desirable proposal would be to offer 'packages' of existing pits *and power stations* to private investors. The close relationship between the coal and electricity supply industries means there is considerable logic in such an idea, and its implementation would avoid an undesirable increase in the buying power of the CEGB (below). Unlike coal, there are some natural monopoly elements in electricity supply (for example, the bulk transmission grid and local distribution of electricity to households). However, power generation itself is not a natural monopoly activity; privately-owned power stations[25] could supply electricity to a state-owned (or private but state-regulated) national grid which would in turn supply distributors.

The offer of pits *and* nearby power stations in the central coalfield areas should be very attractive to private investors, subject to the qualifications mentioned above. It has the advantage of privatising two nationalised industries in one operation, introducing private ownership into those parts of the electricity supply industry where it is most appropriate. Moreover, it would result in a very substantial

---

[24] Alan Burns, Martin Newby and Jonathan Winterton, 'The restructing of the British coal industry', *Cambridge Journal of Economics*, Vol.9, 1985, pp. 93-110.

[25] Private power generation has been made somewhat easier by the provisions of the Energy Act 1983.

reduction in monopoly power in two fuel industries. At present, as we have seen, there is bilateral monopoly bargaining between the CEGB and the NCB over coal supplies for power stations. If the NCB were split into several supply companies with no change in the position of the CEGB, the latter would stand in a very powerful monopsonistic situation as the main customer for the competing suppliers of British coal. To avoid this accretion of power to the electricity supply industry, it seems to us desirable that there should be a move to private ownership of power stations - in some cases, with associated pits - at the same time that coal mining is privatised.

CONCLUSIONS ON THE FORMS OF LIBERALISATION

As we have argued above, some forms of liberalisation would be more straightforward than others. Lifting import restrictions and full privatisation of opencast coal mining would probably be the easiest first steps, although both moves would no doubt be opposed by the NCB and the unions because of possible encroachment on the market for deep-mined British coal.

Privatisation of deep mining raises more complex issues, partly because it would require radical changes to the structure of the coal-mining industry (and, ideally, of the electricity supply industry). It is also obvious that, given the unfortunate history of British coal mining under private ownership, strong emotions are attached to 'public' ownership of the coal mines, even though the present form of ownership gives no transferable property rights to the public but imposes on taxpayers a heavy burden of support to offset mining losses and on consumers unnecessarily high prices. The majority of both management and union members in the coal industry may well perceive their interests to be to hold on to such market power as they now have. Monopolies, however, have a habit of promoting their own demise. Although the NCB has a virtual monopoly of coal mining in Britain and the NUM monopolises most mining labour, coal currently supplies only about one-third of UK energy consumption so that there are other fuels to which consumers can turn. Coal's monopoly power has already waned significantly, as the most recent strike showed. It is a serious indictment of both the NCB and the NUM that, even when oil prices were soaring in the 1970s and early 1980s, they were unable to exploit their much-improved competitive position to promote the expansion of the industry.

Our perception is thus that the monopoly power of both the NCB and the mining unions has been an important factor in the decline of British coal within the British energy market, and thus in undermining their own positions. Liberalisation of the market, far from being against the interests of those employed in the industry, is the one firm hope many of them have of improved prospects in the longer term.

PART IV

TRANSPORT

12

PRIVATISATION AND COMPETITION IN ROAD PASSENGER TRANSPORT

John Hibbs

Director of Transport Studies, City of Birmingham Polytechnic

THE RETURN of the bus and coach industry to market forces, in place of the increasingly *dirigiste* régime in which it had functioned since the 1930s, was a declared policy of the British Governments of 1979 and 1983. The first steps were taken when the 1980 Transport Act abolished price control, deregulated long-distance coach services, and made several less significant changes. From the experience thus gained, and with the contributions from (among others) the Institute of Economic Affairs, the next moves were outlined in a White Paper, *Buses*,[1] published in 1984, and firmly taken in the shape of the Transport Act 1985.

DEREGULATING BUS SERVICES: THE TRANSPORT ACT 1985

This measure extended deregulation to all types of bus service (except in London), subject to a requirement to give notice of the intention to start or end a local service; it also withdrew the previous exemption of the industry from legislation concerning monopolies and fair trading, bringing it within the scope of the Office of Fair Trading (OFT) for the first time. Local authorities were also given various rules to prevent them inhibiting competition. The so-called 'network subsidy', which had amounted to some £691 million in 1982-83 (the major part going to urban operators in public ownership), was prohibited, and in its place local authorities at

[1] Cmnd. 9300, London: HMSO, 1984.

county and regional level were required to call for tenders for the provision of such individual elements, not offered by the market, as they considered socially necessary. (The requirement to register 'commercial' services provided a signalling system whereby they could identify these 'social' bus services.)

The Act also strengthened the system of operator licensing, designed to ensure safety in construction, maintenance and use of buses and coaches, and ended the practice whereby many local authorities restricted the number of taxi licences they were prepared to issue. But its biggest new development was provision for the privatisation of the two-thirds of British buses and coaches that were currently in the ownership of either local authorities or the state (although the process was to be delayed in the case of London Transport and the Scottish holding company).

Privatisation was seen to be a prerequisite for the return of the industry to market forces, since without it the publicly owned operators would be able to exercise a market dominance that would severely constrain the effect of deregulation (this had happened in the case of long-distance services after 1980). Hence the subsidiary companies of the state-owned National Bus Company (NBC) were to be sold individually, contrary to the advice of the NBC board. In the process, there were numerous cases of separation, to produce smaller operating units; and the eventual number of companies successfully disposed of has been about 60, a high proportion of them management buy-outs. In two cases, full staff buy-outs have taken place.

The municipal sector of the industry included 49 bus fleets owned by district councils (regions in Scotland), and ranging from three to 368 vehicles in size. These had been managed by council committees, and in most cases had an effective monopoly of the town's public transport (apart from taxis). The Act set them up as entities under Company Law, with their shares owned by the council, thus producing an arm's-length relationship together with an easy next step to privatisation. In the case of the six English and one Scottish conurbations, the council-owned bus fleets were also transferred to limited-company ownership, but with shares in the hands of a successor body to the former metropolitan county council (in the English examples – the Scottish one (Strathclyde) remaining in the ownership of the Regional council). Here the Act drew back from tackling the problem of size – the average fleet in these seven examples being 1,414 buses in 1982, against an average for the whole industry of 12.6. A subsequent breakdown into smaller units was hinted at for the future, along with the privatisation of the Scottish holding company (with 11 operating subsidiaries) and the extension of the Act to London.

HISTORICAL BACKGROUND

The idea of transport being owned and operated by the state or by municipal authorities is far from new. Gladstone's Act of 1844 provided for the state to acquire any railway authorised after its passage; since much of the system had by then been built, it was a dead letter, but it does not seem to have been highly controversial. The Tramways Act of 1870 gave powers to councils compulsorily to acquire tramways at fixed intervals, for virtually their scrap value – it was Bristol's vacillation about this that kept 1896 tramcars running there until the blitz put them out of their misery in 1941. In 1921 Winston Churchill told the Commons that the Government had contemplated nationalising the railways, but had decided to amalgamate them into four main-line companies; before this, Sir Eric Geddes had persuaded Lloyd George to include powers of compulsory purchase for his proposed Ministry of Ways & Communications – the Commons struck them out, and gave us the Ministry of Transport, with regulatory powers instead. (Why does it no longer require an Act of Parliament to set up a new Ministry?)

By 1939 it seems that support for state ownership of the railways was to be found in all political parties. Public ownership had already appeared in the form of the London Passenger Transport Board, and the Conservative Government had nationalised the airlines, with Sir John Reith in charge, just before war broke out.[2] The Labour Nationalisation Act of 1947 is thus not so revolutionary as it might be made to appear. All that had happened had been the shift from direct state ownership as planned by Geddes to the arm's-length corporations devised by Herbert Morrison. But municipal transport had been circumscribed by the 1930 Licensing Act, and no cities obtained new powers to run trams or buses thereafter.

There is a hint of what may underly this ambiguous history in the effective nationalisation of the railways in both world wars, and the state control of road haulage in the second. Most states with the Civil Code – in contrast to those with the Common Law – seem to regard public transport as a proper function of the administration, which may in some circumstances be opened to private firms to 'exploit' by way of what amounts to a franchise. The beginnings of this are exceedingly ancient: the empires of antiquity seem to have seen transport as a means of social control, and the postmasters in Persia were spies of the central authority. No less an authority than Max Weber sees transport as a direct function of the state in much the same way.

It can be argued that the evolution of transport policy was diverted by the peculiar nature of railways – and also air transport – as requiring a quasi-military discipline, in view of their 'fail-dangerous' nature; the circumstance that if any system failure happens, it is likely to be somewhat disastrous. It is perhaps equally significant that

---

[2] *British Overseas Airways Act*, London: HMSO, 1939, Ch.61.

the railways, before the establishment of commercial motor transport by road in the 1920s, enjoyed something of a technological monopoly, that had in turn led, as theory would predict, to combination, merger and monopoly. Thus it is hardly surprising that the conventional wisdom of the 1920s and 1930s accepted without question the regulation of the bus industry, and the emergence of 'territorial' operators, with considerable monopoly power.

CONSEQUENCES OF REGULATION

The taxonomy of regulation is important. There are three types: *quality*, *quantity* and *price* control. Each of these was introduced by the Road Traffic Act 1930, which set up the system that was substantially reformed by the Transport Acts of 1980, 1981 and 1985.

Quality control concerns the construction, maintenance and operation of mechanical equipment. It is commonly justified by the difficulty faced by consumers in assessing these aspects of road transport and, while it is applied uniformly across an industry, it is by no means economically neutral. For one thing, it is bound to inhibit desirable innovations, and for another, the circumstances that face bus and coach operators are in practice widely different.

On the other hand, *quantity control* intervenes in the structure of an industry, favouring some interests at the expense of others. In classical terms firms already in the market obtain licences to continue (often called 'grandfather rights'), while subsequent attempts to enter the market are either prohibited or faced with considerable expense and difficulty. As a consequence, it provides those inside with a statutory monopoly, and the inevitable consequence is a process of combination and merger. It is significant to note that Griffith-Boscawen, the minor Conservative politician who chaired the Royal Commission on Transport of 1928-30, spoke of road transport regulation as a measure of 'rationalisation leading to nationalisation'.

Finally, *price control* is generally taken to be necessary in monopoly situations where it is feared that suppliers will exploit their position. The perceived technological monopoly of the railways attracted such control in 1835, with consequences that were disastrous when commercial road transport emerged after 1919. Yet the response of both Labour and Conservative Governments was not to free the railways, but to extend price control to the road transport industry, where artificial monopoly was created by statutory quantity control. In practice it could not be made to stick in road haulage, but was undoubtedly one of the prime causes of decline for the bus industry in the 1970s, with massive consequent subsidisation.

A Regulated Market

The three forms of regulation work to create a *regulated market*. In essence, commercial pressures will cause the barriers to leak to some extent, although firms which manage to enter in this way will then support any effort to keep newcomers out. It is important to note that there is a tendency for the transport industry to regulate itself along much the same lines in the absence of statutory intervention. The London omnibus trade in the 19th century exercised its own quantity and price controls through a system of route associations, and something very similar emerged in the wake of deregulation in Chile. The comparison with liner conferences in deep-sea shipping is enlightening.

In contrast, the permeable nature of quality control permits the existence of a contestable market. This is the current situation of the bus and coach industry in Great Britain. But even here distortions can arise from infrastructure scarcities. In air transport, an example is the limited number of airport 'slots' for landing and take-off at peak periods, in the absence of a system of auctioning them to the highest bidder; where buses are concerned, the scarcity of urban road space at certain times and places will be familiar.

The legislation of 1930, then, introduced a regulated market for bus and coach services (though the private hire sector – charter in US terminology – was left contestable). Foreseeing this, the four main-line railway companies, having obtained parliamentary powers to provide road transport, acquired an interest in the provincial bus companies in England, Wales and Scotland, though the shrewdness of J.F. Heaton, manager of the Tilling group of companies, prevented them ever owning more than 49 per cent of the equity in any such business. The railway companies poured money into the emerging road combines, which, after 1929, took advantage of the regulated market and embarked on a programme of expansion by purchase, secure in the knowledge that no new entrant could prevent them from extracting a monopoly profit to recoup their outlay.

Nationalisation and After

The nationalising Act of 1947 brought the railways' shareholding into state ownership, and this was followed by the voluntary sale of two of the ownership trusts that had been built up since the 1920s, the Tilling Group and Scottish Motor Traction, along with a new one that had started to emerge, Red & White United. Only the British Electric Traction group remained in private hands, accepting a state holding of up to 49 per cent in most of its operating companies. The municipal operators were left in the hands of those towns and cities that had operating powers dating from before 1930. But the pressure was upon the administrators and politicians to tidy up the industry, and Barbara Castle's Act of 1968, followed by the re-organisation of local government, achieved this, the BET board by now being prepared to sell its holding in the industry.

From these changes came the National Bus Company (for England and Wales) and the Scottish Bus Group, which set out to rationalise the structure of the industry, still secure in a regulated market. Barbara Castle, then Minister of Transport, had the idea of a series of conurbation transport authorities whose function would have been to co-ordinate land-use and transportation planning. Her successor, Richard Marsh, extended them to produce Passenger Transport Authorities (PTAs), whose scope was extended by making each one responsible for a Passenger Transport Executive (PTE), which was to be a transport operator in its own right. Each PTE was endowed with the local authority bus fleets in its area, and there were powers of compulsory purchase, or of compulsory 'co-ordination', affecting all other bus operators within the same boundary. A consequence was to produce bus undertakings that were monstrously large for an industry where there is general agreement that firms operate under constant returns to scale.[3]

In many ways the 1968 Transport Act can be seen as the culmination of the policy originating in the Road Traffic Act of 1930, and probably it was expected at the time that there would be little further change. It is true that there had been growing problems in the provision of rural bus services, and there private firms with lower costs had been taking over services from the National Bus Company, and were to continue to do so. But a new and radically different climate of thought was already beginning to appear, as may be seen from Table 1.

EVIDENCE OF A NEW APPROACH

Today many trade union officials and managers are willing to admit that there was a lot wrong with the bus and coach industry before 1985, and that the system of regulation was having a debilitating effect. They were supported by the secular decline in carryings, from 80 billion passenger-kilometres in 1952 to 40 billion p-ks 30 years later. On such a trend, nemesis threatened, with zero carryings in the year 2002 – with the alternative (politically attractive in some factions of all parties) of total subsidy, sometimes referred to as 'fares-free'.

Thus the enactments of 1980 and 1985 should not be seen as a sudden *volte-face* in what we have called 'the state of public knowledge', but as the evolution of a new, more market-oriented approach to the provision of bus and coach services. At the same time, the generation of managers that had taken the industry into the regulated market had been replaced by the 1960s with men

[3] A summary of the various studies of scale economies in bus operation will be found in Chapter 9 of my book, *The Bus and Coach Industry, its Economics and Organisation*, London: Dent, 1975.

Table 1

THE STATE OF PUBLIC KNOWLEDGE

1919	Formation of the Ministry of Transport – nationalisation clauses deleted.
1924	London Traffic Act – non-controversial anti-competitive measure
1925	Report of Sir Henry Maybury's Departmental Committee – quantity control for road transport to protect railways and tramways
1929	Second Report of Royal Commission – Maybury policy endorsed
1930	Road Traffic Act – licensing clauses 'tacked on' to controversial road safety Bill, and never debated
1930/50	Period of 'benign neglect', and of consolidation of ownership
1952	Thesiger Report – recommends no change, against a very narrow frame of reference
1967	White Paper, *Public Transport & Traffic*
1968	Transport Act (Barbara Castle's Act) – rationalisation of state and municipal transport undertakings; subsidy powers
1972	Local Government Act – rationalised conurbation areas, and provided for compulsory co-ordination
1980	Transport Act – limited deregulation; price control removed
1984	Local Government Act – abolition of Metropolitan County Councils
1984	White Paper, *Buses*
1985	Transport Act – quantity control removed; tendering for subsidy; OFT introduced; provisions for privatisation as necessary for a contestable market

who accepted regulation as a fact of life, and who, it must be admitted, tended to abuse the monopoly it gave them. It was against their régime that the positive virtues of a market economy for bus operation were to become plain, not only to external proponents of reform, but also to the younger generation which, by the 1980s, was anxious for greater freedom to pursue innovation and both personal and corporate satisfaction.

The three decades after 1950 saw the bus and coach industry fall into a malaise that is well described by the aphorism that the biggest monopoly profit is a quiet life. The trade unions, too, took advantage of the lack of a competitive market, and the satisfaction of management and workers increasingly took the place of the interest of the travelling public. The period was marked by a rapid growth in the number of private cars, yet management did not realise that these were their true competitors, and services were allowed to deteriorate, encouraging more travellers to find their own means of transport. After subsidy was permitted by the Transport Act of 1968 its volume rose rapidly, and, predictably, undermined the motivation of bus managers to achieve financial success.

At a deeper level, the regulated market was having even more serious consequences for the economic health of the bus industry. Protected from the commercial realities, and subject to a policy of price control that D.N. Chester[4] had analysed as far back as 1936, the management of both state-owned and municipal undertakings had neglected to develop any serious techniques for costing – indeed, in the 1950s the state-owned bus companies had resisted the suggestion that the British Transport Costing Service might assist them in this area. The licensing authorities actually imposed a system of standard pricing, logically required by the internal cross-subsidisation that the companies claimed to practise.

Their yardstick for measuring success or failure was to compare average revenue per vehicle-mile with a figure for the firm's total average cost per vehicle-mile derived from the previous year's data. This resulted in a tendency to cut out mileage that, although earning less than average cost, was contributing a surplus above marginal cost, and thereby contributing to overheads. As a consequence, overheads had to be carried by a reduced gross income, thus raising the average cost, and leading to a further round of cuts. A vicious spiral of reduced output ensued, which, ironically, the small private firms in the industry escaped, although it is doubtful whether their proprietors could have expressed their policy in terms of incremental costing.

Thus as we approach the legislation of 1980 and 1985 there are a few conclusions to be drawn. Throughout Great Britain the National Bus Company and the Scottish Bus Group retained company structure, and never sought to evolve a massive bureaucracy. Even in the municipal sector, the county districts that had kept their bus fleets were relatively small, and retained the financial disciplines of traditional municipal trading. The state-owned firms, having been 'rationalised' after 1968, were now made too large for efficiency, but they were still financial entities. Without such profit centres, privatisation would have been more difficult. By the 1980s these companies were starting to attract a new generation of younger, more entrepreneurial managers, while some of the more senior figures were starting to see the threat that heavy subsidy imposed upon freedom of managers to control their operations. For the most part, by the late 1970s, the bus industry was still being managed by people who did not have the debilitating need to seek re-election.

But there remains one perplexing factor. Why were they so slow to recognise that the regulatory system itself was in such urgent need of reform? Leaders of the industry have complained that successive

---

[4] D.N. Chester, *Public Control of Road Passenger Transport*, Manchester: Manchester University Press, 1936.

Secretaries of State never consulted them about the reforms they planned, yet who would have sought the advice of people whose attitude resembled a mixture of the ostrich and the dinosaur? I know how far many of the younger ones welcomed my own critique of the system, but I recall, too, the contumely (it is not too strong a word) with which I was treated by many of the older men, when my work appeared in print.

DEREGULATING AND PRIVATISING: MR FOWLER'S ACT

The initial approach of the Conservative Government elected in 1979 was to move towards the deregulation of the industry. With unprecedented speed (some said haste), Mr Fowler's Transport Act of 1980 began to dismantle the system that had been sacrosanct since 1930. Spokesmen for the industry prophesied doom, while other people said the Act had not gone far enough. For our purposes, there were four significant aspects of Mr Fowler's Act:

- o it swept away price control, subject to reserve powers that have not been used, from all sectors of the industry.
- o it removed quantity control from all long-distance coach services, merely requiring operators to register such services with the Traffic Commissioners.
- o it shifted the burden of proof in contested licence applications from the applicant to the objector.
- o it provided for local authorities to establish 'trial areas' within which quantity control would be removed.

Fares Down, Traffic Up

The results are worth noting. Freeing operators from price control proved a great stimulus to management, and in combination with freeing long-distance services from control, reduced fares on those services substantially, leading to a significant growth of traffic.[5] Not all of this came from British Rail, but a further effect was to encourage BR to improve its marketing in order to hold its own. Shifting the burden of proof had very little effect, largely because the confrontational procedure itself formed a financial and behavioural barrier, inhibiting attempts to enter the market; in a number of cases, such attempts were still not successful, and the regulating authorities appeared unwilling to respond to the change. In the few trial areas that were established, it rapidly became plain that regulation was already a dead letter in 'deep rural' areas, since profits there were seen to be too small to attract new entrants. In Herefordshire the

[5] I. Savage in *The Deregulation of Bus Services*, Gower, 1985, detected a net welfare gain.

effect was to transfer control to the county council by way of subsidy, but there also followed a period of fierce competition on the streets of Hereford. This provided ammunition for opponents of further deregulation, but was never likely to be a widespread phenomenon, given the more effective quality control enacted in 1985.

Moreover, the expected emergence of a competitor for the state-owned franchising agency, National Express, which dominated the long-distance market, proved a damp squib. A consortium of private firms attempted to market a franchised network of their own, but the market dominance of National Express, and its command of the travel agencies, was in the event more effective in holding off this challenge than any serious price war. Commuter coach services, serving London, were the most significant new development springing from coach deregulation, followed by the use of new high-specification coaches by a few private firms, rapidly copied by National Express. In the cities, removal of price control gave rise to the introduction of travel cards, which can be seen to be a powerful way of protecting an operator's monopoly, by tying the holder to one source of supply.

After 1980 a good deal of thought was given to the next step in reform, and it was argued that privatisation was essential if deregulation was to work. In the 1985 Act, Nicholas Ridley, the Secretary of State, showed that this had been accepted, and he is to be congratulated for persuading the Treasury that privatising the public sector operators was a structural rather than a financial priority.

Despite this, the 1985 Act was still partial, and further legislation is expected. Here are its main provisions, for our purpose:

o It swept away all remaining quantity control, except for the area of the new London Regional Transport, requiring instead that operators register their intention to start, modify or abandon a local bus service, giving 42 days' notice.

o It swept away 'network subsidy', thereby removing an open drain for public funds and a powerful incentive to managerial inefficiency. Henceforth, subsidy could only be applied for the provision of specified services by means of open tender.

o It provided for the partial and limited privatisation of the industry, which we will now examine.

- *The National Bus Company* was to be wound up after the disposal of all of its subsidiary companies.
- *The Scottish Bus Group* was not affected by the Act in this way.
- *Public transport in London* was not to be privatised, but London Regional Transport was given powers to put bus services out to tender.
- *The Passenger Transport Authorities* (PTAs), by now *ad hoc* 'residual bodies' with their membership nominated by the district

councils concerned, were left in place, but their Passenger Transport Executives (PTEs) were to be transferred to new companies, formed under Companies Act procedure, and subject to eventual liquidation for insolvency. The PTA can 'rescue' its company (whose shares it holds) once only, in the event of financial difficulty. The PTEs were envisaged as being merged with the PTAs in due course; their remaining functions being the arrangements for obtaining 'unremunerative' services by tender, and the provision of rail transport, either directly as in Tyne & Wear, or by subsidy to British Rail.

- *The municipal undertakings*, outwith the former metropolitan counties, were to be similarly hived off from the councils in Companies Act form.

Immediate Effects of the 1985 Act

Before we attempt to reach any conclusions about the 1985 Act, its immediate consequences should be summarised. The effect of deregulation itself has been patchy, though marked in such places as Manchester, Oxford, Southampton and Glasgow. Some managers have taken steps that seem to indicate a lack of understanding of market behaviour – as one observer has said, 'They seem to think that competition means that Sainsbury's manager goes out every Monday and throws a brick through Tesco's window'. This perhaps should not be unexpected, since the managers of many companies come from a background and ethos of protectionism and must find the new dispensation quite unfamiliar. The industry, after all, has never developed any sophisticated marketing sense, which is now essential for the survival of the firm.

The prohibition of network subsidy coincided with the rate-capping of the local authorities given the duty of identifying socially necessary services, and inviting firms to tender for their provision. Nevertheless, most local authorities reported substantial savings in merely replacing the journeys that had not been commercially registered (under the 42-day rule) by the date (26 October 1986) when the new system came into effect. While in urban areas this process has largely meant the provision of evening and weekend facilities, there has been a different pattern in many parts of the shire counties, where the county council has become the principal provider of bus services, through the tendering process. Some of these councils have required successful tenderers to conform to a corporate image, by painting their vehicles in the livery dictated by the subsidising authority. Some have even required performance bonds. Boundary problems have arisen in urban areas where the subsidising authority – itself inescapably a political entity – has chosen to provide tendered services that compete with commercially registered ones, and in some cases at lower fares. As with rural tendering, this is a problem that demands further examination.

Privatising the NBC

Privatisation of the National Bus Company will have been virtually concluded when this book appears. In its early phases, most of the subsidiaries were sold to management teams, frequently with provision for employee share holdings; in two cases there was a full co-ownership buy-out, similar to that made with such success in the case of the National Freight Consortium. One of these, People's Provincial in Hampshire, has been a remarkable success story. More recently there have been a number of buyers from outside the industry, whose purchasing power has been such as to drive up prices, and deprive several management teams of their hoped-for success. In some cases there has been a suggestion of asset-stripping, where companies, usually in the South, owned valuable sites. Some managers have found their contracts terminated where they did not see eye to eye with their new proprietors. A natural tendency to concentrate upon the re-structuring of the industry may have limited the pace of adjustment to a deregulated environment.

In the case of the free-standing municipal firms, management in many instances has shown itself capable of responding to a competitive market, though rumours persist of some casualties. In some cases shares have been sold to other operators, and in one case (Portsmouth) the whole undertaking has been put up for sale. The situation in the former metropolitan counties is very different. There the successor companies are still extremely large, although capable of trading successfully without the subsidy their predecessors enjoyed. In any case, the Secretary of State is expected to act before long to re-structure these companies, and, presumably, to complete the privatisation of the municipal sector.

The two remaining areas – Scotland and Greater London – are also due for further intervention. The Secretary of State for Scotland has announced his intention to privatise the Scottish Bus Group (SBG) (as with the National Bus Company) by the sale of the subsidiary companies. If the SBG is not restructured, the Scottish bus industry will be subject to a frightening market dominance. London Buses Ltd, on the other hand, is to be broken up into some 15 separate companies, of 200-400 vehicles apiece, which is a bold step in view of the ancient tradition of monolithic ownership in the metropolis.

Finally, it should be recorded that the Traffic Commissioners, freed of their responsibility for quantity control, have proved effective monitors of the quality aspect of regulation, while the Office of Fair Trading, which can now investigate the bus industry, has kept an effective watch on the danger area of 'competing to kill'. There is a general consensus that the 1985 legislation will not be capable of final assessment until some five years have passed, but there is also a general feeling among managers that the new dispensation is an improvement, from which they would not want to retreat. What is more, this view has been expressed by the principal trade union involved. Today's conventional wisdom states that bus deregulation has been a success.

A TRIAL BALANCE

Deregulation and privatisation have turned the world of the bus and coach operator upside-down. It has brought with it a new air of confidence among the new managers (partly no doubt because many of those who found the whole thing unsympathetic took early retirement). Even more, the industry has now been freed from the local councils which, through the mechanism of subsidy, had been usurping the powers of managers to control their own business. There will be problems ahead, some of which can already be foreseen; failures and bankruptcies are to some extent inevitable, and will weed out the weaker elements, and the optimum size of firm in the market environment has yet to become plain. There is a need for further management education, and for better training of 'point-of-sale' staff – drivers, conductors and inquiry staff. The impact of information technology is being felt, and techniques like management by exception need to be more widely understood. Traffic costing, which has been shown to be the Achilles' Heel of the industry under regulation, still requires study, and the practice of charging the same price per mile over the whole of a firm's operations will have to give way to more creative pricing policies.

The present author, in advocating deregulation and privatisation, never ventured to prophesy what the outcome would be, save that things could only improve. So far the evidence is that they have. A commentator, who must remain anonymous, has wittily remarked that the industry has moved from one era to another – BC meaning 'before competition' to AD meaning 'after deregulation'. The analogy is close, for the Law that previously governed every small decision is now replaced by Faith: faith in the beneficial effects of the market and in the freedom that it gives to capable and innovative managers to offer services of the quality and price that consumers will prefer.

In some ways, however, the new dispensation has brought about an increase in regulation, and not just by way of a ncessary tightening of quality control. Freedom is still hedged about with requirements to register one's intentions in advance, and to keep an eye on the Office of Fair Trading, while tendering can inhibit market responses. It is far too soon to attempt any kind of rigorous assessment of the outcome of the Transport Acts 1980 and 1985, but we can usefully remind ourselves of their overall objectives, and look at the consequences to date.

Objectives of the Legislation

To force the bus and coach industry to become market-led, by removing the artificial protection of quantity control.

To free the state-owned companies from central control by means of privatisation.

To move the municipal undertakings nearer to commercial freedom by making them subject to company law.

To reduce the amount of subsidy required for socially necessary bus services.

To replace network subsidy and internal cross-subsidy by a system of subsidy by tender, thereby forcing management to become more commercial.

To erect residual defences of 'the public interest' by making the industry subject to fair trading laws and establishing statutory traffic authorities.

Consequences of the Legislation

- Substantial cost-cutting;
- Initial reduction in subsidy;
- Marginal loss of facilities;
- Initial confusion in some urban areas;
- Marked shift in management objectives;
- Increased central planning in rural areas;
- Net increase in regulation.

PROVISIONAL CONCLUSIONS

The expected 'big bang' on 26 October 1986 never happened. What did happen was that the successor companies to the former PTEs came into existence with a minimum of time to prepare for the new dispensation, because their political masters had forbidden them to plan. The metropolitan county councils, all at the time with Labour majorities, took an ostrich-like attitude, and pretended that 26 October had been abolished in advance. As a result, there was considerable confusion on the streets, which it is not uncharitable to say arose from managerial problems and not from either deregulation, privatisation or rate-capping. Yet the ability of politicians to muddy the waters is illustrated by the remark of one who countered the complaints that he said had 'snowed them under' by claiming that nothing could be done. 'Responsibility for commercial services', he said, 'rested with the private operator and not the authority' – ignoring the fact that the authority was in effect the owner of the private operator.

The smaller municipal operators and the NBC companies were on the whole far more successful in reacting to the Act, as were the SBG subsidiaries in Scotland. (A strange development was fierce competition on the streets of Glasgow between publicly owned firms – the SBG subsidiaries and Strathclyde PTE.) Here and there private firms have succeeded in finding a foothold, either with tendered or commercially registered services. Some new money is now coming into the industry; a lot of old management has taken early retirement; and marketing and pricing have come to the fore as the skills necessary for survival.

The Effect of Privatisation Has yet to Be Fully Felt

Uncertainties as to future ownership have inhibited the development of new management strategies, and the effects of deregulation have still to work their way through, especially in costing and pricing, where the industry has been disastrously backward for so many years. It will be another five years before an adequate assessment can be made. But let me hazard a guess.

Three things appear to emerge from the combined effect of deregulation and privatisation (and from any further steps the Secretary of State seems likely to take in the life of the present Government):

1. Deregulation, leading to a contestable market, seems likely to give rise to a series of companies each holding a territory, defended from potential competition by good service at attractive prices. Those whose competence is sufficient will survive (and managerial competence will be at a premium as never before). In this situation there will tend to be limited and occasional outbreaks of actual competition, but the consumer will benefit from the permanent threat of it. The companies will be relatively small, reflecting the absence of any significant economies of scale, upper limits of size being set by span of control and similar behavioural constraints. The removal of quantity control has placed the bus industry in the situation described by Baumol[6] as a contestable market, where the firm is deterred from exploiting any element of monopoly that it may achieve by the potential entry of new competitors. Deregulation should not be seen as requiring constant confrontations between bus operators on the streets.

2. Privatisation will not necessarily prevent the re-emergence of ownership trusts such as dominated the industry in the period from

[6] W. Baumol, 'Contestable Markets: An Uprising in the Theory of Industry Structure', *American Economic Review*, Vol. 72, 1982, pp.1-15.

1930 to 1980 (whether in private or public sector ownership). But a limit may be set, unexpectedly, by the attractiveness of bus and coach companies to the conglomerates – not because of any outstanding profitability, but because of their strong cash flow. These companies do not have to wait to be paid for their product, and may even be able to collect payment in advance of sales! As the people who have been successful in making management take-overs come to retirement age – or even sooner – a bit of profit-taking will seem attractive, and the ownership pattern may be changing quite rapidly in five to 10 years time.

3. The largest area of uncertainty lies in the remaining provisions for tendering. Two trends seem to be emerging. First, the competent authorities – county councils and PTEs – have been given considerable power to intervene in the market. The Hereford Trial Area transferred effective control of bus services from the Traffic Commissioners to the County Council, and this may not be at all disagreeable to councillors or officials. Some councils, indeed, appear to be emerging as operators 'in disguise', by establishing their own market brand-image for the tendered bus routes. The concept of subsidy by tender was certainly an effective sweetener, in the face of opposition from the Government's own supporters (not least, in the Lords), but it may already be seen as a hostage to fortune. The whole area is a minefield at present, and deserves serious investigation by researchers with no specific interest to defend; this is underlined by the second trend, which some would see to lead to a poor quality of subsidised operation, because of its insulation from market forces. There is also the danger that subsidy will come to be seen as the 'solution' to the problems of insufficient demand, and thereby stifle any market-led innovation that might prove preferable to the consumer.

The most significant conclusion, however, lies in the extent to which the reforms of 1980 and 1985 are regarded within the industry as having been beneficial. Some ill-informed and partial criticism is heard, to be sure, from the consumer lobbies, and there are not a few politicians who regret the loss of their control, especially in the former metropolitan counties. Yet on the whole, the objective expressed in the title of Hobart Paper 95, *Transport without Politics...?* (1982), seems well on the way to being achieved. Not everything is perfect, nor will it be, but the bus and coach industry has emerged from 50 years of protectionism to take its stand *as an industry*, and not as – what it had been rapidly becoming – a channel for subsidy to the carless deprived.

SELECT BIBLIOGRAPHY

1. **General Economic and Managerial Background**

Cole, S., *Applied Transport Economics*, Kogan Page, 1987.

Hibbs, J., *Bus and Coach Management*, Chapman & Hall, 1985.

White, P., *Public Transport, its planning, management and operation* (2nd Edn.), Hutchinson, 1986.

2. **Regulation and Deregulation**

Douglas, N.J., *A Welfare Assessment of Transport Deregulation*, Gower, 1987.

Hibbs, J., *Transport without Politics...?*, Hobart Paper 95, London: IEA, 1982.

Hibbs, J., *Regulation, an international study of bus and coach licensing*, Coachex Ltd., Dyfed: Tregaron, 1985.

Kilvington, R.P. & Cross, A.K., *Deregulation of Express Coach Services in Britain*, Gower, 1986.

Nelson, James C., *Regulation and Competition in Transport*, ed. John W. Fuller, University of British Columbia, 1983.

Ruppenthal, Karl M. & Stanbury, W.T., *Transportation Policy: Regulation, Competition and the Public Interest*, University of British Columbia, 1976.

Savage, I., *The Deregulation of Bus Services*, Gower, 1985.

Glaister, S. & Mulley, C., *Public Control of the British Bus Industry*, Gower, 1983.

3. **A Case-Study of What Went Wrong in the USA**

Jones, David, *Urban Transit Policy: an Economic and Political History*, New York: Prentice-Hall, 1985.

13

BRITISH RAIL: COMPETITION ON THE NETWORK*

David Starkie

Institute for Fiscal Studies and TM Economics

THE PUBLIC SECTOR can be privatised in a number of ways but with British Railways (BR), attention has focussed on the sale to the private sector of assets in non-rail subsidiaries. Hotels have been disposed of and other non-rail activities have been grouped under a holding company – British Rail Investments Ltd – with a view to selling equity in them to private sector shareholders. Suggestions have recently been made for treating similarly the wholly-owned subsidiary, British Rail Engineering Ltd (BREL), which carries out extensive repair work for BR and builds much of its rolling stock.

On the operational side there have been proposals for the private sector to take over railway lines. The two most publicised schemes are from Victoria to Gatwick Airport, and Fenchurch Street to Southend. The Fenchurch Street line runs for about 40 miles through southern Essex and operates very much as a separate part of the rail network. A business consortium has expressed an interest in its purchase.

It is arguable whether such transfers would promote the objective most strongly canvassed by the privatisers – increased efficiency in the supply of services and therefore more benefits to consumers. Efficiency is associated with competition, but it is not necessarily true (even if it seems likely) that a simple transfer of assets to the private sector has the effect of sharpening competitive forces.

Professors Michael Beesley and Stephen Littlechild[1] have argued

---

* This article was first published in the IEA's journal *Economic Affairs*, Vol.5, October-December 1984. It is reproduced by kind permission of the then publisher, Longmans.

[1] 'Privatisation: Principles, Problems and Priorities', *Lloyds Bank Review*, July 1983.

that privatisation without increased competition will, nonetheless, procure benefits. Private firms are able to respond more easily to demand by having better access to capital, and they will have a stronger incentive to produce goods and services in the quantity and variety that consumers prefer, especially where monopoly power is limited by the existence (even when only potential) of close substitutes. But privatisation which enhances competition is more likely to secure a wider range of benefits. The issue is thus what form of privatisation will increase competitive forces within the railway industry.

LARGE FIXED COSTS, NATURAL MONOPOLY ELEMENTS

A major barrier to competition in the railway industry is its large, unavoidable fixed costs of production, which arise because many inputs into the industry are 'lumpy'. To run one train service between two cities, for example, requires a minimum outlay on track formation, motive power, rolling stock and administration. As these inputs are used more intensively, i.e., as more services are run, their cost is spread over more units of output so that average costs fall until the point when the railway is used so intensively that the track becomes congested and management over-stretched. But railways normally operate on the falling segment of their cost curves. Either market demand will have decreased, leaving spare capacity in the system, or new technologies such as centralised traffic control (CTC) will have enabled higher capacities to be achieved from existing plant. Railways therefore are referred to as 'natural' monopolies in the sense that a single, vertically-integrated firm can fulfil market demand more cheaply than two.

Although railways are natural monopolies in this sense, their true monopoly power as means of *transport* has now been all but eliminated by competition from aviation and road transport. But despite this competition BR is not as efficient as it might be. A cost analysis by Stewart Joy[2] (later to become BR's chief economist) during the 1960s suggested that BR was capable of reducing its permanent way costs to a substantial degree. More recently, the Select Committee on Nationalised Industries [3] and the Report of the Serpell Committee[4] have pointed to inefficiencies in the use of both equipment and personnel.

When inefficiency is substantial, falling average costs are not enough to maintain the railway monopolist's inherent advantage. The opportunity exists for a more efficient firm to set up in competition but producing at a lower cost. What prevents this happening is a second important characteristic of many railway assets. Embankments

---

[2] 'British Railways' Track Costs', *Journal of Industrial Economics*, Vol. 13, 1964, pp. 74-89.

[3] *The Role of British Rail in Public Transport*, First Report, Select Committee on Nationalised Industries, Session 1976-77, HC 305, London: HMSO, 1977.

[4] *Railway Finances*, London: HMSO, 1983.

and cuttings, the rail formation and the platforms, etc., are fixed *in situ* – they are sunk, committed irreversibly to a specified market. Consequently potential competitors are faced with substantial risks to enter a particular market in this way. They face BR with equivalent infrastructure written-down or written-off and with the potential to eliminate its inefficiencies that provide the opportunity for a private enterprise company. Once entry is accomplished the inefficiencies of BR might quickly disappear leaving competitors with unamortised assets they are unable to transfer.

It is thus not feasible for the private sector to build new permanent way and terminals in competition with BR. There may be special cases which provide exceptions; for instance, where existing track and terminal capacity is saturated and the particular market still has considerable growth potential (the Victoria-Gatwick Airport service may be in this category). But even in these circumstances, it is most likely that BR will be able to add to its existing infrastructure at a lower cost than a potential rival could build new rights-of-way or terminal facilities.

TOWARDS COMPETITION ON THE TRACKS

If competition from new rail infrastructure is out of the question, private enterprise could take over existing permanent way (at book value) in competition with BR (or other private companies). But BR have eliminated some of the obvious spare capacity in the system established by competing rail companies in the 19th century to achieve precisely these economies of use. Consequently, the opportunities for competing rail services using alternative, existing infrastructure between common centres are few (London-Southend services are an exception).

Similar, but again limited, opportunities for increased competition exist where the permanent way carries multiple tracks so that track ownership can be divided. Although modern CTC makes it feasible to divide double tracks into lengths of single track with two-way operations,[5] more flexibility can be achieved where there are four running tracks with competing companies handling two each (and each having restricted running rights over competitors' lines). However, there is a limited length of quadruple track and the train-control, rail formation and stations would have to remain in single ownership. Although worthy of further investigation (especially where there is not too much mixing of freight, slow passenger and fast passenger traffic), it is probable that in many instances the additional complexities of operation would negate the increased efficiency achieved by competition.

---

[5] Some of the world's busiest lines in terms of tonnages handled are single track (but highly specialised) railways.

STATE TRACK, PRIVATE TRAINS

A more logical way to proceed would be to work with, and not against, the constraints to competition inherent in the technology of railway systems. This approach would recognise that most large-scale effects are inherent in the permanent way, train-control and stations – precisely the assets irretrievably committed to a particular rail market once installed. In contrast, the rail vehicles – locomotives, wagons, carriages – are mobile between markets and economies in their use are well encompassed by the market opportunities available. This distinction begs for wider recognition within the institutional framework.

By distinguishing the ownership of the permanent way from the ownership of the vehicles an opportunity presents itself for having competing trains running on shared track. In other words, one would emulate a practice which is common in road and air transport: public sector buses (National Bus Company) compete against private coach companies on the state-owned motorway system and rival airlines (some in the private sector) utilise airports in separate and often state ownership. The last analogy is the more useful because of the scheduling and safety implications. Airlines arrange for access times to the terminal and runways and immediate air space; in effect, they rent this access. Translated into rail terms, access to lines and terminals would be rented by competing train companies who would then sell services directly to the public.

Such a policy may sound distinctly different from that which we associate with railways in modern Britain but its strength lies in the fact that it represents a further development of what is now happening and what used to happen on a large scale until 1948.

Before nationalisation in 1948, railways in Britain had developed quite complex structures reflecting in some cases a distinction between ownership of track and ownership of rolling-stock.

One example of this was the Cheshire Lines Railway which controlled lines between Manchester and Liverpool and between Chester and Stockport.[6] It was a statutory railway company under its own management but with parent companies (originally three and then two) represented on the Board. Its singular feature was that each year it handled millions of passengers without owning a single locomotive and millions of tons of freight without owning a single wagon. Locomotives were hired from another rail company and wagons came from a variety of sources including non-railway companies. (In the early 1930s there were something like 700,000 private rail wagons.)

The Cheshire Lines Railway disappeared as a separate entity in 1948, at the same time as much of the huge private wagon fleet was incorporated within the nationalised railway. For the private wagon

---

[6] For further details, R.P. Griffiths, *The Cheshire Lines Railway*, Headington, Oxford: Oakwood Press, 1947.

fleets this at least was but a temporary demise: private wagons never disappeared entirely from the network (some specialist wagons were retained by private companies in 1948) and in recent years their role has grown very rapidly.

EXTENDING THE PRIVATE RAIL SECTOR

They now form a substantial component within the rail freight system.[7] In terms of tonne miles, private wagons carried 40 per cent of BR's freight traffic in 1982. If coal and coke tonnage, carried mostly in 'merry-go-round' fleets running between collieries and power stations, were excluded, the private wagon proportion accounted for as much as two-thirds of tonne miles. Within this total, individual companies generate large flows of ore, cement, aggregates, oil as well as general freight and their investment in private wagons is substantial: oil and chemical industries alone have around £300 million invested.

Thus there already exists in the operational railway system a large private sector component and one that is based on a distinction between mobile and sunk assets. The next logical step would be for the private sector to extend into the motive power sector, purchase locomotives, employ or lease crews, and offer train services directly in competition with each other and with British Railways. Some of the large companies generating large volumes of traffic might consider it worthwhile to operate their own freight trains, just as many now operate 'own-account' lorries carrying road freight. But this would depend on their ability to utilise adequately the locomotives. The majority would probably prefer to hire the locomotive and train services (just as in effect they now do) but with the option of buying services from private 'hire and reward' train companies.

Wagon hirers already exist and a number have combined to form the British Wagon Hirers Association. Included is the multinational transport conglomerate, VTG, with a European fleet of 26,000 hire wagons, many of which operate over the BR network. VTG also operates in Europe large petroleum tank terminals and about 100 river-going vessels and an extension into railway locomotives would appear to complement its specialist transport activities. The provision of complete train services on a 'hire and reward' basis might be particularly attractive to transport distribution companies like National Carriers or the new-to-Britain, aggressive, rapidly growing Thomas Nationwide Transport (with experience of chartering company trains in Australia).

The Venice Simplon-Orient-Express Company Ltd, operating private coach stock between Victoria and the Channel Ports, is an example, albeit rather special, of the principle extended into the rail

[7] For further information, *The Future of Rail Freight: An End to Uncertainty*, A Submission to Government by the Private Wagon Federation, London, July 1983.

passenger market. The company agrees with BR the 'train path' in the busy south-east network and hires the locomotive and crew. With a more flexible approach the locomotives and crew could be hired from a private sector company quoting a rate for the job in competition with the state sector.

This extension of the private sector in the operational railway would be facilitated if the assets of BR were divided into two groups. The permanent way, train control, maintenance depots and termini could be vested in one company (the name British Railways remains appropriate), which would also handle overhead functions like general administration.[8] Rolling stock could be vested in a separate, public sector company or companies (which I shall refer to collectively as British Trains – BT). BR's charges to BT and private sector competitors would be based on direct train control cost, track wear and tear, and directly attributable terminal costs, supplemented by additional charges, broadly reflecting judgements of what the market will bear, to assist with covering joint costs. At times when passenger and freight demand is high the train companies would bid against each other for available train paths. The resulting 'rents' accruing to the permanent way company would help to cover the joint and common costs of the network (Figure 4).

THE 'SOCIAL' RAILWAY

The approach assumes that train services, if they operate at all, cover the marginal costs of operation. But there is a large 'social' railway – services considered necessary for social reasons – which fail to cover their direct costs. These would exist alongside competitive services. But there is the danger that the Public Service Obligation (PSO) grant, paid to maintain social services, might be used to cross-subsidise BT's competitive bids for use of BR's system. This could happen, for example, where social and competitive services offered by BT used common rolling stock. To eliminate this possibility, one approach would be to fence in the competitive market to prevent misuse of the PSO grant.

This fencing-in is already taking place in BR's adoption of sector management. BR is now divided into five operating sectors: freight, parcels, London and South East passenger services, other provincial passenger services, and inter-city passenger. Freight and inter-city have been set a commercial quasi-target and it is here that the privatisation proposals outlined would apply more easily. Data in the Serpell Report suggest, for example, that only a small proportion of inter-city train miles (about 10 per cent) was failing to cover direct costs (Figure 5). With competition resulting in higher efficiency, it is likely that the total number of inter-city train miles covering these costs could be increased.

---

[8] There would be some divestment of administration and marketing to train companies.

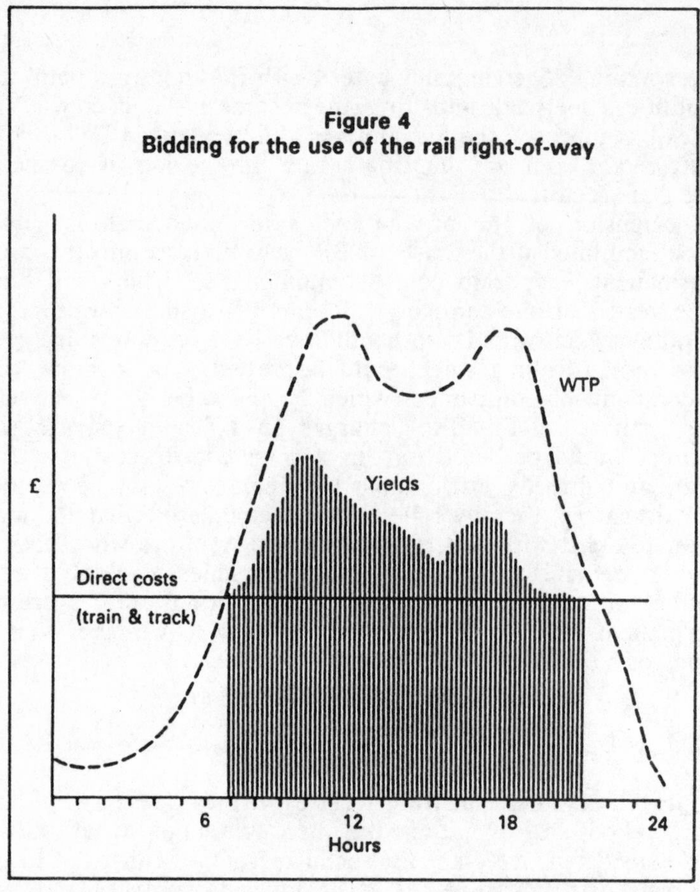

The dashed line in the chart illustrates the aggregate willingness to pay (WTP) for a journey between two towns (at a specified quality of service) at different times of the day. Train operators are not able to expropriate the whole of this because of an inability to perfectly discriminate when charging. The yield to the train company from each service operated is shown by the vertical lines. The amount exceeding direct costs (the latter shown as constant per service) represents the maximum that the permanent way company can expect to extract as a contribution towards the joint and common costs of the right-of-way.

A substantial proportion of train miles in the London and South East network also cover their direct costs, some by a large margin. But there is a minor, but not insignificant, proportion making large operating losses. It is difficult to judge from the information available whether the spur of competition would radically alter this picture without a reduction of services. The size of the positive externalities attached to some of these services (reduced road congestion in London is one example), and the political implications, advises caution. For the time being at least, this sector is better considered,

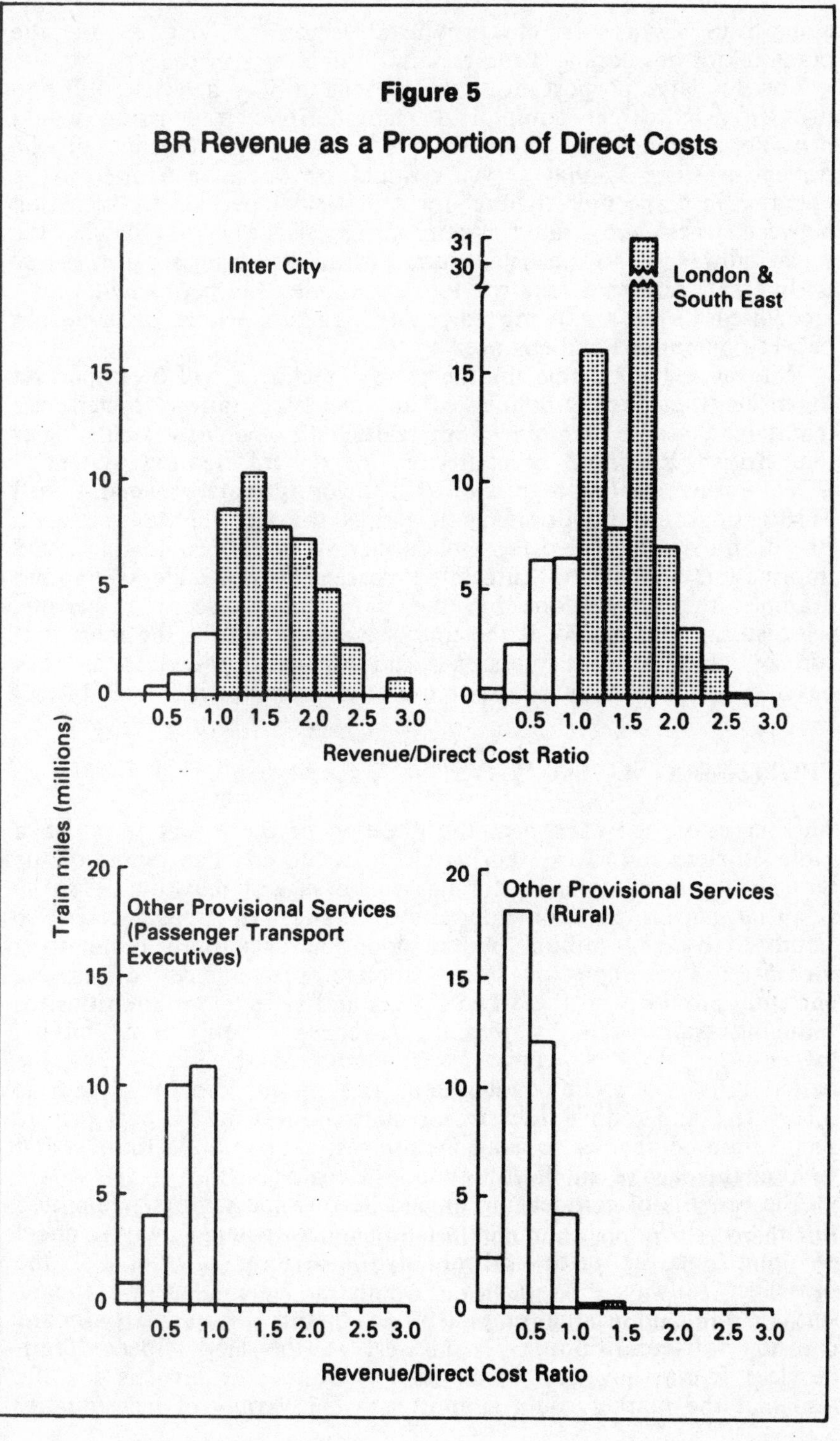
Figure 5
BR Revenue as a Proportion of Direct Costs
Inter City
London & South East
Train miles (millions)
Revenue/Direct Cost Ratio
Other Provisional Services (Passenger Transport Executives)
Other Provisional Services (Rural)
0
5
10
15
20
30
31
0.5
1.0
1.5
2.0
2.5
3.0

along with services in the provincial sector, as lying outside the potential for developing commercially competing services.

For this large proportion of the present railway not susceptible to provision by direct competition, competitive franchising would provide a means of improving efficiency. The essence of the franchising idea is that services would be open for tender to be operated in a specified manner for a particular period. A distinction between 'track' and 'trains' is appropriate also when franchising the social railway. The expertise required to operate train services *per se* is different from that required for maintaining the permanent way – recognised in BR's existing corporate structure which distinguishes between operations and engineering.

With an extended role for the private sector, it will be important to ensure that the economies of an integrated railway system are maintained. These economies are realised through new technologies like British Railways' computerised wagon information system – TOPS – whereby the progress of each wagon (privately owned as well as BR stock) is monitored as it passes through the rail network. Private train companies, too, will need to have access to the TOPS information system. An integrated passenger time-table is another example; the present one includes more than a score of private, seasonal railways aimed at the tourist market (and for the most part run by volunteers). Professional, private sector services as they develop, will need to be incorporated in the system-wide timetable.

PROFIT-MAKING RAILWAYS?

The suggested approach begs the question of the extent to which a more efficient railway system would be achieved. The report of the Serpell inquiry contained estimates which suggest that, by 1986, the financial performance of inter-city rail and rail freight could be improved by £84 million by the adoption of various cost-cutting measures. This figure is based upon improvements to services currently provided by these two sectors and reflects opportunities for reducing train costs by purchasing cheaper equipment (buying low-cost locomotives overseas was mentioned specifically); by the better utilisation of both equipment and labour; and by savings in locomotive and rolling stock maintenance. One would expect private sector train companies to avail themselves of these opportunities and to force the pace of adoption by the state sector railway.

The benefits of competition extend beyond the savings pinpointed in the Serpell Report. Competition in services would have the effect of optimising the price and quality of services offered. For the passenger railway, BR display a tendency to market a standard service with increasing emphasis on quality – speed, on-board catering, air-conditioning – manifest in the High Speed Train Services. It may have judged the market accurately. But it is possible also that the market could support a wider variety of price/quality packages.[9] For example, the private sector may wish to test-market a lower standard of inter-city service based on the new rail-bus technology. Crew savings, lower fuel consumption, reduced vehicle depreciation and less wear and tear on the track could produce a lower ticket price acceptable, despite the slower, less comfortable ride,[10] to a number sufficient to support the service – the young, pensioners, and so on.

A further benefit of the suggested competitive model would be the provision of better guidance for investment in rail infrastructure and the reduction, if not elimination, of the present arbitrary allocation of overhead and joint costs to the inter-city sector. Inter-city rail is expected to earn a surplus on direct and 'indirect' costs equivalent to a 5 per cent discounted cash flow on certain defined capital assets. As Mr Alfred Goldstein, a member of the Serpell Committee, remarked in his Minority Report, the rationale of this test has not been satisfactorily explained. Under the proposed framework for competitive services, the contribution towards costs not attributable to the direct provision of a train service would come from track 'rents'. If these rents fail to cover renewal of infrastructure specific to a competitive sector, the market will have signalled an eventual withdrawal of these services. Conversely, where competitive bidding for train paths pushes up rents, expansion of track and terminus capacity will be called for.

THE SHAPE OF A COMPETITIVE RAILWAY INDUSTRY

Finally, one can speculate on the long-term structure of a competitive railway industry. We might expect an initial increase in the overall size of the freight and inter-city sectors. A wider variety of services and/or lower fares and charges should produce an increase in demand for rail travel. In the longer term, the character of the industry will depend also on the Government's view on the size of the social railway and thus on the amount of infrastructure that the Government is willing to support.

It is difficult to judge whether the public sector's involvement in freight and inter-city services would continue as at present. This depends upon whether there are economies or diseconomies of scale and scope in the provision of train services.[11] Large companies may be able to balance and match rolling-stock to different market

[9] More freedom of entry into airline markets has produced this effect: Peter Forsyth, 'Airline Deregulation in the United States: The Lessons for Europe', *Fiscal Studies*, Vol. 4, November 1983, and David Starkie and Margaret Starrs, 'Contestability and Sustainability in Regional Airline Markets', *Economic Record*, September 1984.

[10] There might be a beneficial effect of smaller trains operating at more frequent intervals. For a discussion of trade-offs between vehicle size and service frequency, Alan Walters, 'Externalities in Urban Buses', *Journal of Urban Economics*, Vol. 11, 1982.

[11] Economies of scale are to be distinguished from economies of utilisation (sometimes referred to as economies of traffic density). Economies of scope refer to the advantages of jointly producing multiple outputs, i.e., different types of services.

demands rather better but at the expense of managerial diseconomies.[12] The most plausible outcome is that the state sector will maintain a substantial presence alongside a range of private sector firms – as it does in today's airline and bus industries.

[12] Recent studies of US railroads have suggested only limited economies of scale. R.H. Spady (*Econometric Estimation for the Regulated Transportation Industries*, New York: Garland, 1979), for example, concludes that there are managerial diseconomies of scale in rail transport.

PART V

THE SELLING OF STATE ASSETS

14

PRIVATISATION: THE FACTS

Howard Hyman

Director of Privatisation Services, Price Waterhouse

IN THE DECADE from 1977 to 1987, privatisation activity in the UK involved the sale of over 13 billion shares, raising £25 billion for the British Government and creating 13 listed companies with a current market capitalisation of over £48 billion (almost £60 billion before the stock market fall in October 1987). Sales to other companies or to management and/or employees raised a further £1 billion (Tables 1 and 2).

In that same period the proportion of Gross Domestic Product attributable to state-owned industry fell from 9 per cent to approximately 5 per cent and almost one million jobs were transferred from the public to the private sector.

In this Chapter a statistical overview of the British Government's privatisation programme is undertaken.[1] In particular the following areas are considered:

- a survey of the sales;
- the revenue generated by privatisation;
- the financial performance of privatised companies;
- arrangements for small investors;
- the methods and results of sales;
- underwriting arrangements;
- costs of privatisation;
- use of a special share for privatised companies.

[1] Unless otherwise stated, the data for this chapter are derived from *Privatisation: The Facts*, London: Price Waterhouse, 1987. All data are those current at the end of March 1988.

Table 1
PRIVATISATION – PUBLIC OFFERINGS, 1977 – 87

Company	Date of Sale	Percent Sold (a) %	Gross Proceeds Company £m.	Government £m.	Total £m.
Amersham Int'l	February 1982	100	6	65	71
Associated	February 1983	51.5	56	(34)	22
British Ports	April 1984	48.5	–	52	52
BAA	July 1987	100	–	1,281	1,281
British Aerospace	February 1981	51.6	100	50	150
	May 1985	59	188	363	551
British Airways	February 1987	100	–	900	900
British Gas	December 1986	97 (c)	(2,286)	7,720	5,434
British Petroleum	June 1977	17	–	564	564
	November 1979	5	–	290	290
	September 1983	7	–	566	566
	October 1987	36.8	1,515	5,725	7,240
British Telecom	November 1984	50.2	1,290	2,626	3,916
Britoil	November 1982	51	–	549	549
	August 1985	48	–	449	449
Cable & Wireless	October 1981	49 (d)	35	189	224
	December 1983	22	–	275	275
	December 1985	31	331	602	933
Enterprise Oil	June 1984	100	–	392	392
Jaguar (b)	July 1984	99	–	294	294
Rolls Royce	May 1987	100	283	1,080	1,363
		Total:	1,518	23,998	25,516

(a) May total more than 100% due to rights issues or less than 100% due to shares retained for loyalty bonus of employees.

(b) Proceeds to the Rover Group (then known as British Leyland); indirectly to HM Treasury via a lower public sector borrowing requirement for Rover.

(c) Sufficient shares retained to satisfy loyalty bonus arrangements.

(d) A further 1% went directly to the Employee Share Ownership Plan.

A SURVEY OF THE SALES

The Conservatives' First Term: 1979-84

The Conservative Government's drift toward a privatisation programme started slowly in 1979 with the sale of 5 per cent of its share in British Petroleum for £290 million. This was the first

Table 2
PRIVATISATION – PRIVATE SALES, 1979 – 87

	Date	Method	Gross Proceeds £m.
British Shipbuilders Warship Yards			
Brook Marine	May 1985	MBO	0.1
Yarrow Shipbuilders	June 1985	TS	34.0
Vosper Thornycraft	November 1985	MBO	18.5
Swan Hunter Shipbuilders	January 1986	MBO	5.0
Hall Russell	March 1986	TS	+
Vickers Shipbuilding & Engineering	March 1986	MBO	60.0*
British Technology Group (NEB)			
ICL	December 1979	TS	37.0
Fairey	June 1980	TS	15.0
Ferranti	July 1980	TS	43.0
Inmos	August 1984	TS	95.0
National Bus Company	August 1986– March 1988	MBO/ TS	325.0
National Freight Company	February 1982	MBO	7.0
Rover Group			
Unipart	January 1987	MBO	30.0*
Leyland Bus	January 1987	MBO	4.0
British Leyland Trucks	April 1987	Merger	–
DAB	May 1987	MBO	7.0
Istel	June 1987	MBO	26.0
British Rail			
British Rail Hotels	March 1983	TS	45.0
Sealink	July 1984	TS	66.0
British Airways			
International Aeradio	March 1983	TS	60.0
British Airways Helicopters	September 1986	TS	13.5
British Gas Wytch Farm	May 1984	TS	80.0*
Royal Ordnance – Leeds tank factory	October 1986	TS	15.4
– remainder	April 1987	TS	190.0
			1,326.5

+ = Not disclosed

* Initial proceeds only; additional proceeds contingent on future activity for Vickers (£40m.), Unipart and Wytch Farm (£135m. plus profit share).

MBO = Management buy-out (including management/employee consortia).

TS = Trade sale.

reduction of the Government's holding in a major state-owned enterprise to under 50 per cent of the equity. It was followed by sales of several significant investments of National Enterprise Board ('NEB'): ICL, Fairey and Ferranti. The NEB was a holding company established by the previous Labour Government to own new and/or ailing companies which required financial assistance. With the change of Government in 1979, and the subsequent Industry Act 1980, the NEB's function was altered to that of a catalyst for investment in high technology industries and in partnership with the private sector. It was encouraged to dispose of its investments wherever possible in order to increase private sector involvement.

It was not until February 1981 that the next public offering took place – 51 per cent of British Aerospace. Several more public offerings followed in the Government's first term – Cable & Wireless (49 per cent), Amersham International (100 per cent), Associated British Ports (51.5 per cent) and Britoil (51 per cent). Britoil was the first issue in the privatisation programme to exceed £500 million, the first to use a tender offer and the first sale which 'failed' in the sense that only 27 per cent of the shares were bought by the public.

Both the Amersham International sale and, to a lesser extent the British Aerospace and Cable & Wireless sales, led to a general concern that the Government had underpriced the companies sold. Accusations were made that the taxpayer had 'lost' significant sums because the initial trading of these shares was at prices substantially above the price at which they were sold to the public. This led to the use of a tender offer for Britoil, i.e. where buyers bid for the shares rather than the Government setting the selling price. During the course of the offer of Britoil shares, between the time the minimum price was announced and applications were submitted, Sheik Yamani successfully obtained an agreement among members of the OPEC cartel to lower the price of oil. As a result, institutional investors bid for only 1 per cent of Britoil shares which were applied for, and the Government failed to sell all the shares.

The Government's fiscal year 1983 ended with the sales of British Rail Hotels (by British Rail) and International Aeradio (by British Airways) to private investors (so-called 'trade sales') rather than by the issue of shares to the public at large.

The Conservatives' Second Term: 1984-87

The Government's second term began with the sale of a further 7 per cent of British Petroleum by tender, this time fully subscribed. Within the next year four more public and three major trade sales occurred – 22 per cent of Cable & Wireless (a tender offer, again under-subscribed), the remaining 48.5 per cent of Associated British Ports, all of Enterprise Oil and of Jaguar, and trade sales of British Gas's onshore oil assets (Wytch Farm), Sealink and Inmos (owned by the NEB).

Enterprise Oil, created from the oil interests of British Gas, was the Government's second tender sale in the volatile oil industry. Once again, the public failed to buy all the shares, this time because both oil prices and the stock market generally fell significantly before the sale. Only 17 per cent of the shares were bought by the general public with Rio Tinto Zinc bidding for 49 per cent of the offer. The Government restricted RTZ's purchase to 10 per cent, leaving 73 per cent with the underwriters. Enterprise Oil's articles of association place restrictions on ownership of shares or voting rights to 15 per cent (unlike many privatised companies), but the Government stated that each applicant would be restricted to a maximum of 10 per cent of total shares in order to promote its objective to establish a new *independent* British oil company. Jaguar, Wytch Farm and Sealink were not sold directly by the Government but by the state-owned enterprises of which they were a part – Rover Group (formerly British Leyland), British Gas and British Rail respectively.

In 1984 a significant change to the privatisation programme occurred with the sale of 51 per cent of British Telecom to the public. At the time this was the largest equity offering ever made anywhere in the world, raising £3.9 billion. It has subsequently been exceeded by two UK privatisation offers, British Gas (1986) and British Petroleum (1987). The sale by the Japanese Government of Nippon Telephone and Telegraph in December 1986 for 2,000 billion yen (£8.5 billion) holds the record as the largest single sale of shares.

British Telecom was unique in several other respects. It was the Government's first sale of a public utility and raised concerns over privatising a monopoly. The result was the creation of a regulatory régime, supervised by a new regulatory 'watchdog' – The Office of Telecommunications (OFTEL). There was also a fear that the capital markets would be unable to absorb such a large issue. 14 per cent of the shares were allocated to investors outside the UK and payment for the shares was in three instalments, extending over almost two years. The Government also linked this sale with the objective of wider share ownership. A mass marketing effort was directed towards individual investors, and preference was given to the sale of small parcels of shares to these investors. New techniques to encourage first-time share owners, such as loyalty bonuses, were developed. These techniques are discussed in more detail below (pp.202-4).

The BT sale was extremely successful. The general public applied for four times the shares available to them, leading to over 2.3 million shareholders. The value of these partly paid shares immediately increased by 85 per cent, providing these new shareholders with a substantial return on their initial investment. One of the principal reasons for this dramatic increase was the return to the London stock market of most of the shares initially sold to overseas investors.

In 1985 and 1986 the remaining Government holdings in British Aerospace, Britoil, Cable & Wireless, British Shipbuilders Warship Yards (by British Shipbuilders) and BA Helicoptors (by British Airways) were sold. In December 1986 the sale of British Gas raised total proceeds of nearly £8 billion (combining a £5.5 billion share sale with the creation of £2.25 billion in debt).

The privatisation of the National Bus Company took place against the background of deregulation of the industry in 1986.[2] The primary objective of this privatisation was to promote competition. The 70 subsidiaries of NBC were sold separately and four of the largest subsidiaries were split up to provide greater competition in the industry. Management buyouts were encouraged – over half of the sales took place this way. The sale of the NBC raised over £300 million, more than the total estimated for the sale of NBC as a single entity and some three times the original estimates of the proceeds if it were split up.

In 1987 there were further sales of three companies to the public – British Airways, Rolls-Royce and BAA (100 per cent in each case) – and five private sales – Unipart, Leyland Bus, DAB and Istel (all by Rover Group), and Royal Ordnance.

The Conservatives' Third Term: 1987-

In October 1987, the Government sold its remaining holding in British Petroleum. This could not have been more unfortunately timed for the underwriters since the offer had already been underwritten when the stock market 'crashed'. The Government was therefore assured of its money while the underwriters were required to buy-in BP shares at substantially below their market value. Some individuals who applied for shares quickly (before the crash) lost money on the BP sale, and those who still held shares from previous privatisation issues experienced the risks of stock market ownership for the first time.

No new public sales were planned for late 1987/early 1988, and the only significant transaction since the BP offering has been the private sale of the Rover Group to British Aerospace. Work continues on preparations for the next group of privatisations. The privatisation of British Steel has been launched with a public offering in late November 1988. Bids for the purchase of Girobank were received in August 1988, with a final decision also expected by November. The electricity and water supply industries are heavily involved in re-structuring and planning for sales which are expected (according to press reports) in late 1989/1990 respectively. The Government still owns 49 per cent of British Telecom, which it will eventually sell.

PRIVATISATION PROCEEDS IN PERSPECTIVE

Figure 6 summarises the cash received by central government from privatisations for the fiscal years 1979/80 to 1987/88 (estimated). (These figures do not, however, include proceeds received directly by state-owned enterprises from sales of their subsidiaries or other parts of their business.)

---

[2] For more detailed analysis, see Hibbs's and Beauman's chapters in this volume.

FIGURE 6 PRIVATISATION PROCEEDS CENTRAL GOVERNMENT RECEIPTS

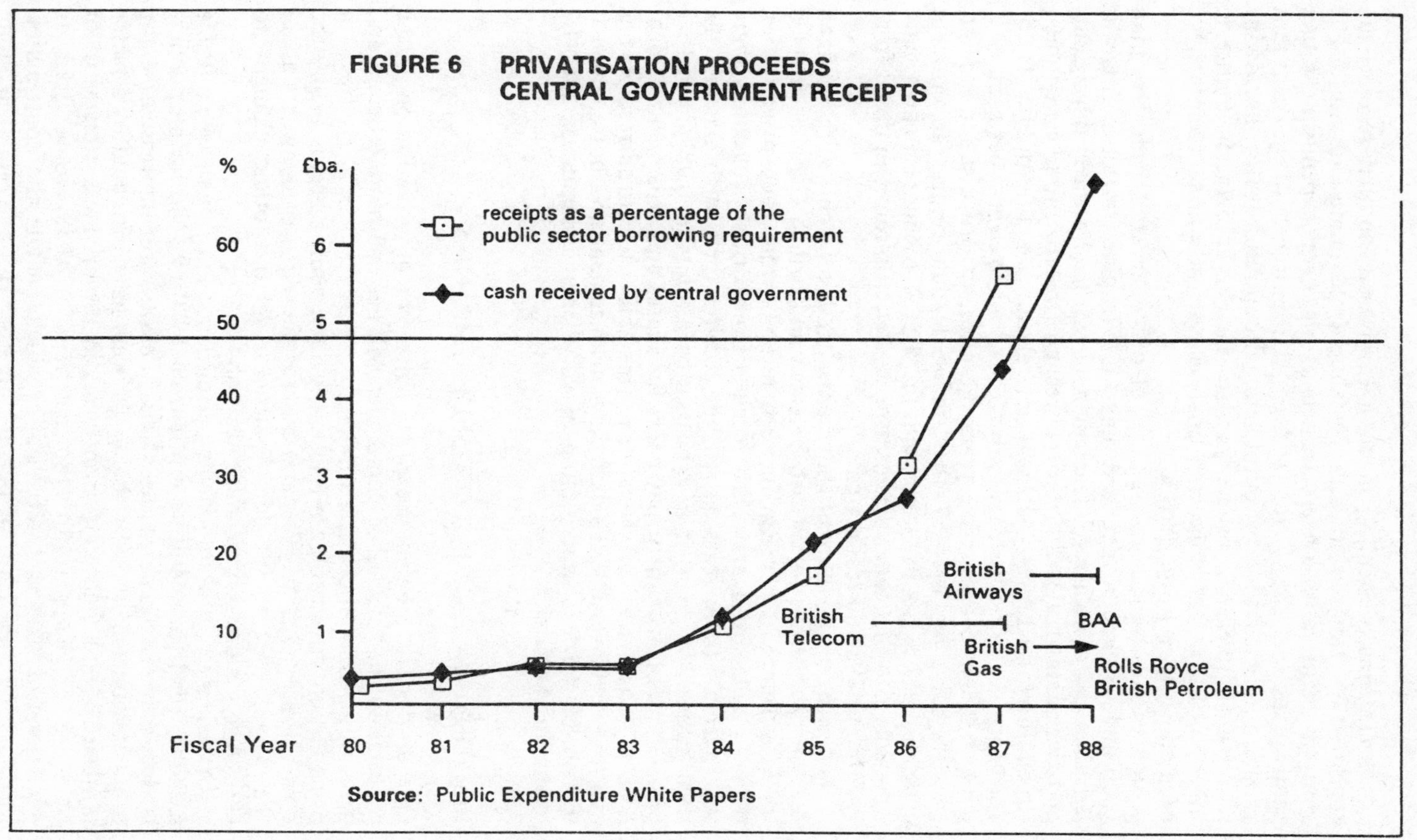

Source: Public Expenditure White Papers

Government accounting is on a cash basis, so that receipts are spread over the period that instalment payments are due. The proceeds of privatisation are treated as 'negative' expenditure rather than revenue. They thus reduce the amount of government expenditure in official figures and the public sector borrowing requirement ('PSBR') which measures the public debt. In Figure 6, for purposes of the following analysis, privatisation receipts have been added back to the PSBR.

In the Government's first term of office, receipts were less than £500 million in each year, and only £1,757 million in total. This was less than the annual total reached by 1985/86. Proceeds during this period remained a steady 0.4 per cent of total central government expenditure and grew slightly in relation to the public sector borrowing requirement from under 3 per cent to over 5 per cent.

Over the subsequent five years the effect of privatisation receipts grew rapidly; by 1986/87 they reduced total central government expenditure by 2.6 per cent and the PSBR by more than a half. Appendix I to this paper discloses privatisation receipts in detail from 1979/80 to 1987/88 (estimated).

The use of instalment payments, and of debt with a fixed repayment schedule for British Telecom and British Gas, has enabled the Government to spread its cash receipts from each privatisation over a number of years. Cash receipts from British Telecom's share sales spanned three years, as will the receipts for British Gas and the final British Petroleum sale. Privatisation receipts for 1987/88 include £2.5 billion of instalment payments for shares and repayment of debt from previous years' privatisations. This ability to spread receipts has assisted the Government's cash flow management and has enabled it to control the level and timing of very large demands on the UK capital markets.

PERFORMANCE OF PRIVATISED COMPANIES

One of the Government's explicit objectives of privatisation is the expectation that privatised companies will become more efficient and profitable than their nationalised predecessors. The effect of privatisation on a company's efficiency and profits begins before the point of privatisation. Preparations for the change of ownership to the private sector include re-structuring and other changes to encourage a more commercial operation.

One measure of a company's performance is profits earned. Table 3 shows trends in operating profit from 1980 to 1986 for all publicly traded privatised companies. Some results are impressive – the profits of Amersham and Cable & Wireless have increased by a factor of about five in their first seven years in the private sector. Most of Cable & Wireless's profits (85 per cent in 1988) come from its operations in Asia and the Pacific, which include the contribution from its 79 per cent ownership of the Hong Kong Telephone

Table 3
PERFORMANCE OF PRIVATISED COMPANIES' OPERATING PROFIT

	(b) 80/81	81/82	82/83	83/84	84/85	85/86	86/87
Amersham International	6 ■	10	12	15	19	20	24
Associated British Ports	(a)	(a)	(a) ■	15	(7)	19	26
BAA	n/a	n/a	74	89	110	129	131 ■
British Aerospace	112 ■	128	156	144	196	211	217
British Airways	(95)	13	185	268	292	198 ■	173
British Gas (current cost)	381	311	663	844	662	706 ■	1,001
British Petroleum ■	3,392	3,086	2,999	3,146	4,022	4,189	1,458
British Telecom	663	1,007	1,565 ■	1,531	1,856	2,118	2,349
Britoil	321	462	573 ■	625	719	756	149
Cable & Wireless	54 ■	62	108	140	207	242	268
Enterprise Oil	–	–	–	81 ■	130	97	48
Jaguar	(44)	(31)	10	51 ■	87	108	107
Rolls Royce	n/a	126	122	74	162	211	273 ■

n/a = not available

(a) Major restructuring of ABP prior to privatisation makes previous results not comparable.

(b) 31 December/31 March year ends.

■ Point of privatisation.

Source: Annual Reports and Accounts.

Company, acquired in 1984.

British Aerospace's profits have doubled in six years and Rolls-Royce's have almost trebled, with a steady growth in profits except for 1983 when the beginning of the world airlines' recession was felt.

Jaguar has shown a significant turn around from a £44 million loss in 1980 to a profit of £107 million in 1986, but had a difficult year in 1987 with new model introductions and an unfavourable US dollar exchange rate. British Airways has also emerged from a loss-making position with steadily rising profits. This was temporarily halted by re-allocation of routes to British Caledonian in 1985/86 (particularly Saudi Arabia) and loss of traffic due to international terrorism in 1986/87, but showed a recovery in 1987/88 with a significant increase in passenger load factors for the first time since 1984/85.

Associated British Ports' record is patchy, and reflects the disruption caused by the coal strike and related dock workers' strike in 1984. Nonetheless, the overall trend is one of an improvement in profits.

BAA's profits have shown steady growth over the six years of its existence, the result of aggregate increases in passenger and cargo business. The oil companies' profits all reflect dramatic changes in the world price of oil.

British Gas's current cost operating profits (historical cost figures are not available on a consistent basis for this period) in 1987/88 are almost three times those in 1980/81. A steady increase was interrupted in 1984/85, primarily as a result of higher prices for gas supplied from more distant and expensive North Sea fields. Fluctuations in profits reflect movements in the cost of buying gas, linked to the price of oil.

British Telecom's profits have grown both in the years before and after privatisation. A price control formula under the regulatory régime has restricted its ability to raise prices since privatisation to 3 per cent below the rate of inflation, so some measure of increased efficiency is indicated.[3]

For those companies sold by trade sales, one, the National Freight Corporation (NFC), has demonstrated a particularly impressive performance since privatisation. NFC's shares, held by its management and workers and valued quarterly by Phillips and Drew, have increased in value by 62 times since privatisation in 1982, and its profits have increased by over 12 times in the same period. Employee shareholder commitment is given as one of the primary reasons for success. The company is now preparing to apply for a Stock Exchange listing. Based on the current share price determined by trading in its internal market for shares, the company is valued at £360 million. However, analysts estimate it may be worth up to £500 million if the shares were traded in the Stock Exchange. There are plans to raise up to £100 million through a share issue after the Stock Exchange listing.

Another measure of a company's performance is the movement of its share price relative to the movement in the Financial Times Actuaries Index for the relevant industry sector. Table 4 shows the movement in share price for those privatised companies which are publicly quoted, from their first day of trading until 31 March 1988 (adjusted for stock splits, rights issues and future instalment payments), as compared to the movement in the relevant FT index over the same period. The newly created Telephone Network sector consists of only Cable & Wireless and British Telecom, making comparison against the sector relatively meaningless. This is why they have been compared to the wider Industrials sector index.

[3] This is discussed by Professor Bryan Carsberg, Director General of Telecommunications, in his contribution to this volume (pp.81-95).

Table 4

PRIVATISED COMPANIES' SHARE PRICE MOVEMENT, AT 31 MARCH 1988

	Share price change	Sector	Proportion of index	Sector change
	%		%	%
Amersham International	262	Health & Houshold Products	1	515
Associated British Ports	739	Shipping & Transport	43	330
BAA	(14)	Shipping & Transport	12	(21)
British Aerospace	275	Mechanical Engineering	8	223
British Airways	103	Shipping & Transport	13	104
British Gas	120	Oil & Gas	14	120
British Telecom	143	Industrials	*	165
Britoil	255	Oil & Gas	6	243
Cable & Wireless	544	Industrials	*	347
Enterprise Oil	176	Oil & Gas	2	165
Jaguar	184	Motors	16	243
Rolls Royce	(42)	Mechanical Engineering	10	(20)

Source: Financial Times

Several of the privatised companies have significantly out-performed their sectors. Associated British Ports' success is largely due to its expansion into property development; as a government corporation it was allowed to engage only in docks-related activity. It is also interesting to note that two-thirds of the Shipping & Transport sector index is now composed of privatised companies.

British Aerospace's share price has been affected by the acquisition of Royal Ordnance and Rover Group and also by the recent UK arms deal with Saudi Arabia, of which it is expected to win a major share.

Cable & Wireless has expanded worldwide – ranging from the UK where its subsidiary Mercury Communications Ltd. was licensed to compete with British Telecom in 1982 (trading profitably by the end of the year to 31 March 1988), to Hong Kong where its 79 per cent-owned subsidiary, acquired in 1984, contributes over half of Cable & Wireless's profits.

Table 5
ARRANGEMENTS FOR SMALL INVESTORS

	Number of instalments	Months to 2nd/ 3rd instalment	Loyalty bonus shares
Associated British Ports 1984	2	3	–
BAA	2	2	200
British Aerospace 1985	2	4	–
British Airways	2	6	400
British Gas	3	6/16	500*
British Petroleum 1979	2	3	–
1983	2	4	–
1987	3	10/18	150
British Telecom	3	7/19	400*
Britoil 1982	2	5	–
1985	2	3	–
Cable & Wireless 1983	2	2	–
1985	2	3	–
Enterprise Oil	2	3	–
Rolls Royce	2	4	–

* or bill vouchers of up to £250 (British Gas) or £216 (British Telecom).

Note: for 2nd and 3rd issues existing shareholders were also given preferential consideration.

There were no special arrangements for Amersham International, Associated British Ports 1983, British Aerospace 1981, Cable & Wireless 1981 or Jaguar.

Enterprise Oil's share price reflects its acquisition of ICI's upstream oil and gas interests in January 1987 and its discovery of oil in the North Sea in March 1988. It has also been the subject of intense bid speculation - its special share is due to be redeemed on 31 December 1988.

In the six years since its privatisation, Amersham International's share price has increased by only half as much as its sector, but that sector's movement is dominated by Glaxo, whose share price has increased more than ten fold.

Other share price movements have generally been in line with the respective sectors.

ARRANGEMENTS TO ENCOURAGE INVESTMENT BY SMALL INVESTORS/EMPLOYEES

One of the Government's major objectives has been to encourage individual and employee share ownership through the subsidised and preferential purchase of shares. It has developed a number of techniques in the course of the privatisation programme to encourage small investors to buy and to hold shares in privatised companies. Instalment payments, loyalty bonuses and special arrangements for employees have all been used to attract new individuals to the idea of shareholding.

Table 5 summarises arrangements offered to small investors in each public sale.

Instalment Payments

Instalment payments can provide several benefits. They allow a small investor with little spare cash to make a larger investment than could be done if full payment of the issue price were required immediately, and they give the Government the ability to manage its receipt of cash. In several privatisations (e.g., British Airways, British Gas and British Telecom) full dividends were paid during the period that shares were partly paid, giving the shareholder an initial higher dividend yield.

Instalment payments magnify the initial premium the market puts on the offer price, resulting in a much larger percentage return for those who sell their shares immediately. For example, if shares are priced at 100p payable in two equal instalments, and the 50p paid shares start trading at 75p, the market premium is 25p on the offer price. This is actually a 25 per cent premium, but the investor who sells before the second payment makes a 50 per cent gain because he has had to pay only 50p in cash for the shares. This incentive increases public interest in the sales and contributes to the heavy over-subscription which most issues have experienced. It may not, however, contribute to the Government's objective of wider share ownership if many who buy the shares are motivated only by the prospect of short-term profits from the immediate re-sale of allocated shares.

Payment by instalment was first introduced in 1979 as part of the first British Petroleum sale. This pattern of payment in two instalments only several months apart was repeated up to the BT sale. For the British Telecom, British Gas and British Petroleum (1987) sales, payment was in three instalments paid at intervals up to 19 months apart. Amersham International, Jaguar and the first issues of Associated British Ports, British Aerospace and Cable & Wireless shares were the only sales not to use instalment payments.

Loyalty Bonuses

Loyalty bonuses, established to encourage individual investors to retain their shares, entitle individual shareholders to one free share for every 10 held for three years. They were first used in the 1982 Britoil sale where they were available only to investors who applied for 2,000 or fewer shares. In subsequent sales where loyalty bonuses were offered (British Telecom, British Gas, British Airways, BAA, and the 1987 sale of BP shares), all individual investors were eligible, but a maximum number of bonus shares was set.

British Telecom and British Gas also offered vouchers to induce individual shareholders to keep their shares. This gave shareholders who were also consumers discounts on their telephone/gas bills and were an alternative to bonus shares. The (partial) benefits of these vouchers were available six months after the flotation rather than the three years investors had to wait for the benefit of loyalty bonuses.

EMPLOYEE SHARE ARRANGEMENTS

All public offerings of shares have included special arrangements for employees (Table 6). For each initial offering (except for Enterprise Oil and Jaguar, and British Petroleum which was already publicly traded) the Government offered each employee a number of free shares and matched a further number of shares to those purchased by employees. In the Cable & Wireless (1981) sale a block of free shares was offered directly to the Employee Share Ownership Scheme. All free and matching shares offered to individual employees have also been required to be held in Employee Share Ownership schemes and therefore have not been available for immediate sale.

Employees have received preferential consideration in each public sale of shares, with as much as 10 per cent of the total shares (British Telecom) reserved for various employee and pensioner arrangements. For the British Telecom sale there was no limit on the number of shares each employee could acquire under the preferential arrangement. In all subsequent sales except British Airways there has been a limit on individual employee purchases. In four sales, British Telecom, British Gas, British Airways and Rolls-Royce, employees were also offered a further discount of 10 per cent for a specified number of shares if held until the final instalment was paid.

Employee take-up of the offers has ranged from 19 per cent for Jaguar (only preferential consideration) to 99 per cent for Amersham International, British Gas and Cable & Wireless (1981) and 96 per cent for British Telecom (free and matching shares). Two offers with free and matching shares, British Aerospace (1981) and Britoil (1982), had a lower employee take-up (74 and 72 per cent respectively).

Table 6
SPECIAL ARRANGEMENTS FOR EMPLOYEES

	Free Shares	Matching Shares	Priority each	Priority total	% of Employees Participating
Amersham International	35	350	*	5%	99
Associated British Ports 1983	53	225	*	3%	90
1984	–	–	1,000	–	–
BAA	41	82 (a)	4,802	5%	n/a
British Aerospace 1981	33	600	*	2.5%	74
1985	–	–	10,000	2%	–
British Airways	76	120 (a)	*	9.5% (b)	90
British Gas	52	111 (a)	20,000	5% (b)	99
British Petroleum 1979	–	137	137	–	43
1983	–	–	250	–	–
1987	–	–	1,000	–	–
British Telecom	54	77 (a)	*	10% (b)	96
Britoil 1982	28	186	11,500	–	72
1985	–	–	10,000	3%	–
Cable & Wireless 1981	(c)	–	*	5%	99
1983	–	–	1,000	–	–
1985	–	–	5,000	1%	–
Enterprise Oil	–	–	13,500	–	71
Jaguar	–	–	10,000	7.5%	19
Rolls Royce	41	88 (a)	5,882	5% (b)	n/a

n/a = not available

* no limit

(a) The Government matched each share purchased with a further 2 shares.

(b) Also 10% discount on up to 1,600 shares (British Airways and British Telecom), 1,481 shares (British Gas) and 1,176 shares (Rolls Royce) per employee if held until final instalment paid.

(c) 285,833 were made available free of charge to the trustees of the Employee Share Schemes.

METHODS AND RESULTS OF SALES

The choices

As has already been indicated, there are a number of ways the Government can sell state-owned enterprises. The first choice is between a *public offering* (the sales of shares to the public) and a *trade sale* (the sale of the company privately to another company or investor) or a *management/employee buy-out*. If a public offering is to be used, there is a further choice between a *fixed-price offer* and a *tender offer*. A tender offer requires the applicant to apply at any price at or above a stated minimum price set by the Government.

One of the most difficult decisions which the Government must take is at what level to set the price of the shares. A fixed-price offer is the easiest for the investing public to understand. The price is set by the Government and its financial advisers and publicised; the investor only has to decide whether or not to buy.

Tender Offers

A tender offer is more difficult. It transfers the judgement as to price from the informed adviser to the (relatively) uninformed investor, subject to the floor bid set by the minimum price. Although the financial press will express opinions as to the likely price in the light of the commercial factors surrounding the company, the unsophisticated investor may feel unable to invest in a tender, or may select an unrealistically high price.

A partial solution to this difficulty is the use of a *striking price*, as was done in all tender sales except BAA. The striking price is selected from the range of tender offers which will sell all shares (the price at which there are sufficient offers at or above to sell all of the shares) and all investors pay that striking price. In each of the tender offers so far provision has been made for smaller applications to be made 'at the striking price', thus removing the need for the small investor to make a decision on the appropriate price at which to bid for shares.

In a true tender, investors whose applications are accepted pay at the price they have tendered. Applications are accepted beginning with the highest price tendered and continue in descending order until all of the shares have been allocated. Investors are allowed to make as many applications as they wish at differing prices.

A mixture of approaches has been used in the 20 public sales so far. Tenders for the entire offer have been used five times, in an 18-month period from November 1982 to June 1984. Only the first, Associated British Ports, used a fixed-price offer in that period.

Three of the five tenders were not fully taken up by the public – two in the volatile oil industry (Britoil and Enterprise Oil, discussed

Table 7
PREMIUMS ON NEW ISSUES

	Offer/ Striking Price	Price at one week*	Premium %
Amersham International	142	192	35
Associated British Ports	112	141	26
BAA (fixed price portion of offer)	245	280	14
British Aerospace	150	178	19
British Airways	125	169.5	36
British Gas	135	149.5	11
British Telecom	130	172.5	33
Britoil (tender)	215	189	(12)
Cable & Wireless	168	198	18
Enterprise Oil (tender)	185	186	–
Jaguar	165	177	7
Rolls Royce	170	288	34

* grossed up for all future instalment payments.

above) and the second tranche of Cable & Wireless. The Cable and Wireless under-subscription was a surprise both to the Government and the City. There was speculation in the press that sub-underwriters (who are also institutional investors) saw a cheaper way of getting the shares they wanted by not applying at a (higher) tender price and accepting shares at the minimum tender price in their role as sub-underwriters.

The other two tenders, both for companies already traded, were successful. The British Petroleum (1983) sale was 1.3 times subscribed with a striking price 7 per cent above the minimum tender (435p against 405p); Associated British Ports' (1984) striking price also exceeded the minimum – by 8 per cent (270p against 250p) – and the offer was 1.6 times subscribed.

Fixed-Price Offers

The alternative to tender offers is the traditional fixed-price offer. The shares sold in this way have subsequently been traded at a premium (Table 7).

This is frequently the case. Most new offers, not just privatisation issues, are priced to trade at a premium after the initial allocation of shares. One reason for this is that market quotations are for sales of relatively small parcels of shares, as are normally traded on the Stock Exchange. Privatisations involve very large amounts of shares and would be expected to have a lower per share price than for the subsequent trading of smaller parcels of shares for the same reason that bulk purchases of most goods attract discounts. Similarly, secondary offers are priced at a discount to the current market price.

The premiums set by the market on the offer price (fully paid equivalents) ranged from 7 per cent (Jaguar) to 36 per cent (British Airways). Investors in issues with instalment payments who sold their shares while still partly paid made immediate returns of up to 83 per cent (British Airways) and 85 per cent (British Telecom) before dealing costs, because of the instalment payment effect.

Combined Fixed-Price and Tender Offers

A new approach to privatisation was used for two sales in 1987, BAA and British Petroleum (1987): a combined fixed-price and tender offer. For the BAA sale this was further refined by the use of a true tender (see above) for 25 per cent of the shares – no striking price, but acceptance at the price tendered in descending order. The remaining shares were offered at the fixed price. Both the fixed-price offer and the tender were over-subscribed (by 10 and 6 times respectively), and the average accepted tender price, at 290p, raised an additional £56 million for the Government. Initial trading, although at a healthy premium to the fixed price, was well below the higher tender prices paid.

The British Petroleum (1987) sale was a totally different type of combined offer. The tender offer (which reverted to the use of a striking price) was restricted to institutional and overseas investors and was separate from the fixed offer made to the general public.

Results of sales

The degree of over-subscription and the total number of applications received for some sales indicate the popularity of privatisation (Table 8). Two of the highest levels of over-subscription, Amersham International and Associated British Ports (ABP) (1983), were of the two smallest sales. British Airways had a similar degree of over-subscription. It was a much larger issue than Amersham or ABP, but still smaller than the British Telecom and British Gas which had by then taken place, and it received a mass marketing effort similar to that of the larger sales.

Beginning with the British Telecom sale there was a change in the structure of the offers. Only part of the offer was available to the general public and employees, with up to 60 per cent placed with institutional investors (see discussion of priority applicants under

Table 8

RESULTS OF SALES OFFER TO GENERAL PUBLIC AND EMPLOYEES

	No. of times subscribed	Applications received '000	Shares applied for (million)
Amersham International	24.0	264	n/a
Associated British Ports 1983	34.0	156	660
1984	1.6	8	n/a
BAA - fixed price	10.0	2,160	n/a
- tender offer*	6.0	88	n/a
British Aerospace 1981	3.5	155	350
1985*	12.0	260	790
British Airways*	32.0	1,194	7,800
British Gas*	4.0	4,550	6,600
British Petroleum 1979	1.5	n/a	n/a
1983	1.3	79	n/a
1987	–	n/a	n/a
British Telecom*	9.7	2,300	11,321
Britoil 1982	0.3	35	70
1985*	10.0	450	n/a
Cable & Wireless 1981	5.6	157	n/a
1983	0.7	35	n/a
1985*	2.0	219	n/a
Enterprise Oil	0.7	13	n/a
Jaguar	8.3	320	1,480
Rolls Royce*	9.6	2,000	3,150

n/a = not available

* Information related only to the UK public offer (shares offered to the general public and employees).

'Underwriting arrangements' below). As a result the degree of over-subscription appears to have been higher than it would have been if total applications were compared to total shares on offer.

Five public sales of shares have had over 1,000,000 applications each: British Telecom, British Gas, British Airways, Rolls-Royce and BAA. British Telecom attracted an estimated 1 million individuals who had never owned shares before; British Gas another 2 million.

How many investors have retained their shares? The National Audit Office reports indicate that six months after the sale, 80 per cent of British Telecom investors and 70 per cent of British Gas investors still owned their shares. However, three years after the sale only 40 per cent of British Telecom's original shareholders were still investors, less than 10 per cent of Amersham's were still there after five years and almost 35 per cent of British Airways' had deserted within six months.

Despite the drop-out rate, research in 1987 by Dewe Rogerson showed that the total number of shareholders in Britain had trebled from 3 million in 1979 to over 9 million today. More than 75 per cent of individual shareholders hold shares in privatised companies or the TSB and 44 per cent only in privatised companies or the TSB. Mass marketing campaigns, the perception of guaranteed profits and ease of application have all combined to make millions of individuals see privatisation as something they want to participate in.

Underwriting arrangements

The underwriter's role in a public offer of shares is to guarantee, for a fee, that all of the shares will be purchased at the price which has either been set or agreed with the underwriters, i.e., to ensure that privatisation takes place. Those shares not purchased by the public are taken up by the underwriter. In this way the seller, in this case the Government, eliminates the risk of not selling the shares.

Underwriting is traditionally arranged in two layers – a primary underwriter who arranges the deal and takes the risk until sub-underwriting is arranged, and sub-underwriters who each agree to underwrite a portion of the shares. The primary underwriter may also act as sub-underwriter for some of the shares.

The underwriting arrangements for successive privatisations have been refined. Competitive bids for primary underwriting were introduced in the 1985 Cable & Wireless sale, and have reduced primary underwriting rates dramatically in each subsequent sale from highs of 0.5 per cent for British Aerospace (1981), Cable and Wireless (1981) and Jaguar to a low of 0.018 per cent for the British Petroleum (1987) sale (Table 9). All sales up to that of Jaguar (July 1984) used a traditional sub-underwriting arrangement, with sub-underwriting commission at a (traditional) rate of 1.25 per cent. The use of priority applicants was introduced for the British Telecom sale and eliminated traditional sub-underwriting, until its return for the British Petroleum 1987 sale.

Priority applicants (institutional investors whose applications for shares are arranged in advance of the public offer) serve several purposes. They ultimately perform a sub-underwriting function, in that they apply to purchase all of the shares if not taken up by the general public. They also ensure that the offer is fully taken up since they have technically applied to purchase all of the shares.

The shares applied for by the priority applicants are split into three categories (Table 10):

Table 9

UNDERWRITING RATES AND ARRANGEMENTS

	UK primary underwriting commission %	UK sub-underwriting commission %
British Petroleum 1979	.125	1.25
British Aerospace 1981	.500	1.25
Cable & Wireless 1981	.500	1.25
Amersham International	(a)	(a)
Britoil 1982	.200	1.25
Associated British Ports 1983	.425	1.25
British Petroleum 1983	.125	1.25
Cable & Wireless 1983	.125	1.25
Associated British Ports 1984	.505	1.25
Enterprise Oil	.300	1.25
Jaguar	.500	1.25
British Telecom	.375	)
British Aerospace 1985	.425	)
Britoil 1985	.425	)
Cable & Wireless 1985	.263	)(b)
British Gas	.175	)
British Airways	.111	)
Rolls Royce	.061	)
BAA	.053	)
British Petroleum 1987	.018	1.00

(a) The shares in Amersham International were sold to NM Rothchild and Morgan Grenfell who in turn offered them for sale. They received fees totalling £1,287,000 (approximately 1.8%) and in turn paid underwriting commissions of 1.25% plus brokers' fees.

(b) Priority applicants received placing commission ranging from 0.25 to 1.5% – Table 10.

- o *firm placing shares* – those which the priority applicants are guaranteed to receive;
- o *provisional placing shares* – the priority applicants will receive these unless the offer of shares to the public is over-subscribed by a predetermined amount, in which case they will be 'clawed back' and allocated to the public, and;
- o *commitment shares* – to be taken up by the priority applicants only if not applied for by the general public.

The clawback of provisional placing shares, which was to occur if the public subscribed for four times the shares available to it, did *not* occur in the Cable and Wireless sale. Lower levels of about two times subscribed were set for British Gas, British Airways and Rolls-Royce, and clawback did take place. The BAA provisional placing shares

Table 10
PRIORITY APPLICANT ARRANGEMENTS

	Placing Commission				
		Provisional		Proportion Allocated	
	Firm &	Commitment	Firm	Provisional	Commitment
	%	%	%	%	%
British Telecom	1.50	1.25	55	–	45
British Aerospace 1985	1.50	1.25	55	–	45
Britoil 1985	1.50	1.25	50	–	50
Cable & Wireless 1985	0.50	1.25	34	3	63
British Gas	0.50	1.25	30	20	50
British Airways	0.50	1.25	48	12	40
Rolls Royce	0.25	1.25	50	10	40
BAA	0.25	1.25	25	25	50

were to be clawed back to the extent that applications under the tender offer were accepted and were ultimately all absorbed by the tender offer. Estimates of the degree of over-subscriptions are shown in Table 8 (as disclosed in National Audit Office Reports). These figures are based only on the commitment shares (those available to the public).

More recent sales with priority applicants have led to lower sub-underwriting costs. Initially, priority applicants were paid a higher commission for firm placing shares (1.5 per cent as compared with the traditional sub-underwriting rate of 1.25 per cent) but this fell dramatically to 0.5 per cent for the Cable & Wireless (1985) sale and to 0.25 per cent for the Rolls-Royce sale.

Costs of Privatisation

The costs of selling state-owned enterprises to the public to date (Table 11) have totalled over £660 million, half of which have been underwriting costs. The companies concerned have borne £145 million of these costs as disclosed in their prospectuses, £70 million alone was borne by British Petroleum in the 1987 sale. Costs to the Government have not been systematically disclosed. In some cases they can, however, be found in various House of Commons replies or other Government statements.

Underwriting costs have averaged about 1.6 per cent of the gross proceeds up until the Cable & Wireless (1985) sale. They then decreased significantly to average about 1 per cent for the most recent five sales, as both primary underwriting rates and firm placing share commissions fell.

Some costs other than underwriting costs have been disclosed in House of Commons written answers and National Audit Office reports, but these vary in the amount of detail given. Table 11 shows

Table 11

PRIVATISATION COSTS

	Paid by HM Government £m.			Estimated Total Costs	
	U/w Costs	Other Fees and Commisions	Advertising Costs	% of Proceeds	£m.
British Petroleum 1979	4	2	)	2.4	7
British Aerospace 1981	2	2	)	4.0	6
Cabe & Wireless 1981	4	1	)	3.1	7
Amersham International	1	1	)	4.2	3
Britoil 1982	9	3	)	3.1	14 (d)
Associated British Ports 1983	1	1	)n/a	9.1	2
British Petroleum 1983	7	3	)	1.8	10
Cable & Wireless 1983	4	1	)	1.8	5
Associated British Ports 1984	1	1	)	1.9	1
Enterprise Oil	6	3	)	2.8	11
Jaguar	5	n/a	)	2.0	6
British Telecom	84	14	10	3.9	152 (d)
British Aerospace 1985	6	3	2	3.3	18
Britoil 1985	7	1	3	3.3	15
Cable & Wireless 1985	7	3	2	n/a	n/a
British Gas	70	10	21	3.2	175 (d)
British Airways	10	3	6	3.3	30 (d)
Rolls Royce	11	n/a	2	2.1	29 (d)
BAA	14	n/a	5	3.4	43
British Petroleum 1987	73	n/a	18	2.0	114
	325				

n/a = not available

Note: underwriting costs exclude amounts for shares offered by the company in the British Aerospace 1985 sale (approximately £3 million) and the Cable & Wireless 1985 sale (approximately £8 million) which were paid by the company.

(d) excludes costs of employees, free shares and discounts, bonus shares and vouchers; Britoil 1982 £3 million, for others see Table 12.

Source: House of Commons written answers.

those costs which have been disclosed for all issues to date: underwriting costs, other fees and commissions and advertising costs for the last nine sales, as incurred by the Government. Estimated total costs, paid by the Government and the company, have also been disclosed. Table 12 contains detailed cost information available for only four of the sales: British Telecom, British Gas, British Airways and Rolls-Royce.

UK underwriters have received £257 million of the total underwriting costs paid (£246 million from the Government and a further £11 million directly from companies), which may be

Table 12

DETAILS OF COSTS FOR CERTAIN PRIVATISATIONS

£m.

	British Telecom	British Gas	British Airways	Rolls-Royce
UK offer				
Underwriting/placing commissions	74	60	8	13
Selling commissions	13	9	3	4
Clearing bank costs	20	45	8	11
Marketing (includes advertising)	14	40	6	4
Adviser's fees	6	5	4	2
Overseas offer	30	23	5	–
	157	182	34	34
Less				
paid by company	(1)	–	–	–
interest on application money	(4)	(7)	(4)	(5)
	152	175	30	29
Add (maximum) incentive costs				
Bill vouchers	23	63	–	–
Bonus shares	88	122	13	–
Employee free shares/discounts	56	37	15	14
	319	397	58	43

Source: National Audit Office reports.

contrasted with an estimated £450 million paper loss that they experienced as of the first day of trading on the British Petroleum sale which occurred during the Stock Market crash of October 1987.

Advertising and marketing costs have also been a major factor beginning with the mass marketing of British Telecom shares. British Gas's 'Tell Sid' advertising campaign cost the Government about £21 million in advertising out of the total marketing costs of £40 million. The estimated advertising costs disclosed for the recent British Petroleum sale indicate that the trend of rising advertising costs has continued.

Another significant cost which has affected some sales is the implicit cost of 'free' bonus shares and the actual cash cost of vouchers. Britoil's 1982 bonus shares cost £3 million, and for the British Telecom and British Gas sales the combined cost of bonus shares and vouchers has been estimated at over £100 million each.

Use of a Special Share

The Government has taken the view that many of the companies privatised have a significant national interest and that it was necessary to protect that interest. This has been accomplished by use of a special share in 10 of the 13 companies privatised. British Petroleum, Associated British Ports and British Airways have no special share. However, because various air services agreements with other countries require that British Airways be substantially owned and effectively controlled by the British Government or its nationals to be classified as a 'national carrier', British Airways' articles give its directors the ability, with the agreement of the Secretary of State, to impose a limit of not less than 25 per cent on the number of shares held by non-UK nationals if necessary to protect its operating rights.

The special share (sometimes referred to as a 'Golden Share') is held by the Government and entrenches certain provisions laid down in the privatised company's articles of association, which cannot be changed without the special shareholder's permission. Restrictions have included some or all of the following:

- Prohibition on one person having an interest in 15 per cent or more of the voting shares of the company.
- Prohibition of total foreign ownership exceeding 15 per cent.
- Restriction on the issue of shares with voting rights different from those of ordinary shares.
- Requirement that the chief executive be a British citizen.
- Prohibition of the removal of government-appointed directors.
- Restriction on the disposal of the whole or a material part of the assets of the group ('material' deemed to be 25 per cent).
- Restriction on the voluntary winding up or dissolution of the company.

Effectively, the special share provides the Government with indirect control in the event of a takeover threat by requiring the special shareholder's permission to change those articles of association which control the ownership of the company. Table 13 outlines the principal restrictions entrenched by the special share for each privatised company. All the various routes by which control could be obtained – ownership of a significant amount of existing shares, creation of new types of shares (possibly with voting control), or transfer of a significant portion of the company to another company (sale of assets) – may require the Government's permission.

The restrictions on voting differ somewhat for Britoil and Enterprise Oil and the effect can be seen in the recent take-over of Britoil by British Petroleum. These companies have no restriction in their articles on the concentration of ownership, rather the special shareholder may acquire temporary majority voting rights if someone attempts to gain control of the company. The exercise of these voting rights requires an active step by the Government to block a take-over compared to the restriction on the size of individual shareholding

Table 13

PRINCIPAL RESTRICTIONS ENTRENCHED BY SPECIAL SHARE

Company	15% voting restrictions	15% restriction on foreign ownership	Restriction on issue of new voting shares	British chief executive	Government appointed directors	Disposal of assets	Restriction on winding up or dissolution
Amersham International	✓		✓			✓	✓
British Gas	✓		✓				
British Telecom	✓		✓	✓	✓		
Rolls Royce	✓	✓	✓*	✓		✓	✓
Britoil	(1)		✓				✓
BAA (2)	✓						✓
British Aerospace		✓		✓+	✓		
Jaguar	✓					✓	✓
Cable & Wireless	✓		✓	✓		✓	✓
Enterprise Oil	(1)		✓				✓

Special Clauses

(1) Temporary majority of votes where person seeks to obtain control.

(2) Provision concerning the ownership or control of the designated airports (Heathrow, Gatwick and Stansted).

* For two years

+ All Directors

which is a passive protection. In the case of Britoil, the Government chose not to exercise its special voting rights.

The special share does not, however, give the Government any say in the running of the business or participation in its profits. In only two cases, British Telecom and British Aerospace, does the Government have its own directors on the Board. In the case of British Telecom, this is to represent the Government's 49 per cent ownership and these directors are empowered to vote only on issues relating to contracts in which the Crown has a direct interest. The Government's right to appoint a director to the British Aerospace Board exists only so long as the Government has a contingent liability in respect of the Airbus programme.

The special share is not always intended as a permanent arrangement. It has been redeemed for Amersham International in July 1988 and in two cases has a finite life defined in the company's articles of association. Enterprise Oil's special share is to be redeemed on 31 December 1988 and Jaguar's on 31 December 1990. In all other cases the special share may be redeemed at the request of the special shareholder.

APPENDIX I

PRIVATISATION PROCEEDS: CONTRIBUTION TO GOVERNMENT SPENDING

COMPANY	1979-80	1980-81	£ million 1981-82
Amersham International	–	–	64
Associated British Ports	–	–	–
BAA	–	–	–
British Aerospace	–	43	–
British Airways	–	–	–
British Gas – sale of shares	–	–	–
– redemption of debt	–	–	–
Britoil – sale of shares	–	–	–
– repayment of debentures	–	–	–
British Petroleum	276	–	8
British Telecom – sale of shares	–	–	–
– redemption of loan stock and preference shares	–	–	–
Cable & Wireless	–	–	182
Enterprise Oil	–	–	–
Rolls Royce	–	–	–
Other share sales	60	83	51
Sale of property/oil licences	34	279	107
Sale of commodity stocks/ oil stockpiles	–	–	82
Total	370	405	494
Public Sector Borrowing Requirement (before privatisation receipts)	12,600	13,100	9,100
Receipts as a % of PSBR	2.9	3.1	5.4
General Government expenditure (before privatisation receipts)	90,138	108,699	120,566
Receipts as a % of general government expenditure	0.4	0.4	0.4

Note: These amounts represent cash inflows to central government and are net of related costs. Only properties sold directly by the government are included. Properties sold by state-owned enterprises (e.g. BR Hotels, Sealink, Jaguar) are accounted for by the industry and reduce its borrowing requirement.

(a) Guaranteed cash inflows from instalment payments and debt repayment schedules as well as completed sales.

(b) Net of disclosed underwriting and advertising costs only; other costs not yet available.

APPENDIX I (Continued)

					£ million
1982-83	1983-84	1984-85	1985-86	1986-87	1987-88 (est.) (a)
–	–	–	–	–	–
46	–	51	–	–	–
–	–	–	–	–	478 (b)
–	–	–	346	–	–
–	–	–	–	435	415
–	–	–	–	1,796	1,811
–	–	–	–	750	250
246	293	–	426	–	–
88	–	–	–	–	–
–	543	–	–	–	2,537 (b)
–	–	1,352	1,246	1,084	–
–	–	44	61	303	23
–	263	–	571	4	–
–	–	382	–	–	–
–	–	–	–	–	1,319
–	–	142	30	34	–
68	28	155	22	16	–
40	15	6	–	–	–
488 (c)	1,142 (d)	2,132 (e)	2,702 (f)	4,422	6,841
9,400	10,900	12,300	8,500	7,800	n/a
5.2	10.5	17.3	31.8	56.7	n/a
132,979	141,266	152,116	160,902	169,261	n/a
0.4	0.8	1.4	1.7	2.6	n/a

(c) Excludes British Rail Hotels (£30m.) and International Aeradio (£60m.).

(d) Excludes British Rail Hotels (£15m.).

(e) Excludes Jaguar (£297m.), British Gas Wytch Farm (£82m.) and Sealink (£40m.).

(f) Excludes British Shipbuilders Warship Yards (£75m.) and Sealink (£26m.).

Source: Public Expenditure White Papers 1985-88.

15

COMPETITION AND FLOTATION

Christopher Beauman

Director,
Morgan Grenfell Group

THERE IS a conflict between the conditions for effective competition and those of flotation. In this short note I will deal with the conflict between competition and flotation, and with the meaning of competition, and with the implications for wider share ownership.

It is essential to inject into the debate on privatisation and competition what investors really want. Professor Hibbs's paper gives an excellent analysis of the revolution in the transport industry with particular reference to buses. It is no coincidence that there are no flotations in buses. The changes in the bus industry are too difficult, too radical, too exciting for investors. If you were introducing real competition for the first time, then courage is required from investors and as much control as possible.

The champion of competition in telecommunications, Mercury Communications Ltd., has been losing large amounts of money. Even when it begins to make money it will still have vast capital commitments. Two of Mercury's original corporate investors, BP and Barclays Merchant Bank, sold their stakes to avoid becoming liable for the continuing capital investment required. The remaining investor, Cable and Wireless, has acquired total control and is now carrying the burden of capital investment. In the USA, MCI, a publicly quoted company and the principal challenger to AT & T, made a large loss last year due to write-offs; the US regulatory system is now being adjusted to try and assist it and others to remain effective competitors. In the UK airline industry British Caledonian's problems are well-known, and Professor Hibbs has demonstrated what happens to the competitors to National Express's buses.

COMPETITION WILL BE TOUGH

It is tough coming in to compete in a newly opened market, and in a capital-intensive industry the only entrants will be large companies with cash who must make strategic moves to survive. Those large companies face a changing world in which they will become obsolete if they do not search out bold new opportunities. They, therefore, are prepared to accept high risks for the prospect of high rewards.

But institutional investors and personal investors do not have to make such strategic moves. They have the choice of investing in an enormous range of quoted bonds and equities both in the UK and overseas. Why should they take excessive risks? The institutional investor may sometimes take a larger risk on a controlled basis, but the bulk of personal investors should be seeking securities with a reasonably predictable future. Therefore, if government wants to spread wider share ownership it has to create a situation in which there are minimum risks.

The first flotation in the UK privatisation programme was that of British Aerospace whose prime business was, if not a monopoly, a dominant position in the UK defence contracting industry. The second flotation was Cable and Wireless whose business was based on long-standing telecommunications franchises in the ex-colonies. By contrast, when Royal Ordnance, which had been groomed for flotation, faced real competition from Vickers in tanks the plans for flotation immediately collapsed and the company was sold not to investors but to a corporate buyer, British Aerospace.

Investors also want to see a profit record, and indeed the Stock Exchange insists on a five-year record. The major exception was the issue of shares in Eurotunnel which was given special dispensation by the Stock Exchange. Eurotunnel may be regarded as a relatively safe and straightforward investment, and is not comparable to a new or radically re-structured company in a newly competitive industry.

For these reasons there is a sharp and inescapable conflict between the requirements of competition and those of flotation in previously monopoly industries.

LEARNING AND DISCOVERY

There is still, however, a need to be more precise about what meaning we give to the word 'competition'. I favour the view, associated both with Adam Smith and with Austrian economists,[1] that competition is a process of learning and discovery. It has little to do with the world of micro-economic textbooks, common in British schools and universities, which are based on a framework of perfect competition and known facts about market opportunities. Therefore

---

[1] S.C. Littlechild, *The Fallacy of the Mixed Economy*, Hobart Paper 80 (2nd edn.), London: IEA, 1986.

the sort of system we have to design is one where people will learn by doing.

This means, first of all, that you should be very wary of simply throwing out an existing industrial structure which has, within whatever statutory framework, evolved, and the people in it do know something; it is a justification for a relatively conservative approach. Secondly, you should not expect the whole thing to happen in one great streak of lightning, as if one day you have a wicked, publicly owned, inefficient industry and the next morning an effective, privately owned competitive industry.

Competition is a process over time, and the art is to design something which will develop over time. That means in many cases, and probably in the electricity industry, a wedge approach. In the case of Mercury it is remarkable how much effect this relatively small company has had on competition in the telecommunications industry. If, however, we are trying to implement a process which will work over time, we are calling for the most extraordinary skilled government intervention of the decade.

I have worked in the steel industry which has been a regular victim of disastrous government intervention since the war. I now work in the financial industry whose shape has been completely revolutionised by recent government intervention ('Big Bang'), and which will be a test of the effectiveness of another form of government intervention (the Financial Services Act 1986).

FAILURE OF GAS PRIVATISATION A WARNING

In the energy industries, future direction will come from the department responsible for the privatisation of British Gas, which was not an example of introducing new and effective competition. The key to such competition is the possibility of attractive enough rewards to encourage private companies to enter. These should be primarily corporate investors (as in the case of Mercury) if there is to be real competition and hence major risks and uncertainties.

It will not be hard to do better than the Energy Act 1983. Even when that Act was designed there was the example of the Public Utilities Regulatory Programme Act in the USA as a more effective framework for encouraging competition. The Energy Act failed to provide a framework which positively encouraged competition, let alone a regulatory agency with the responsibility for making it work.

We should be less concerned with the immediate structure of the electricity industry and more concerned with how to structure an OFTEL-type body to preside over the lengthy process of promoting competition with a cumulatively powerful effect. Again the credibility of this body will be crucial for any new entrants.

These objectives must take priority over those of wider share ownership *per se*. The privatisation programme has had a dramatic effect in widening, if not deepening, share ownership. Millions of UK investors now hold shares in British Telecom and British Gas. From their viewpoint the next step should be to diversify into companies in the competitive production sector of the economy.

Large flotations of utilities will still be necessary to achieve privatisation in water and electricity. But these may be the least important part of the process. The important part is the commitment to high-risk investments by those who themselves bring new competition into the industry.

CONCLUSIONS

My conclusions are:

- we need courageous, large companies as new entrants to those capital-intensive industries where competition can be introduced. These could well include non-UK companies, bringing in a different expertise and management;
- an aggressive regulatory body to promote competition (as achieved in OFTEL) is essential to ensure that improvement through competition develops cumulatively over time; and
- in this context wider share ownership should be a means, not an end, so that the constraints of flotation do not take precedence over the necessity to achieve an industry structure which enhances competition.

SELECT BIBLIOGRAPHY

SELECT BIBLIOGRAPHY

Abromeit, H., *British Steel: An Industry between the State and the Private Sector*, Leamington Spa: Berg Publishers Ltd., 1986.

Albon, R., *Privatising the Post*, London: Centre for Policy Studies, 1987.

Ascher, K., *The Politics of Privatisation – Contracting Out Public Services*, London: Macmillan, 1987.

Ashworth, M. & P. Forsyth, *British Airways – Civil Aviation Policy and the Privatisation of British Airways*, IFS Report Series No.12, London: Institute for Fiscal Studies, 1984.

Bailey, R., 'Gas Privatization and the Energy Strategy', *National Westminster Bank Quarterly Review*, August 1986, pp. 2-12.

Beesley, M.E., *Liberalisation of the Use of British Telecommunications' Network*, London: HMSO, 1981.

Beesley, M.E. & S.C. Littlechild, 'Privatisation: Principles, Problems and Priorities', *Lloyds Bank Review*, Vol. 149, 1983, pp. 1-20.

Bös, D., 'A Theory of the Privatisation of Public Enterprises', *Journal of Economics*, (Z. Nationalöökon), Supplementum 5, 1986, pp. 17-40.

Bös, D., 'Privatisation of Public Enterprises', *European Economic Review*, Vol. 31, 1987, pp. 352-360.

Bös, D. & M. Rose, *Welfare and Efficiency in Public Economics*, Berlin: Springer Verlag, 1988, esp. Ch. 3.

Boyd, C.W., 'The Comparative Efficiency of State-owned Enterprises', in A.R. Negandhi *et. al.* (eds.), *Multinational Enterprises and State-owned Enterprises – A Challenge to International Business*, Greenwich, Conn.: JAI Press, 1980.

Boyfield, K., *Privatisation in the Third Term: A Background Briefing Paper*, London: Centre for Policy Studies, 1987.

Boyfield, K., *Put Pits Into Profit*, London: Centre for Policy Studies, 1985.

Bradley, I. & C. Price, 'The Economic Regulation of Private Industries by Price Constraints', *Journal of Industrial Economics*, Vol. 37, 1988, pp. 97-106.

Brittan, S., 'Privatisation – A Comment: An Examination the Government Did not Sit', *Economic Journal*, Vol. 96, 1986, pp. 33-38.

Brittan, S., 'The Politics and Economics of Privatisation', *Political Quarterly*, Vol. 55, 1984, pp. 109-128.

Bruce, A., 'State to Private Sector Divestment: The Case of Sealink', in J. Coyne & M. Wright (eds.), *Divestment and Strategic Change*, Oxford: Philip Allan, 1986.

Buckland, R., 'The Costs and Returns of the Privatization of Nationalized Industries', *Public Administration*, Vol. 65, 1987, pp. 241-257.

Buckland, R. & E.W. Davis, 'Privatisation Techniques and the PSBR', *Fiscal Studies*, Vol. 5, 1984, pp. 44-53.

Butler, S.M., *Privatising Federal Spending – A Strategy to Eliminate the Deficit*, New York: Universe Books, 1985.

Byatt, I., 'Market and Non-Market Alternatives in the Public Supply of Public Services: British Experience with Privatisation', in F. Forte and A.T. Peacock (eds.), *Public Expenditure and Government Growth*, Oxford: Blackwell, 1985.

Carsberg, B., 'Regulating Private Monopolies and Promoting Competition', *Longrange Planning*, Vol. 19, 1986, pp. 75-81.

Carsberg, B. & S. Lumby (eds.), 'Privatising British Airports Authority – Policies, Prospects, Procedures', *Public Money*, Vol. 5, 1985.

Cook, P. & C Kirkpatrick, *Privatisation in Less Developed Countries*, Brighton: Wheatsheaf Books, 1988.

Curwen, P., *Public Enterprise: A Modern Approach*, Brighton: Wheatsheaf Books, 1986.

Davies, D.G. & P.F. Drucato, 'Property Rights and Transaction Costs: Theory and Evidence on Privately-Owned and Government-Owned Enterprises', *Journal of Institutional and Theoretical Economics*, Vol. 143, 1987, pp. 7-22.

Davis, E.H., 'Express Coaching Since 1980: Liberalisation in Practice', *Fiscal Studies*, Vol. 5, 1984, pp. 76-86.

Department of Energy, *Sale of Government Shareholding in British Gas, National Audit Office, Report of the Comptroller & Auditor General*, HC Paper 22, Session 1987-88, London: HMSO, 1987.

Department of Environment, *The National Rivers Authority – The Government's Proposals for a Public Regulatory Body in a*

Privatised Water Industry, London, July 1987.

Department of the Environment, *Privatisation of the Water Authorities in England and Wales*, Cmnd. 9734, London: HMSO, 1986.

Department of Transport, *Airports Policy*, Cmnd. 9542, London: HMSO, 1985.

Department of Transport, *Airline Competition Policy*, Cmnd. 9366, London: HMSO, 1984.

Department of Transport, *Economic Regulation of the British Airports Authority plc.*, London, July 1986.

The Development of Cable Systems and Services, Cmnd. 8866, London: HMSO, 1983.

Director General of Telecommunications, *The Regulation of British Telecom's Prices: A Consultative Document*, London: Oftel, 1988.

Domberger, S. & J. Piggot, 'Privatization Policies and Public Enterprise: A Survey', *Economic Record*, Vol. 62, 1986, pp. 145-62.

Domberger, S., S. Meadowcroft & D. Thompson, 'The Impact of Competitive Tendering on the Cost of Hospital Domestic Services', *Fiscal Studies*, Vol. 8, 1987, pp. 39-54.

Domberger, S., S. Meadowcroft & D. Thompson, 'Competitive Tendering: The Case of Refuse Collection', *Fiscal Studies*, Vol. 7, 1986, pp. 69-87.

Dunleavy, P., 'Explaining the Privatisation Boom: Public Choice versus Radical Approaches', *Public Administration*, Vol. 64, Spring 1986, pp. 13-34.

Eckel, C.C. & T. Vermaelen, 'Internal Regulation: The Effects of Government Ownership on the Value of the Firm', *Journal of Law & Economics*, Vol. 19, 1986, pp. 381-403.

EPAC, *Efficiency in Public Trading Enterprises*, Canberra: Economic Advisory Council, 1987.

The Financial and Economic Obligations of the Nationalised Industries, Cmnd. 1337, London: HMSO, 1961.

Foreman-Peck, J. & M. Waterson, 'The Comparative Efficiency of Public and Private Enterprise in Britain: Electricity Generation Between the Wars', *Economic Journal*, Vol. 95 (Supplement), 1985, pp.83-95.

Foreman-Peck, J. & D. Manning, 'Liberalisation as an Industrial Policy: The Case of Telecommunications Manufacturing', *National Westminster Bank Quarterly Review*, November 1986, pp. 20-33.

Forrest, R. & A. Murie, *Selling the Welfare State: The Privatisation of Public Housing*, London: Routledge, 1988.

Forsyth, P.J., 'Airlines and Airports: Privatisation, Competition and Regulation', *Fiscal Studies*, Vol. 5, 1984, pp. 61-75.

Foster, C.D., 'Privatising British Airports: What's to be Gained?', *Public Money*, Vol. 3, 1984, pp. 19-22.

Future of Telecommmunications in the UK, Cmnd. 8610, London: HMSO, 1982.

Gist, P.D. & S. Meadowcroft, 'Regulating for Competition: The Newly Liberalised Market for Private Branch Exchanges', *Fiscal Studies*, Vol. 7, 1986, pp. 41-66.

Glade, W. (ed.), *State Shrinkage: Comparative Inquiry into Privatisation*, Austin: University of Texas Press, 1985.

Gritten, A., *Reviving the Railways: A Victorian Future?*, London: Centre for Policy Studies, 1988.

Grout, P., 'Employee Share Ownership and Privatisation: Some Theoretical Issues', *Economic Journal*, Vol. 98, 1988, pp.97-104.

Grout, P., 'The Wider Share Ownership Programme', *Fiscal Studies*, Vol. 8, 1987, pp. 59-74.

Hammond, B., D. Helm & D. Thompson, 'British Gas: Options for Privatisation', *Fiscal Studies*, Vol. 6, 1985, pp. 57-65.

Hanke, S.H. (ed.), *Privatisation and Development*, New York: International Center for Economic Growth, 1988.

Hanke, S.H. (ed.), *Prospects for Privatisation*, New York: Academy of Political Science, 1987.

Hawkings, F., 'Selling British Telecom', *Policy Studies*, Vol. 7, 1987, pp. 1-20.

Hazlewood, A., 'The Origin of the State Telephone Service in Britain', *Oxford Economic Papers*, Vol. 5, 1953, pp. 13-25.

Heald, D., *Public Expenditure: Its Defence and Reform*, Oxford: Martin Robertson, 1983.

Heald, D., 'Privatising Public Enterprises: An Analysis of the Government's Case', *Political Quarterly*, Vol. 53, 1982, pp. 333-349.

Heald, D. (ed.), *Privatisation: Policies, Methods and Procedures*, Manila: Asian Development Bank, 1985.

Heald D., 'Will Privatisation of Public Enterprises Solve the Problem of Control?', *Public Administration*, Vol. 63, 1985, pp. 7-22.

Heald, D. & D. Steele, 'The Privatisation of UK Public Enterprises', *Annals of Public and Cooperative Economy*, Vol. 52, 1981, pp. 351-367.

Helm, D., 'RPI Minus X and the Newly Privatised Industries: A Deceptively Simple Regulatory Rule', *Public Money*, Vol. 7, 1987, pp. 47-51.

Helm, D. & G. Yarrow, 'The Assessment: The Regulation of Utilities', *Oxford Review of Economic Policy*, Vol. 4, June 1988, pp. i-xxxi.

Hemming, R. & R.M. Mansoor, 'Privatization and Public Enterprises', *Occasional Paper*, No. 56, Washington DC: International Monetary Fund, 1988.

Henney, A., *Privatise Power – restructuring the electricity supply industry*, London: Centre for Policy Studies, 1987.

Hensher, D.A., 'Privatisation: An Interpretative Essay', *Australian Economic Papers*, Vol. 25, 1986, pp. 147-74.

HM Treasury, 'The Public Sector for the Public', *Economic Progress Report*, Vol. 145, 1982, pp. 1-4.

Holmes, A., J. Cheshire & S. Thomas, *Power on the Market: Strategies for Privatising the UK Electricity Industry*, London: Financial Times Business Information, 1987.

House of Commons, *Regulation of the Gas Industry – Memorandum*, HC Paper 15(i), London: HMSO, 1985-86.

House of Commons, *The Structure, Regulation and Economic Consequences of Electricity Supply in the Private Sector*, Memoranda Energy Committee, HC Paper 307, London: HMSO, 1987-88.

House of Commons, *34th Report from the Committee of Public Accounts: Control and Monitoring of Investment by BSC in Private Sector Companies*, HC Paper 307, Session 1984-85, London: HMSO, 1985.

House of Commons Committee of Public Accounts, *The Handling and Sale of the Government's Shareholdings in British Gas plc and British Airways plc – Minutes of Evidence*, London: HMSO, 1987-88.

Howell, D., *The New Capitalism: Personal Ownership and Social Progress*, London: Centre for Policy Studies, 1985.

Jaffer, S.M. & D. Thompson, 'Deregulating Express Coaches: A Reassessment', *Fiscal Studies*, Vol. 7, 1986, pp. 45-68.

James, M. (ed.), *Restraining Leviathan – Small Government in Practice*, Sydney: Centre for Independent Studies, 1987.

Jenkinson, T. and C. Mayer, 'The Privatisation Process in France and the UK', *European Economic Review*, Vol. 32, 1988, pp. 482-490.

Johnson, C., 'Privatisation and Ownership', *Lloyds Bank Annual Review*, Vol. 1, 1988.

Kay, J. A. & D.J. Thompson, 'Privatisation: A Policy in Search of a Rationale', *Economic Journal*, Vol. 96, 1986, pp. 18-32.

Kay, J.A., C. Mayer & D. Thompson (eds.), *Privatisation and Regulation: The UK Experience*, Oxford: Oxford University Press, 1986.

Kay, J.A. & A. Silberston, 'The New Industrial Policy – Privatisation and Competition', *Midland Bank Review*, Spring 1984, pp. 8-16.

Kay, J.A., *The State and the Market: The UK Experience of Privatisation*, Occasional Paper 23, London: Group of Thirty, 1987.

Keating, G., 'The Macroeconomic Impact of the BT Flotation', *LBS Financial Outlook*, September 1984, pp. 1-4.

Le Grand, J. & R. Robinson (eds.), *Privatisation and the Welfare State*, London: George Allen & Unwin, 1984.

Letwin, O., *Privatising the World*, London: Cassell, 1988.

Levitt, M.S. & M.A.S. Joyce, *The Growth and Efficiency of Public Spending*, Cambridge: Cambridge University Press, 1987.

Littlechild, S.C., 'Economic Regulation of Privatised Water Authorities and Some Further Reflections', *Oxford Review of Economic Policy*, Vol. 4, 1988, pp. 40-68.

Littlechild, S.C., *Economic Regulation of Privatised Water Authorities*, London: HMSO, 1986.

Littlechild, S.C., *The Fallacy of the Mixed Economy*, Hobart Paper 80, 2nd. edn., London: Institute of Economic Affairs, 1986.

Littlechild, S.C., *Regulation of British Telecommunications' Profitability*, London: HMSO, 1983.

Littlechild, S.C., 'Ten Steps to Denationalisation', *Economic Affairs*, Vol. 2, October 1981, pp. 11-19.

MacLachlan, S., *The National Freight Buy-out*, London: Macmillan, 1983.

Matthews, D., 'Laissez Faire and the London Gas Industry in the Nineteenth Century', *Economic History Review*, Vol. 39, 1986, pp. 281-94.

Mayer, C., 'Public Ownership: Concepts and Applications', *Centre for Economic Policy Research Working Paper*, Vol. 182, 1987.

Mayer, C. & S. Meadowcroft, 'Selling Public Assets: Techniques and Financial Implications', *Fiscal Studies*, Vol. 6, 1985, pp. 42-56.

Millward, R. & R. Ward, 'The Costs of Public and Private Gas Enterprises in Late 19th Century Britain', *Oxford Economic Papers*, Vol. 39, 1987, pp. 719-737.

Millward, R. & D.M. Parker, 'Public and Private Enterprise: Comparative Behaviour and Relative Efficiency', in R. Millward *et al.* (ed.), *Public Sector Economics*, London: Longman, 1983.

Millward, R., 'The Comparative Performance of Public and Private Ownership', in Lord Roll (ed.), *The Mixed Economy*, London: Macmillan, 1982.

Milne, R. G., 'Competitive Tendering in the NHS: An Economic Analysis of the Early Implementation of HC(83) 18', *Public Administration*, Vol. 65, 1987, pp. 145-60.

Molyneux, R. & D. Thompson, 'Nationalized Industry Performance: Still Third-Rate?', *Fiscal Studies*, Vol. 8, 1987, pp. 48-82.

Monopolies and Mergers Commission, *British Airways plc and British Caledonian Group plc: A Report on the Proposed Merger*, London: HMSO, 1987.

Monopolies and Mergers Commission, *Manchester Airport plc*, London: Civil Aviation Authority, 1987.

Monsoor, A.M., 'The Budgetary Impact of Privatization', in M.I. Blejer, and K.-Y. Chu (eds.), *Measurement of Fiscal Impact – Methodological Issues*, Occasional Paper 59, Washington DC: International Monetary Fund, 1988, pp. 48-56.

Moore, J., 'Privatisation in the United Kingdom', speech given to the Institute of Directors, London, 17 April 1986.

Moore, J., *The Success of Privatisation*, London: HM Treasury Press Office, 1985.

Moore, J., *Why Privatise?*, London: HM Treasury, 1983.

Mullery, C. & M. Wright, 'Buy-outs and the Privatisation of National Bus', *Fiscal Studies*, Vol. 7, 1986, pp. 1-24.

National Audit Office, *Report on the Sale of Government Shareholding in British Airways*, House of Commons Paper 37, London: HMSO, 1987.

National Audit Office, *Department of Energy: Sale of Government Shareholding in British Gas plc*, London: HMSO, 1987.

National Audit Office, *Department of Trade and Industry: Sale of Government Shareholding in British Telecommunications plc*, London: HMSO, 1985.

National Audit Office, *Department of Transport: Sale of Government Shareholding in British Airways plc*, London: HMSO, 1987.

National Audit Office, *Department of Transport: Sale of Government Shareholding in BAA plc*, London: HMSO, 1988.

National Audit Office, *Department of Trade and Industry: Sale of Government Shareholding in Rolls-Royce plc*, London: HMSO, 1988.

The Nationalised Industries, Cmnd. 7131, London: HMSO, 1978.

Nationalised Industries: A Review of Economic and Financial

Objectives, Cmnd. 3437, London: HMSO, 1967.

NEDO, *A Study of UK Nationalised Industries*, London: National Economic Development Office, 1976.

Neuberger, J., *Privatisation...Fair Shares for All or Selling the Family Silver*, London: Macmillan, 1987.

Newman, K., *The Selling of British Telecom*, Eastbourne: Holt, Rinehart & Winston, 1986.

Ofgas, *Competition in Gas Supply*, Office of Gas Supply, London, 1987.

Ohasi, T.M. & T.P. Roth, *Privatisation – Theory and Practice*, Vancouver: Fraser Institute, 1988.

Osborne, M. & M. Costello, 'Selling off the Public Estate: A Broker's View', *Public Money*, Vol. 3, 1984, pp. 57-59.

PAC, *Report from the House of Commons Public Accounts Committee: Sales of Government Shareholdings in Publicly-Owned Companies*, HC Paper 243(i), London: HMSO, 1984.

PAC, *Tenth Report from the Committee of Public Accounts*, HC Paper 189, London: HMSO, 1982.

Pack, J.R., 'Privatisation of Public-Sector Services in Theory and Practice', *Journal of Policy Analysis & Management*, Vol. 6, 1987, pp. 523-40.

Papps, I., 'Deregulation and Privatisation', in A.C. Darnell & L.J. Evans (eds.), *Contemporary Economics*, Oxford: Philip Allan, 1988.

Peacock, A.,'Privatisation in Perspective', *Three Banks Review*, Vol. 144, 1984, pp. 3-25.

Pirie, M., *Privatisation – Theory, Practice and Choice*, Aldershot, Hants.: Wildwood House, 1988.

Poole, R.W. (ed.), *Federal Privatization: Toward Resolving the Deficit Crisis*, Santa Monica: Reason Foundation, 1988.

Price, C., 'Competition in UK Gas Distribution', *Energy Policy*, Vol. 13, 1985, pp.37-50.

Price Waterhouse, *Privatisation: The Facts*, London, 1987.

'Privatisation – Everybody's Doing It. Differently', *The Economist*, 21 December 1985.

Prosser, T., *The Nationalised Industries and Public Control – Legal, Constitutional and Political Issues*, Oxford: Blackwell, 1986.

Pryke, R., 'The Comparative Performance of Public and Private Enterprises', *Fiscal Studies*, Vol. 3, 1982, pp. 68-81.

Pryke, R., 'Privatising Electricity Supply', *Fiscal Studies*, Vol. 8, 1987, pp. 25-88.

Public Finance Foundation, *Privatisation in the Water Industry – Proceedings of a Foundation Seminar*, July 1985.

Ramanadham, V.V. (ed.), *Privatisation in the UK*, London: Routledge, 1988.

Rees, R., 'Is There an Economic Case for Privatisation?', *Public Money*, Vol. 5, 1986, pp. 19-26.

Rees, R., 'Inefficiency, Public Enterprise and Privatisation', *European Economic Review*, Vol. 32, 1988, pp. 422-31.

Report of the President's Commission on Privatization, *Privatization – Toward More Effective Government*, Washington DC: White House, 1988.

Robinson, C. & E. Marshall, *Can Coal Be Saved?: A Radical Proposal to Reverse the Decline of a Major Industry*, Hobart Paper 105, London: Institute of Economic Affairs, 1985.

Robinson, C. & A. Sykes, *Privatise Coal – Achieving International Competitiveness*, London: Centre for Policy Studies, 1987.

Robinson, C., 'A Liberalised Coal Market?', *Lloyds Bank Review*, April 1987, pp. 16-35.

Robinson, C., 'Competition in Electricity', *IEA Inquiry*, No. 2, London: Institute of Economic Affairs, 1988.

Roth, G., *The Private Provision of Public Services in Developing Countries*, Oxford: Oxford University Press, 1987.

Rowley, C.K. & G.K. Yarrow, 'Property Rights, Regulation and Public Enterprise: The Case of the British Steel Industry 1957-75', *International Review of Law & Economics*, Vol. 1, 1981, pp. 63-96.

Savage, I., *The Deregulation of Bus Services*, London: Gower, 1985.

Savas, E.S., *Privatization – The Key to Better Government*, New Jersey: Chatham House, 1987.

Senior, I., *The Postal Service: Competition or Monopoly?*, IEA Background Memorandum 3, London: Institute of Economic Affairs, 1970.

Senior, I., *Liberating the Letter – A Proposal to Privatise the Post Office*, Research Monograph 38, London: Institute of Economic Affairs, 1983.

Shackleton, J.R., 'Privatisation: The Case Examined', *National Westminster Bank Quarterly Review*, May 1984, pp. 59-73.

Starkie, D. & D. Thompson, *Privatising London's Airports*, London: Institute for Fiscal Studies, 1985.

Starkie, D. & D. Thompson, 'The Airports Policy White Paper: Privatisation and Regulation', *Fiscal Studies*, Vol. 6, 1985, pp. 30-41.

Steele, D.R. & D. Heald (eds.), *Privatising Public Enterprises: Options and Dilemmas*, London: Royal Institute of Public Administration, 1984.

Steele, D.R. & D. Heald, 'The Privatisation of Public Enterprises 1979-83', in P.M. Jackson (ed.), *Implementing Government Policy Initiatives – The Thatcher Administration 1979-1983*, London: Royal Institute of Public Administration, 1985.

Swann, D., *The Retreat of the State – Deregulation and Privatisation in the UK and USA*, Hemel Hempstead: Harvester/Wheatsheaf, 1988.

Sykes, A. & C. Robinson, *Current Choices: Good Ways and Bad to Privatise Electricity*, London: Centre for Policy Studies, 1987.

Thompson, P., 'The NFC Buy-out – A New Form of Industrial Enterprise', *Longrange Planning*, Vol. 18, 1985, pp. 19-27.

Veljanovski, C., *Selling the State: Privatisation in Britain*, London: Weidenfeld & Nicolson, 1987; Revised Paperback Edition, 1988.

Vickers, J. & G.K. Yarrow, 'Regulation of Privatised Firms in Britain', *European Economic Review*, Vol. 32, 1988, pp.465-472.

Vickers, J. & G.K. Yarrow, *Privatization: An Economic Analysis*, London: MIT Press, 1988.

Vickers, J. & G.K. Yarrow, *Privatization and the Natural Monopolies*, London: Public Policy Centre, 1985.

Walker, M. (ed.), *Privatisation: Tactics and Techniques*, Vancouver: Fraser Institute, 1988.

Webb, G.R. & J.C. McMaster, 'Privatisation in Asia and South East Asia', *National Australia Bank Monthly Summary*, June 1987, pp. 15-16.

Wiltshire, K., *Privatisation: The British Experience*, Melbourne: Longman Cheshire, 1987.

Wright, M., 'Government Divestment and the Regulation of Natural Monopolies in the UK', *Energy Policy*, Vol. 15, 1987, pp. 193-216.

Yarrow, G.K., 'Privatization in Theory and Practice', *Economic Policy*, Vol. 4, 1986, pp. 323-377.

THE AUTHORS

THE AUTHORS

Christopher Beauman is Deputy Head of Planning at the Morgan Grenfell Group. After degrees in History (Cambridge) and Economics (Columbia) he joined Hill Samuel's Corporate Finance Department in 1968 before becoming a Director of Guinness Mahon in 1973. He was Adviser to the Chairman of British Steel (1976-81) concerned with Strategic Planning and Relations with Government over the period of major restructuring and closures; and then a member of the Government's Central Policy Review Staff (1981-83). At Morgan Grenfell since 1983 he has had responsibilities for privatisation, the development and regulation of investment management business, and strategic planning.

Bryan Carsberg has been Director General of the Office of Telecommunications since 1984. He qualified as a Chartered Accountant in 1960. After four years in private practice, he became a lecturer in accounting at the London School of Economics and Political Science (LSE) and a visiting lecturer at the University of Chicago. He gained an M.Sc. (Econ) at the London School of Economics in 1967. In 1969 he was appointed Professor of Accounting and Head of the Department of Accounting and Business Finance, University of Manchester, and later Dean of its Faculty of Economic and Social Studies. From 1978 to 1981 he was Assistant Director of Research and Technical Activities and Academic Fellow with the Financial Accounting Standards Boards, USA. In 1981 he became Arthur Andersen Professor of Accounting at the LSE and part-time Director of Research for the ICA. He is the author of numerous accountancy publications and has also undertaken various consultancy assignments in accounting and financial economics.

Ray Evans was born in Melbourne and graduated in Electrical and Mechanical Engineering from the University of Melbourne. He worked as a junior engineer in the electricity supply industry in Victoria before going into engineering academic life. In 1982 he moved from Deakin University, where he was Deputy Dean of the Engineering School, to Western Mining Corporation, one of the world's leading gold and nickel producers, where he advises on economic and political developments. He has published numerous essays and reviews in *Quadrant*, the leading Australian journal of opinion, and has edited a number of small magazines. He is currently Vice President of the H.R. Nicholls Society, an association devoted to labour market reform in Australia.

John Hibbs is Professor and Director of Transport Studies at the City of Birmingham Polytechnic. His career was first in bus and rail management, giving him first-hand experience. He has for many years advocated the reform of bus and coach licensing, first in his Hobart Paper, *Transport for Passengers* (1963, 2nd edn. 1971), and renewed (along with privatisation) in another Hobart, *Transport without Politics...?* (1982). Other publications include *The History of British Bus Services* (1968), and *Bus and Coach Management* (1985). He has also published a study of bus and coach regulation worldwide, *Regulation* (1985).

Howard Hyman is Price Waterhouse's Director of Privatisation Services and is currently advising the UK Electricity and Water Industries on all aspects of their privatisation. He also led the team responsible for the audit of share applications for the BAA flotation, directed a viability study of British Rail Engineering Limited in anticipation of possible privatisation, and advised the Rover Group on its privatisation until its acquisition by British Aerospace. From September 1984 to February 1987 he was seconded to HM Treasury as a specialist adviser on privatisation. He is the author of *The Implications of Privatisation for Nationalised Industries* (1988).

Stephen Littlechild has been Professor of Commerce, University of Birmingham, since 1975. He was formerly Professor of Applied Economics, University of Aston, 1973-75, and sometime Consultant to the Ministry of Transport, Treasury, World Bank, Electricity Council, American Telephone & Telegraph Co., and Department of Energy. He is author or co-author of *Operational Research for Managers* (1977), *Elements of Telecommunication Economics* (1979), and *Energy Strategies for the UK* (1982). For the IEA he wrote *The Fallacy of the Mixed Economy* (Hobart Paper 80, 1978), and contributed to *The Taming of Government* (IEA Readings 21, 1979) and *Agenda for Social Democracy* (Hobart Paperback 15, 1983). He has been a Member of the IEA Advisory Council since 1982. He was commissioned by the Department of Industry to consider proposals to regulate the profitability of British Telecom. His Reports, *Regulation of British Telecommunications' Profitability*, and *Economic Regulation of Privatised Water Authorities*, were published in 1983 and 1986.

Eileen Marshall was born in Romford, Essex, educated at Brentwood Ursuline Convent High School, and pursued a career in stockbroking for nine years. She took a First Class Honours degree in 1978 at the

University of Surrey, where she then became a Lecturer in the Department of Economics. In 1984 she was appointed a Lecturer in the Department of Industrial Economics and Business Studies at the University of Birmingham. She has co-authored a number of books with Colin Robinson including *What Future for British Coal?* (IEA Hobart Paper 89, 1981), *Can Coal Be Saved?* (IEA Hobart Paper 105, 1985), *Oil's Contribution to UK Self-Sufficiency* (1984), *The Economics of Energy Self-Sufficiency* (1984).

Walter J. Primeaux is the IBE Distinguished Professor of Business Administration at the University of Illinois. After a successful business career, he undertook graduate studies leading to M.A. and Ph.D. in Economics from the University of Houston. He was Professor of Economics, University of Mississippi, prior to joining the University of Illinois in 1974. He is Vice-President of the Association of Managerial Economics and Associate Editor of *Managerial and Decision Economics*, the managerial economics journal of academic economists. Professor Primeaux's area of expertise is Business Economics. His research interests have concentrated on public utility economics, with special emphasis on direct electric utilities competition. He has recently published *Direct Electric Utility Competition: the Natural Monopoly Myth* (1986). He has published in many leading academic journals on electricity competition, public utility regulation, market structure and management.

Colin Robinson was born in Stretford, Lancashire, and educated at Stretford Grammar School and the University of Manchester, from which he graduated with a First in Economics. He then worked for 11 years as a business economist. In 1968 he was appointed to the chair of economics in the University of Surrey, where there is now a substantial research group in energy economics. He is a member of the Electricity Supply Research Council and of the Secretary of State for Energy's Advisory Council for Research and Development in Fuel and Power (ACORD). Professor Robinson has written widely on energy including *A Policy for Fuel?*(IEA Occasional Paper 31, 1969), *Competition for Fuel* (Supplement to Occasional Paper 31, 1971), *The Energy 'Crisis' and British Coal* (IEA Hobart Paper 59, 1974), (with Jon R. Morgan), *North Sea Oil in the Future* (1978), and (with George F. Ray), *The European Energy Market in 1990* (1982).

Ian Senior was born in 1938 and educated at Sedbergh School and Trinity College, Oxford, where he was a scholar in modern languages. Later he took an MSc (Econ.) at University College, London. His career began with four and a half years at Post Office headquarters where he was latterly private secretary to the Junior Minister. Following two years at Liberal Party headquarters, he became a business consultant and is now managing director of an economic consultancy. Mr Senior's previous contributions to the IEA have been

The Postal Service – Competition or Monopoly? (Background Memorandum 3, 1970), *Liberating the Letter* (Research Monograph 38, 1983), and a commentary in *Bureaucracy: Servant or Master?* (Hobart Paperback 5, 1973).

David Starkie was born in 1942 and took his degree at the London School of Economics. He is now Chairman of TM Economics, a London-based economic consultancy, and an Associate of the Institute for Fiscal Studies. His broadly based career includes full-time employment in the public service and academic world, latterly as Research Professor, Department of Economics, University of Adelaide. He has also been adviser to the House of Commons Select Committees for various inquiries, such as the UK motor industry and airline competition. He has advised the governments of Argentina, Western Australia and South Australia. He is the author of several books on environmental economics, transport policy, and privatisation issues.

Irwin M. Stelzer is Director of Harvard University's Energy and Environmental Policy Center; U.S. economic correspondent for *The Sunday Times*; and Associate Member of Nuffield College, Oxford. He founded National Economic Research Associates, Inc. (NERA) in 1961 and served as its President until a few years after its sale in 1983 to Marsh & McLennan. He was a Managing Director of Rothschild Inc., investment bankers, and is now a Director of Putnam, Hayes & Bartlett, Inc. Dr Stelzer has served on numerous government committees investigating the regulated industries and competition policy and as a consultant to most of America's regulated companies. He has been named to the Advisory Panel of the President's National Commission for the Review of Antitrust Laws and Procedures. He has published work on competition in regulated industries, the organisation of cable broadcasting and antitrust economics. He has served as Economic Editor of the *Antitrust Bulletin*, is a member of the Editorial Board of *Telematics*, and is the author of *Selected Antitrust Cases: Landmark Decisions* (7th edition, 1986).

Cento Veljanovski joined the IEA as Research & Editorial Director in January 1988. Prior to that he was in private practice, Lecturer in Law & Economics, University College, London (1984-87), and Junior Research Fellow, Centre for Socio-Legal Studies, Oxford (1978-84). He has held visiting posts at a number of North American universities and worked for a short period after graduation with the Australian Treasury. He was educated in Australia and the UK holding several degrees in law and economics (B.Ec., M.Ec., D.Phil.). He has advised government and industry on privatisation and regulation and is a director of Putnam, Hayes and Bartlett, regulatory consultants. He is the author of *Selling the State – Privatisation in Britain* (1987), (with W. Bishop) *Choice by Cable* (Hobart Paper 96,

1983), and several books on law and economics.

Jack Wiseman is Emeritus Professor of Economics, University of York, and an adjunct Research Associate at the Center for Study of Public Choice, George Mason University, Virginia. He was formerly Director of the Institute of Social and Economic Research, University of York. He has written numerous books and articles concerned primarily with the economic problems of the public sector and with industry and trade. He has had a long-standing interest in economic problems of education, finance and social services generally; his first paper on the economics of education was delivered to the British Association in 1958. He has been retained as a consultant, expert and rapporteur by UN organisations: European Office of Social Affairs and FAO. He has had a long-standing association with Professor Sir Alan Peacock, resulting in a series of joint publications in public finance and welfare services, including *The Growth of Public Expenditure in the UK, 1840-1955* (1961).

George Yarrow is Fellow and Tutor in Economics at Hertford College, Oxford, and University Lecturer in the Economics of the Firm. After graduating from St John's College, Cambridge, he held appointments at the Universities of Warwick and Newcastle upon Tyne before moving to Oxford. He is an editor of the *Journal of Industrial Economics* and the *Oxford Review of Economic Policy*, and his published work has concentrated largely on problems in industrial organisation, theory of the firm, and privatisation, most recently with J. Vickers, *Privatization – An Economic Analysis* (1988).

THE INSTITUTE OF ECON

Recently Published

FINANCIAL REGU
or OVER-REGULA

Authors

CHARLES GOODHART, Professor of Banking and
School of Economics

JOHN KAY, Professor of Industrial Policy and Di
Centre for Business Strategy, London Business Scho

KATE MORTIMER, Director of N.M. Rothschild, formerly
Policy, Securities and Investments Board

ANDREW DUGUID, Head of Regulatory Services, Lloyd's of Lo

Introduced by **Dr Cento Veljanovski**,
Research & Editorial Director, IEA

Edited by **Arthur Seldon**, Vice-President, IEA

As a result of the dramatic transition that the City of London's financial markets have undergone in the last two years, a deep controversy is raging in financial circles about the structure and costs of the new legal framework that has been created.

In view of the Financial Services Act effective from April 1988, **FINANCIAL REGULATION – or OVER-REGULATION?** is both timely and provocative. It is the first book to question both the economic and regulatory implications of the Act and its expert contributors not only examine the key questions but present radical answers and solutions.

IEA Readings 27   viii + 68 pages   ISBN 0-255 36209-9 £5.00

All IEA titles may be ordered from bookshops or from the Institute. Sample copy of the IEA's bi-monthly magazine *Economic Affairs*, catalogue of 200 titles and details of the Institute's subscription service available on request.

THE INSTITUTE OF ECONOMIC AFFAIRS
2 LORD NORTH STREET, WESTMINSTER, LONDON SW1P 3LB
TELEPHONE 01-799 3745